Minoritized Women Reading
Race and Ethnicity

Feminist Studies and Sacred Texts Series

Series Editor
Susanne Scholz (sscholz@mail.smu.edu)

Advisory Board
Naomi Appleton, Tamara Cohn Eskenazi, Lynn Huber,
Sa'diyya Shaikh, and Sharada Sugirtharajah

Feminist Studies and Sacred Texts makes available innovative and provocative research on the interface of feminist studies and sacred texts. Books in the series are grounded in religious studies perspectives, theories, and methodologies, while engaging with the wide spectrum of feminist studies, including women's studies, gender studies, sexuality studies, masculinity studies, and queer studies. They embrace intersectional discourses such as postcolonialism, ecology, disability, class, race, and ethnicity studies. Furthermore, they are inclusive of religious texts from both established and new religious traditions and movements, and they experiment with inter- and cross-religious perspectives. The series publishes monographs and edited collections that critically locate feminist studies and sacred texts within the historical, cultural, sociological, anthropological, comparative, political, and religious contexts in which they were produced, were read, and continue to shape present practices and discourses.

Titles in the Series

Minoritized Women Reading Race and Ethnicity: Intersectional Approaches and Early Christian (Con)Texts, edited by Mitzi J. Smith and Jin Young Choi
Rape Culture and Religious Studies: Critical and Pedagogical Engagements, edited by Rhiannon Graybill, Beatrice Lawrence, and Meredith Minister
Jewish Feminism: Framed and Reframed, by Esther Fuchs
Feminist Theory and the Bible: Interrogating the Sources, by Esther Fuchs
Unraveling and Reweaving Sacred Canon in Africana Womanhood, edited by Rosetta E. Ross and Rose Mary Amenga-Etego

Minoritized Women Reading Race and Ethnicity

Intersectional Approaches to Constructed Identity and Early Christian Texts

Edited by
Mitzi J. Smith
Jin Young Choi

LEXINGTON BOOKS
Lanham • Boulder • New York • London

Published by Lexington Books
An imprint of The Rowman & Littlefield Publishing Group, Inc.
4501 Forbes Boulevard, Suite 200, Lanham, Maryland 20706
www.rowman.com

6 Tinworth Street, London SE11 5AL, United Kingdom

British Library Cataloguing in Publication Information Available

Library of Congress Cataloging-in-Publication Data

Names: Choi, Jin Young, editor. | Smith, Mitzi J. (Mitzi Jane), editor.
Title: Minoritized women reading race and ethnicity : intersectional approaches to constructed identity and early Christian texts / edited by Jin Young Choi, Mitzi J. Smith.
Description: Lanham : Lexington Books, [2020] | Series: Feminist studies and sacred texts | Includes bibliographical references and index. | Summary: "This book consists of cutting-edge analyses of constructions of racial/ethnic identities in early Christian texts and contemporary contexts from the perspectives of minoritized nonwhite women New Testament scholars. The range of intersectionality comprises gender/sexuality, class, patriarchy, slavery, religion, and empire."—Provided by publisher.
Identifiers: LCCN 2019056196 (print) | LCCN 2019056197 (ebook) | ISBN 9781498591584 (cloth) | ISBN 9781498591591 (epub) | ISBN 9781498591607 (pbk)
Subjects: LCSH: Bible. New Testament—Socio-rhetorical criticism. | Bible. New Testament—Feminist criticism. | Race—Religious aspects—Christianity. | Ethnicity in the Bible. | Ethnocentrism—Religious aspects—Christianity. | Identification (Religion)
Classification: LCC BS2380 .M56 2020 (print) | LCC BS2380 (ebook) | DDC 225.6082—dc23
LC record available at https://lccn.loc.gov/2019056196
LC ebook record available at https://lccn.loc.gov/2019056197

Contents

Introduction

Mitzi J. Smith and Jin Young Choi

Undisputedly, all people belong to the human race or kind (Greek: *genos*). "Race" and "racism" as construed and practiced in modern racialized societies are social constructions. Yet bias based on skin color, physical characteristics, or somatic differences, as well as the idea of ethnicity, existed in the ancient world. The fifth century B.C.E. Greek historian Herodotus referred to an ancient theory connecting black-skinned peoples and semen color: "The Indians have skin nearly identical to the Ethiopians. The semen of the Indians, the seed they ejaculate into their women, is not white like that of other men [how would he know this?], but is black like their skin. This is the same as the semen of the Ethiopians."[1] Herodotus's statement presumes that all white men will have the same color semen and all black men will have black semen.

Gay Byron demonstrates that ethno-political rhetoric in ancient Christian texts includes "both pejorative and idealized representations" of Egyptians/Egypt, Ethiopians/Ethiopia, and blacks/blackness.[2] Sometimes a doctrine of racial superiority appears absent, but it does not "necessarily imply behavioral tolerance in the relations between peoples of somatically different groups."[3] If the concept of the Other in the ancient world served to "shape their understandings of appropriate practices, beliefs, and values," Egyptians/Egypt, Ethiopians/Ethiopia, and blacks/blackness represent "extremes within early Christianity" or a distant sense of Christian identity.[4] Egyptians, Ethiopians, and blacks were considered distinctive *genos*.

Representing a dominant view of Jews and Syrians as inferior, Cicero regards these ethnic groups as "born to be slaves." Josephus also presents a perception of Jews who "have long learned to be slaves (*mathousi douleuein*) to others."[5] The person or people with the ink, the authority and power, to tell the story of other peoples with distinct physiognomy generally engage in a project of othering that includes prejudice, disparagement, and vilification, constructing the identity of the other in opposition to one's self, perhaps with a sense of superiority.[6] Early Christian writers also constructed their own identity based on the dichotomous division of peoples (*laos* and *genos*) as Jew/Judean (*Ioudaios*) or Gentile (*ethnos;* Greeks, *Hellenos*), as either one kind or the other, but never both.[7]

In his book *Hellenicity: Between Ethnicity and Culture,* Jonathan Hall provides a definition of Greek ethnicity that many Greek and Roman historians as well as scholars of ancient Judaism and early Christianity have adopted. Hall's definition is as follows:

> Biological features, language, religion or cultural traits may appear to be highly visible markers of identification but they do not ultimately define the ethnic group. They are . . . secondary. . . . Ultimately, the definitional criteria or 'core elements' which determine membership in an ethnic group—and distinguish the ethnic group from other social collectivities—are a putative subscription to a myth of common descent and kinship, an association with a specific territory and a shared history. . . . Ethnicity often emerges in the context of migration, conquest, and appropriation of resources by one group at the expense of another.[8]

Modern ideas about ethnicity similarly have to do with culture or enculturation, self-naming and self-definition, a sense of shared ancestry, a common myth of origins, common historical experiences of conquest, colonization, and postcolonialism, particularly when one's culture is threatened or the entire ethnic group is under attack. The ethnic group is not always the most salient aspect of identity, but the ethnic group tends to take on greater significance when "the integrity of the ethnic group is threatened."[9] Nomenclature is also often imposed upon ancient and modern groups that share the characteristics that Hall delineates. The ethnic group may later adopt pejorative nomenclature imposed by others, like "Jews" and "Black people."

Ethnic groups are neither static nor monolithic; they are dynamic in that they are subjected to processes of assimilation and differentiation in relation to other groups. Ethnic group identity is one among other social identities and roles that people invoke in a range of circumstances to achieve specific goals or objectives.

Ideas about ethnicity or ethnic group identity, like race, sometimes overlap in the ancient and the modern world. Scholars also impose modern ideas about ethnic identity or ethnicity onto ancient texts, and the reverse is true in that ancient notions of ethnicity derived from reading ancient texts may impact how we understand contemporary ethnic identity or components of it, particularly in the study of religion and among Christians. This is similarly the case with the phenomena we categorize as "religion." All translation, of texts and cultures, is interpretation informed by what came before and by the cultural presuppositions of the modern interpreter. This is why the interpreter needs to locate herself in the present context, especially in the racialized society of the U.S., while reading early Christian texts and paying attention to the constructions of race/ethnicity in those texts.

The history of race in the U.S. is about the socio-political construction and racialization of otherness. Beginning in the sixteenth century, the desire and need for free labor to plant, harvest, and build an alternative life and society in a new land, the inability to enslave the indigenous native peoples, and the access to black bodies from the continent of Africa (first among those who immigrated and then by forced removal from their homelands) led white colonizers (most of whom were Christians) to practice bias against Africans. Unjust legal penalties for miscegenation and other so-called crimes were imposed and some were sentenced to enslavement in perpetuity, and finally racialized laws were enacted to support the unjust practices.[10] The modern racialization of peoples beginning in the New England colonies created a dichotomous biracial classification of peoples as white and nonwhite. The legal perpetual enslavement of Africans and scientific claims about the bio-logical or genetic inferiority of Africans constructed black bodies as inferior, peculiar property, and particularly suited for enslavement. Frantz Fanon stated the following relative to human beings constructed as "black":

> For not only must the black man be black; he must be black in relation to the white man. . . . The black man has no ontological resistance in the eyes of the white man. Overnight the Negro has been given two frames of reference within which he has had to place himself. His metaphysics, or, less pretentiously, his customs and the sources on which they are based, were wiped out because they were in conflict with a civilization that he did not know and that imposed itself on him.[11]

The colonized and enslaved were forced to adapt, improvise, synthesize, and reconstruct their identities, in freedom and independence, individually and collectively.[12] The understanding of race as a modern social construct "stands for the conception or the doctrine that nature produced humankind in distinct groups, each defined by inborn traits that its members share and that differentiate them from the members of other distinct groups of the same kind but of unequal rank."[13] Racism is also a social construct founded upon the concept of race, but the difference between the two, as Karen Fields and Barbara Fields argue, is that while race is a construct like the "the evil eye, . . . racism is like genocide."[14] The ideology of race/racism, upon which the modern enslavement of Africans in the colonies and in the American South is predicated, aimed to erase all memory of or attachments to the enslaved Africans' social-cultural origins, and land or locatedness. It was a strategic forced dehumanizing socio-cultural exile or social death, as Orlando Patterson calls it.[15] All slave societies, including the Roman Empire and the

American South, uprooted and forcibly exiled peoples into foreign lands and cultures. The enslaved were extracted from their homelands and the continuum with the past was socially severed and denied, with the intent to erase the past in exchange for a new identity as human chattel and implements to be used to build and expand kingdoms and colonies.

Along with the extremely painful history of African slavery, one also needs to recover the histories of other racially oppressed people. For instance, American history obscured the forced migration of Asians as indentured laborers through the coolie trade beginning in the mid-sixteenth century. They were used to displace indigenous workers and replace African slavery, working at sugar plantations in Hawaii and constructing infrastructures such as the transcontinental railroad and working in the gold mines on the West Coast. After exploiting their labor, the U.S. controlled Asians' immigration and citizenship through systemic exclusion, enacting restrictive laws and policies.[16] Similarly, with the increase of Latino/a immigration since 1970, new processes of racialization—a social process by which meanings and attributions are assigned to inherited characteristics, usually in order to exploit and exclude—have emerged that impact the social and economic well-being of Latinx people in the U.S., forcing them to the bottom of the socioeconomic ladder.[17] Of course, we cannot forget the near genocide of the Native Americans who were forced from their lands onto reservations and their children often extracted from their parents and placed in so-called Christian boarding schools. Enid Logan states that "if a person is known to have any West African 'blood' or ancestry, then they have been socially and legally defined as black." People of African descent were needed essentially for their labor, and hypodescent expanded the number of people considered to be permanently unfree laborers, and later, exploitable second-class citizens, into perpetuity. Logan states that "Indigenous people, on the other hand, have faced a fundamentally different dynamic of racialization in the US, as they needed to *decrease* in number, or disappear entirely, in order to justify the expropriation of their land."[18]

The racialization and exploitation of other bodies—nonwhite, black, and brown bodies—are characteristic of U.S. society, historically and in the present. Race was to replace and displace "ethnicity" in enslavement and in freedom. Nonwhite formerly enslaved and/or colonized bodies were emancipated or gained their independence "sprawled out, distorted, recolored, clad in mourning in that white winter day."[19] Thus, the contemporary understandings of the relationship between ethnicity and race have changed: ethnicity is treated as a subset of race. This conception accounts for the hyphenation of "race-ethnicity." Within the socio-political and constructed framework of race/racism, people are expected to "self-ascribe" and "self-identify" with an ethnicity. In modern racialized societies like the U.S., people are categorized as white and nonwhite/black; "black" people "self-identify" by race as being of African descent or as black of Hispanic ethnicity in the U.S. census. Ethnicity is construed broadly to include countless social, cultural, and physical characteristics. The two ethnic categories that the U.S. officially recognizes are Hispanic/Spanish and non-Hispanic/Spanish.[20] We see a cross-pollination between "ethnicity" and "race."

Employing the category of ethnicity or ethnic identity as an analytical category for reading Christian texts is less contested than using race/racism as a legitimate category of analysis or as a hermeneutical framework. Cain Hope Felder states that "we must constantly remind ourselves that *in antiquity, there existed no elaborate ideologies, theories, or definitions of race based on physical features and behavioral patterns.* Nevertheless, . . . there is evidence to suggest that, by modern standards of race, the indigenous Pharaohs of the Eighteenth to the Twenty-fifth Dynasties (circa 1500–653 B.C.) were for the most part probably Black" (emphasis author's).[21] Felder's objective is to demonstrate how the Bible is relevant to black faith and the black struggle for freedom and, as he argues, "to determine implications for the problem of racism and ethnocentrism that still bedevil both Church and society in many nations today, including those of the Third World."[22] As stated previously, we find some overlap between modern ideas or constructions of race in the biblical text. Felder asserts, "Ancient authors of biblical texts did have color and race consciousness (they were aware of certain physiological differences), but this consciousness of color and race was by no means a political or ideological basis for enslaving or otherwise oppressing other peoples."[23]

The boundaries of race and ethnicity have always been and remain permeable and contested in human history and in the biblical texts. We acknowledge that concepts like "Christian," "religion," and "church," as well as race/racism, in the modern sense can be anachronisms. However, Denise Kimber Buell maintains "gender, ethnicity, and religion are no less anachronistic than race or whiteness if we mean that our discursive and material productions of these concepts differ significantly from ancient formations."[24] In bringing modern understandings and experiences of race/racism and ethnicity into conversation with early Christian texts, we can highlight the similarities and differences between the ancient text and our current context. We demonstrate how ancient, foundational texts and their rhetorical strategies, not just interpretations, can be and are used to justify, support, and engender oppression in our present contexts. Our readings in *Minoritized Women Reading Race and Ethnicity* focus on the perennial human practice of othering, on the subordination of the "weak" or "conquered" who are constructed as the evil, sinners, and villains, and on how the bodies of the minoritized within a majority constitute contested sites in the struggles for authority.

The contributors intentionally, strategically, and heuristically use their perspectives and experiences of race/racism and ethnicity as interpretive, dialogical frameworks to interpret historical and rhetorical constructions of race and ethnicity in ancient texts and contexts.[25] From our cultural locations, we analyze how the identity of the Other is constructed. As our identities as minoritized or nonwhite women biblical critics are intersectional in that we experience the world simultaneously in terms of our gender, sexuality, race/ethnicity, nation, and, religion, we necessarily use intersectional approaches to examine race/ethnicity, the construction of identity *in* or *and* early "Christian" texts. Patricia Hill Collins and Sirma Bilge describe "[i]ntersectionality as an analytical tool [that] examines how power relations are intertwined and mutually constructing. Race, class, gender, sexuality, dis/ ability, ethnicity, nation, religion, and age are categories of analysis, terms that reference important social divisions. But they are also categories that gain meaning from power relations of racism, sexism, heterosexism, and class exploitation."[26]

A number of volumes that deal with race, ethnicity, and religion in antiquity and early Christianity have recently been published.[27] The authors, mostly white-critical scholars, not only analyze how race/ethnicity is constructed *in* classical and early Christian texts but also demonstrate how the ideologies of race/ethnicity are involved or inscribed in scholarly interpretation and discourse. Moreover, as it is recognized that early Christian identities cannot be viewed as fixed or monolithic, a few works employ intersectional approaches to connect early Christian origins, their group identities, and power relations.[28] Recognizing white-critical scholars' contributions to relating race/ethnicity to early Christian texts and scholarly reproduction of racial/ethnic discourse, however, our volume, *Minoritized Women Reading Race and Ethnicity*, is distinct as the contributors are all nonwhite women New Testament scholars who read from our various individual and collective racialized/ethnicized experiences, histories, and traditions.

We are African American, Asian American, and Asian women. Our experiences as nonwhite women, who have earned terminal degrees in New Testament studies, include those of racialization, racial discrimination, and sexism in both society and ecclesial and/or educational institutions. In addressing (re)constructions of race/ethnicity *and* early Christian texts, our interpretations reflect our social locations, experiences, and struggles. Our voices, as nonwhite New Testament scholars, have been absent from conversations about constructions of race/ethnicity *in* or *and* early Christian texts and contexts. This volume fills epistemological and cultural voids, which is significant considering that nonwhite women (i.e., Native indigenous; African; African American; East, South, and Southeast Asian; Asian American; and Latina/Chicana) are primary subjects and objects of social constructions of race/ethnicity and reside at the intersection of race/ethnicity and gender/ sexuality. We bring embodied and located epistemological perspectives to bear on or in conversation with early Jesus movement texts.

Birthing this project offered certain challenges. We reached out to about twenty potential contributors. When Lexington Press accepted our book proposal, sixteen women had submitted abstracts and committed to contributing essays to this volume. They included one Native indigenous, two Latina/ Chicana, two Asian American, two South Asian/Indian, three East Asian, and six African American women. Minoritized women biblical scholars often suffer invisibility or exclusion, but they are also overburdened. Living and working at multiple intersections, we carry too much. When nonwhite or minoritized women in New Testament studies are few, the dearth greatly impacts our ability to do collective work. While we become more discerning about what we are called to do and where to place our priorities that further the work our individual souls must have, we are not apologetic about the number and composition of contributors—three African American and three women of Asian/Korean descent, who have been persistent, valuing our collective work. This is where we are; it still matters who reads and how we read.

Given our small numbers in the academy and specifically in biblical studies, this book gives voice to a "critical mass" of minoritized women New Testament scholars. According to the 2019 Society of Biblical Literature Member Profile Report, minoritized scholars constitute less than 15 percent of the active membership. If we consider that women are 24.77 percent of all members, it would not be so difficult to count the number of minoritized women in Bible, and particularly in New Testament, studies. Biblical scholarship is overwhelmingly white and male.[29] The interpretation of 85 percent or more scholars (including nonwhite scholars who believe that their interpretations preclude their ethnic identity) is "unmarked." White biblical scholarship deracializes biblical studies by normalizing whiteness to the extent that whiteness becomes invisible. Even as they believe that race/ethnicity do not exist in the text and that interpretation should be detached from the interpreter's prejudice and interest, they construct or reinscribe race/ethnicity—whiteness in(to) the biblical text in certain ways.

Susan Abraham argues, "The erasure of whiteness as a racial marker is performed across the board, and white feminists are often guilty of such erasure."[30] When our analysis of race/ethnicity employs intersectionality as an analytic category of other subcategories of gender, race, and empire, this means that gender should be a marked category, though flexible and negotiable.[31] Ultimately, this project offers a critique of dominant epistemologies about race and ethnicity in early Christian studies, challenging unmarked white scholarship and unmarked feminism and their production. The contributions provide provocative, innovative, and critical cultural and ideological insights into (re)constructions of race/ethnicity and intersectionality, *as well as* ancient canonical, noncanonical, and contemporary contexts and texts. We privilege our own cultural location.

This work is transgressive because we stayed the course long enough to produce a work that disrupts constructions of race/ethnicity in/and early Christian texts currently monopolized by white scholars. Our collective perseverance is performative and the fruit of our labor is performance. Our work is embodied performance that is enacted in our frustration, joy, and hope, as well as throughout the process of conception, writing, revisions, edits, proofing, and then publication and circulation where the performance is repeated. Each encore is a unique performance as diverse readers participate and perhaps mimic the choreography and are inspired to create their own performance.

CHOREOGRAPHY OF THE PERFORMANCE

Jin Young Choi examines the construction of ethnicity in the Gospel of Matthew, considering the intersection of gender and empire. In light of Greco-Roman understandings of ethnicity, she argues that the identity of the Jews as a people (*ethnos*) both in the diaspora and in Palestine was not monolithic or exclusive. Given the "fictive" nature of ethnicity, Choi argues that Jesus's ethnic identity (as an *Ioudaios*, refugee, returnee, Galilean, and king of the *Ioudaioi*) is constantly constructed and deconstructed in the gospel narrative. While Matthew's construction of Jesus's identity based on descent, kinship, and territorial allegiance is inevitably androcentric, patriarchal, and kyriarchal, an intersectional rereading of the Gospel leads Choi to trace a matriarchal lineage of Rachel and other mothers who weep over their lost children and unwaveringly refuse to be consoled. Their mourning in the public square evokes collective memories of displacement, estrangement, and deaths, which include Jesus's own. Choi brings these memories and mourning—a form of historical/social knowledge of the people's root—to the present context of *minjung* in which we are called to join in the mothers' resistance to the "global economy of fear."

The following four essays employ intersectional approaches to Paul's construction of race/ethnicity, gender, and power, situating their readings in conversation with contemporary contexts. In her analysis of Galatians 3:28 focusing on identity differences, Jennifer T. Kaalund employs a theoretical framework combining postcolonial, feminist, and psychoanalytical theorists, and a womanist hermeneutic that privileges the experiences of the African American community. As African American/black identity has been constructed as the other, Kaalund calls attention to the material implications for differences—differences inscribed on their bodies. Kaalund suggests a reading of difference that does not begin with understanding diversity as a deficit but rejects binaries and celebrates what others may debase. The Galatians, defined by their geography and ethnicity, refused Paul's imposition of the "in

Christ" identity similarly seen in the so-called "in the world" identity. According to Kaalund, to be "of Jesus Christ" has multiple meanings, one of which may include belonging to the family of Jesus in the sense of kinship—perhaps biological as opposed to being "in Jesus Christ" whereby Jesus is the object of the identity. Critical of Paul's control over Galatian bodies through a rhetoric that names difference but simultaneously subsumes it under an identity, Kaalund reconstructs how the Galatians talk back and identify themselves as both in Christ and of Christ—both spirit and flesh.

Whereas Kaalund's essay highlights Paul's imposition of the "in Christ" identity that erases the Galatians' (construction of) difference, Mitzi J. Smith's reading of Galatians 3:28 focuses on how Paul rhetorically constructs the identity of the Galatian believers on the "back" of slavery/enslavement in order to regain and defend his apostolic authority and to destroy the spell that the preachers of the *heteron euangelion* (other/different gospel) have over the Galatians. Reading Galatians from an African American and a womanist perspective, Smith asserts that Paul employs counterterror discourse of (re)enslavement to (1) construct his fellow preachers as enemies of *the* truth, troublemakers, dabblers in witchcraft, and enslavers; (2) respond to intra-group conflict using the enslaved/enslavement-freed/freeborn dichotomy as the framework for constructing an *in Christ* identity; and (3) support his moderate anti/proslavery stance, identifying himself as a *doulos Christou* (slave of Christ) who proclaims a liberating gospel. Smith's intersectional reading also critiques the Sarah/Hagar allegory as part of Paul's counterterror strategy whereby he argues that by accepting the *heteron euangelion* (and submitting to circumcision), the Galatian believers become Hagar's children and not sons of Abram. Hagar's children, Smith asserts, still *ain't* free from the oppression and stigma of enslavement. Smith's womanist back talk reveals Paul's counterterror discourse as insensitive to the cruel material realities of enslavement. She places in dialogue her reading of Galatians as counterterror narrative and the voices of Linda Brent and Frederick Douglass, through their slave narratives, and contemporary accounts about how Ivy League schools and institutions of theological education built, survived, and thrived on the backs of enslaved persons.

Both essays of Angela N. Parker and Jung H. Choi discuss women prophets in the *ekklēsiai* that Paul founded and in later churches and the processes of feminization and racialization/ethnicization. Parker addresses the feminization/minoritization of Paul, and Choi discusses racialization/ethnicization and how Paul's rhetoric by way of Origen has been used to feminize/paganize women prophets in Korean and Korean-American churches.

Parker's reader response and ideological analysis based on black feminist and womanist politics of empowerment places the relational power of the cross within the context of the Corinthian women's freedom as opposed to Paul's view of the cross that establishes the hierarchal order. Parker argues that while Paul rhetorically feminizes his Jewish masculine body as an enslaved female body over against the liberating stance of the Corinthian women prophets in 1 Corinthians 11, he actually exercises power employing mimetic language that forces the women prophets to bear the cross. Exposing Paul's rhetoric that dismisses the lived realities of the women's embodied identities, she then explores where the Corinthian woman prophets engage and push back against Paul's matrix of domination. This critical analysis of Paul and the Corinthian women prophets is extended to critiquing Western scholarship's epistemological viewpoint that promotes Paul's mimetic power and the ensuing "Europeanization" of Paul. Thinking through power, Parker's minoritized womanist interpretation displays activism and resistance, as well as contemporary black women's experience of power differential and unequal treatment.

Drawing on feminist and postcolonial biblical scholarship, Jung H. Choi explores how discussions of race, ethnicity, and gender are intertwined with discourses about prophecy in the New Testament and other early Christian texts and in contemporary Korean and Korean-American Christianity. She contends that discussions of prophecy in early Christianity served as a means of constructing identity, negotiating and renegotiating boundaries, and thus legitimizing or illegitimating certain religious practices. First, she examines Origen's discussions that associate "improper" prophecy with women and pagans, two lesser-than categories. The most common techniques for controlling prophetic practice in early Christianity are (1) the process of ethnic reasoning that constructs masculine Christianity as the moral/rational prophets, and (2) feminizing and paganizing the competing prophets as the Other. While feeling that she does not belong to either ecclesiastical worlds as a diaspora, Choi discovers that those techniques of feminization and paganization to oppress women prophets have been similarly used in the contemporary Korean and Korean-American churches, reinforced by colonial contexts.

Janette H. Ok's reading of 1 Peter 3:1–6 puts the experiences of first-century women in mixed marriages and that of Asian immigrant women in interracial marriages together in conversation. Ok argues that in 1 Peter 3:1–6 injunctions are given to Gentile Christian wives who face stereotypes of being family haters as a way to alleviate potentially violent conflict between the wives and their pagan husbands. In doing so, the author of 1 Peter attempts to disrupt essentializing Christian women as threats to their family's cohesion by exhorting them to be more chaste, virtuous, and family oriented than their Greco-Roman counterparts, while offering them the honorary status as "children of Sarah," a new ethno-religious identity through which a sense of agency emerges. While reading the Petrine household code as challenging the essentializing of negative stereotypes of Christian women through the idealizing and ethnicizing of certain behaviors, Ok also addresses the particular challenges of Asian immigrant women married to white

American men. As their identities are often homogenized and exoticized, such imposition leads them to construct their own idealized identities as opposed to white American women and the cultural stereotypes the dominant culture has of them. However, Ok argues that, unlike Christian wives in 1 Peter, idealizing and ethnicizing certain behaviors as a way to disrupt stereotypes and give a sense of personal agency may ironically lead to the essentializing of gender and idealization of whiteness and patriarchy.

The six contributors, from their own social locations as minoritized or nonwhite women biblical critics, engage early Christian texts and the historical narratives of their ancestors/ancestresses, contemporary, domestic, ecclesial/religious, sociopolitical, and global contexts in which minoritized women's bodies and identities are objectified, essentialized, and exploited, but also allow our stories and voices to be heard, to talk back, and to name and resist oppression.

Minoritized Women Reading Race and Ethnicity as choreographed performance does not end with publication. Our writing as embodied performance is enacted as readers engage our work. Every time an instructor creates a syllabus or teaches a course where the only voices represented are white and white performativity is treated as the authoritative norm, students of religious studies and biblical studies are bound more inextricably to systemic inequality and the ideology of white supremacy. An appropriate definition of performance relative to "cultural practice and the materiality of bodies—hence a displayed enactment of ideology and enfleshed knowledge—[is] influenced and motivated by the politics of race, gender, power, and class in the forms of folklore, ritual, spectacle, [creative] resistance, and protest."[32] In seminaries and divinity schools, in the study of religion, classrooms, syllabi, and libraries are sites of struggle where performance is choreographed as public event. Understanding performance in this way "invites investigations of performance as political struggle and resistance."[33] Our embodied written and read performance disrupts the normativity and de facto universality of dominant and mainstream epistemologies and their concomitant ideologies. "[I]deology is performatively constituted."[34] Our volume is unapologetically and overtly ideological. As "ethnic and racial minorities [we] insist on reading with . . . [our] own eyes and making . . . [our] own voices heard."[35] We hope our performance challenges readers and that it is performative in classrooms and churches.

NOTES

1. Herodotus, *Histories* 3.101.2, in *Race and Ethnicity in the Classical World. An Anthology of Primary Sources in Translation*, eds. and trans. Rebecca F. Kennedy, C. Sydnor Roy, and Max L. Goldman (Indianapolis: Hackett, 2013), 54.
2. Gay L. Byron, *Symbolic Blackness and Ethnic Difference in Early Christian Literature* (London: Routledge, 2002), 1.

3. Orlando Patterson, *Slavery as Social Death. A Comparative Study* (Cambridge, MA: Harvard University Press, 1982).

4. Byron, *Symbolic Blackness*, 1.

5. Cicero, *De Provinciis Consularibus,* 5:10; Josephus, *Jewish War,* 6.37–42. See Warren Carter, *The Roman Empire and the New Testament* (Nashville, TN: Abingdon Press, 2006), 10.

6. Byron, *Symbolic Blackness*, 39–44.

7. Buell maintains that in the second through early third centuries C.E. being a Christian was regarded as the new race in the Shepherd of Hermes, Clement of Alexandria, and Origen. Denise Kimber Buell, *Why This New Race: Ethnic Reasoning in Early Christianity* (New York: Columbia University Press, 2005). Sechrest argues that Paul created a third race within the context of Second Temple Judaism; Paul no long saw himself as a Jew, though this argument may be challenged by scholars who view the debates regarding Jews and the Gentiles in the Pauline churches, as well as the Jesus movement, within Judaism. Love L. Sechrest, *A Former Jew: Paul and the Dialectics of Race* (New York: T&T Clark, 2009).

8. Jonathan M. Hall, *Hellenicity: Between Ethnicity and Culture* (Chicago: University of Chicago Press, 2002), 9–10. Hall argues that a common consciousness of Greek ethnic, cultural identity was a relatively late development, reaching maturity after the Persian wars and through the unifying construction of the stereotype of the non-Greek barbarian.

9. Hall, *Hellenicity*, 9–10.

10. Paula Giddings, *Where and Where I Enter: The Impact of Black Women on Race and Sex in America* (New York: William Morrow, 1984).

11. Frantz Fanon, *Black Skin, White Masks* (New York: Grove, 1967), 113.

12. We find these similar social categories and processes in ancient texts. The ancients conquered, enslaved, colonized, and categorized peoples.

13. Karen E. Fields and Barbara Fields, *Racecraft: The Soul of Inequality in American Life* (London: Verso, 2014), 16.

14. Fields and Fields, *Racecraft*, 129.

15. Orlando F. Patterson, *Slavery and Social Death: A Comparative Study* (Cambridge, MA: Harvard University Press, 1982), 420 n. 14.

16. See Avtar Brah, *Cartographies of Diaspora: Contesting Identities* (London: Routledge, 1996); Madeline Y. Hsu, *Asian American History: A Very Short Introduction* (Oxford: Oxford University Press, 2017).

17. Sandra Bucerius, Michael Tonry, and Douglas S. Massey, "The Racialization of Latinos in the United States," in *The Oxford Handbook of Ethnicity, Crime, and Immigration*, eds. Sandra M. Bucerius and Michael Tonry (Oxford: Oxford University Press, 2014).

18. Enid Logan, "Rethinking Race. The Sociology of American Indian Identity," *Sociology*, August 16, 2019. https://cla.umn.edu/sociology/news-events/story/rethinking-race-sociology-american-indian-identity .

19. Fanon, *Black Skin, White Masks*, 110.

20. Joan Ferrante and Prince Browne, Jr., *The Social Construction of Race and Ethnicity in the United States*, 2nd ed. (Upper Saddle River, NJ: Prentice-Hall, 2001), 215.

21. Cain Hope Felder, *Troubling Biblical Waters: Race, Class, and Family* (Maryknoll, NY: Orbis, 1993), 10–11.

22. Felder, *Troubling Biblical Waters*, 37.

23. Felder, *Troubling Biblical Waters*, 37.

24. Denise Kimber Buell, "Anachronistic Whiteness and the Ethics of Interpretation," in *Ethnicity, Race, and Religion: Identities and Ideologies in Early Jewish and Christian Texts, and in Modern Biblical Interpretation*, eds. Katherine M. Hockey and David G. Horrell, 149–67 (New York: T&T Clark, 2018), 158.

25. See Mitzi J. Smith, "Paul, Timothy, and the Respectability Politics of Race: A Womanist Inter(con)textual Reading of Acts 16:1–5," *Religions* 10.3 (2019): 190.

26. Patricia Hill Collins and Sirma Bilge, *Intersectionality* (Cambridge, UK: Polity, 2016), 7. The term "intersectionality" was coined by legal expert and social activist Kimberlé Crenshaw ("Mapping the Margins: Intersectionality, Identity Politics, and Violence against Women of Color," *Stanford Law Review* 43 [1991]: 1241–99).

27. For example, Hockey and Horrell's edited volume addresses historical constructions of ethnicity and race in antiquity, particularly in relation to the identities of Jews and Christians, as well as critical analysis of scholarly ideologies and racial assumptions that have shaped biblical studies. Katherine M. Hockey and David G. Horrell, *Ethnicity, Race, Religion and Ideologies in Early Jewish and Christian Texts and in Modern Biblical Interpretation* (London: T&T Clark, 2019).

28. See Laura Nasrallah and Elisabeth Schüssler Fiorenza, eds. *Prejudice and Christian Beginnings: Investigating Race, Gender, and Ethnicity in Early Christianity* (Minneapolis: Fortress, 2009). The editors of this volume argue that scholars feel relatively comfortable discussing ethnicity in contrast to race and gender as modern categories but often fail to address "the question of how race and gender are involved in social and ideological constructions of Christianity" (5). They focus on exclusions of multiple marginalized subjects from feminist and antiracist work. Similar to this volume, the contributors to *Destabilizing the Margins* primarily read constructions of marginal biblical figures, like slaves, widows, the Ethiopian eunuch, rebellious widows, and the Pythian slave girl through the intersection of gender, sexuality, race/ ethnicity, and class, employing memory theory to analyze identity, injustice, violence, and inclusion/exclusion. Marianne Bjelland Kartzow, *Destabilizing the Margins: An Intersectional Approach to Early Christian Memory* (Eugene, OR: Wipf and Stock, 2012).

29. The report indicates that persons of African descent (men and women) in the U.S. constitute 4.2 percent of the members who responded to the survey; Asian descent, 3.39 percent; Latin American descent, 3.73 percent; Native or First Nations, 2.87 percent; and Native Hawaiian and Ocean descent, 0.23 percent. Society of Biblical Literature, 2019 SBL Membership Data, January 2019, https://www.sbl-site.org/assets/pdfs/sblMemberProfile2019. pdf. At the time of the survey, there were 8,324 active members with 67 percent completing it.

30. Abraham, "Critical Perspectives on Postcolonial Theory," in *The Colonized Apostle: Paul in Postcolonial Eyes*, ed. Christopher Stanley (Minneapolis: Fortress, 2011), 27.

31. Elizabeth A. Castelli, Gary A. Phillips, and Regina M. Schwartz, eds., *The Postmodern Bible: The Bible and Culture Collective* (New Haven, CT: Yale University Press, 1995), 239. Unmarked feminism is characterized by "white, middle-class, heterosexual, U.S woman as the norm."

32. Bryant K. Alexander, Gary L. Anderson, and Bernardo P. Gallegos, "Introduction: Performance in Education," in *Performance Theories in Education: Power, Pedagogy and the Politics of Identity*, eds. Bryant K. Alexander, Gary L. Anderson, and Bernardo P. Gallegos (Mahwah, NJ: Lawrence Erlbaum, 2005), 2.

33. Elyse Lamm Pineau, "Teaching Is Performance: Reconceptualizing a Problematic Metaphor," in *Performance Theories in Education. Power, Pedagogy and the Politics of Identity*, eds. Bryant K. Alexander, Gary L. Anderson, and Bernardo P. Gallegos, 33.

34. Peter L. McLaren, "On Ideology and Education: Critical Pedagogy and the Cultural Politics of Resistance," in *Critical Pedagogy, the State and Cultural Struggle*, eds. Henry Giroux and Peter L. McLaren (Albany: State University of New York Press, 1989), 191.

35. Fernando F. Segovia, *Decolonizing Biblical Studies: A View from the Margins* (Maryknoll, NY: Orbis, 2000), 167.

WORKS CITED

Abraham, Susan. "Critical Perspectives on Postcolonial Theory." In *The Colonized Apostle: Paul in Postcolonial Eyes*, edited by Christopher Stanley, 24–33. Minneapolis: Fortress, 2011.

Brah, Avtar. *Cartographies of Diaspora: Contesting Identities*. London: Routledge, 1996.

Buell, Denise Kimber. "Anachronistic Whiteness and the Ethics of Interpretation." In *Ethnicity, Race, and Religion: Identities and Ideologies in Early Jewish and Christian Texts, and in Modern Biblical Interpretation*, edited by Katherine M. Hockey and David G. Horrell, 149–67. New York: T&T Clark, 2018.

———.*Why This New Race: Ethnic Reasoning in Early Christianity*. New York: Columbia University Press, 2005.

Byron, Gay L. *Symbolic Blackness and Ethnic Difference in Early Christian Literature*. London: Routledge, 2002.

Carter, Warren. *The Roman Empire and the New Testament*. Nashville, TN: Abingdon, 2006.

Castelli, Elizabeth A., Gary A. Phillips, and Regina M. Schwartz, eds. *The Postmodern Bible: The Bible and Culture Collective*. New Haven, CT: Yale University Press, 1995.

Cicero. *Orations: Pro Caelio*. De Provinciis Consularibus. Pro Balbo, translated by R. Gardner, LCL, no. 447. Cambridge, MA: Harvard University Press, 1958.

Collins, Patricia Hill, and Sirma Bilge. *Intersectionality*. Cambridge, UK: Polity, 2016.

Crenshaw, Kimberlé. "Mapping the Margins: Intersectionality, Identity Politics, and Violence against Women of Color." *Stanford Law Review* 43 (1991): 1241–99.

Fanon, Frantz. *Black Skin, White Masks*. New York: Grove, 1967.

Felder, Cain Hope. *Troubling Biblical Waters: Race, Class, and Family*. Maryknoll, NY: Orbis, 1993.

Ferrante, Joan, and Prince Browne, Jr. *The Social Construction of Race and Ethnicity in the United States*. 2nd ed. Upper Saddle River, NJ: Prentice-Hall, 2001.

Fields, Karen E., and Barbara Fields. *Racecraft: The Soul of Inequality in American Life*. London: Verso, 2014.

Giddings, Paula J. *When and Where I Enter: The Impact of Black Women on Race and Sex in America* . New York: William Morrow, 1984.

Hall, Jonathan M. *Hellenicity: Between Ethnicity and Culture*. Chicago: University of Chicago Press, 2002.

Herodotus. *Histories* 3.101.2. In *Race and Ethnicity in the Classical World: An Anthology of Primary Sources in Translation*, edited and translated by Rebecca F. Kennedy, C. Sydnor Roy, and Max L. Goldman, 54. Indianapolis: Hackett, 2013.

Hockey, Katherine M., and David G. Horrell. *Ethnicity, Race, Religion and Ideologies in Early Jewish and Christian Texts and in Modern Biblical Interpretation*. London: T&T Clark, 2019.

Hsu, Madeline Y. *Asian American History: A Very Short Introduction*. Oxford: Oxford University Press, 2017.

Kartzow, Marianne Bjelland, ed. *Destabilizing the Margins: An Intersectional Approach to Early Christian Memory*. Eugene, OR: Wipf and Stock, 2012.

Kennedy, Rebecca F. C., Sydnor Roy, and Max L. Goldman, eds. and trans. *Race and Ethnicity in the Classical World: An Anthology of Primary Sources in Translation*. Indianapolis: Hackett, 2013.

Logan, Enid. "Rethinking Race. The Sociology of American Indian Identity." *Sociology*, August 16, 2019. https://cla.umn.edu/sociology/news-events/story/rethinking-race-sociology-american-indian-identity .

Massey, Douglas S. "The Racialization of Latinos in the United States." In *The Oxford Handbook of Ethnicity, Crime, and Immigration*, edited by Sandra M. Bucerius and Michael Tonry, 21–39. Oxford: Oxford University Press, 2014.

McLaren, Peter L. "On Ideology and Education: Critical Pedagogy and the Cultural Politics of Resistance." In *Critical Pedagogy, the State and Cultural Struggle*, edited by Henry A. Giroux and Peter L. McLaren, 174–202. Albany: State University of New York Press, 1989.

Nasrallah, Laura, and Elisabeth Schüssler Fiorenza. *Prejudice and Christian Beginnings: Investigating Race, Gender, and Ethnicity in Early Christianity*. Minneapolis: Fortress, 2009.

Patterson, Orlando. *Slavery as Social Death: A Comparative Study*. Cambridge, MA: Harvard University Press, 1982.

Pineau, Elyse Lamm. "Teaching Is Performance: Reconceptualizing a Problematic Metaphor." In *Performance Theories in Education. Power, Pedagogy and the Politics of Identity*, edited by Bryant K. Alexander, Gary L. Anderson, and Bernardo P. Gallegos, 15–39. Mahwah, NJ: Lawrence Erlbaum Associates, 2005.

Sechrest, Love L. *A Former Jew: Paul and the Dialectics of Race*. New York: T&T Clark, 2009.

Segovia, Fernando F. *Decolonizing Biblical Studies. A View from the Margins*. Maryknoll, NY: Orbis, 2000.

Smith, Mitzi J. "Paul, Timothy, and the Respectability Politics of Race: A Womanist Inter(con)textual Reading of Acts 16:1–5." *Religions* 10, no. 3 (2019): 190.

Society of Biblical Literature, 2019 SBL Membership Data, January 2019, https://www.sblsite.org/assets/pdfs/sblMemberProfile2019.pdf.

Chapter One

Weren't You with Jesus the Galilean?

An Intersectional Reading of Ethnicity, Diasporic Trauma, and Mourning in the Gospel of Matthew

Jin Young Choi

Biblical scholars' interest in ethnicity and ethnic terminology is not an entirely recent phenomenon, having emerged after World War II. Biblical scholarship on ethnicity came about in the 1980s only after ethnicity studies became an established field of study within the social sciences in 1970s.[1] Works on ethnicity in the Gospel of Matthew appeared beginning in the mid-1990s, mostly addressing how to understand Jewish and Christian identities or how to translate Greek words like *ethnē* ("Gentiles" or "nations") and *Ioudaioi* ("Jews" or "Judeans").[2] Much work has been done regarding the ethnic constitution of the Galileans, through providing historical and archeological evidences of the region.[3] These historical, exegetical, and archaeological interpretations using the interpretive framework of ethnicity do not, however, preclude the interpreters' agendas and interests. For example, the translation of *Ioudaioi* as "Jews" or "Judeans" is related to whether "religion" or "ethnicity" is primary and addresses an interest in the dis/continuity "between ancient *Ioudaioi* and modern Jews."[4]

In approaching the construction of race/ethnicity in the Gospel of Matthew, my basic assumption is that the "Jews" are never a monolithic entity. While Jesus is identified as a person from Nazareth (*Nazōraios*, 2:23; 26:71) or a Galilean (*Galilaios*, 26:69), he is also titled the King of the Jews or Judeans (*tōn Ioudaiōn*, 2:2; 27:11, 29, 37) in the gospel narrative. If Judea appears to be distinguished as a region from other places like Galilee and Samaria, the question is how Jesus's identities as a Galilean and as the king of the Judeans are negotiated. While more scholars now argue that even the

1

term "the Jews" is not merely a religious identity but an ethnic identity, how Matthew engages the construction of ethnicity, particularly in his description of "Galilee of the Gentiles" (*Galilaia tōn ethnōn*), has geopolitical, demographical, and linguistic significance.

In this chapter, I explore the shifting identities of Jesus, who was born an *Ioudaios* in Bethlehem, was displaced as a refugee in Egypt, relocated as a returnee in Nazareth, undertook a prophetic ministry in Galilee, and died as a king of the *Ioudaioi*. As the formation of one's ethnic identity in the ancient Greco-Roman society is inherently androcentric and patriarchal, Matthew's construction of Jesus's identity is not an exception. However, Jesus's ethnic identity based on genealogy, territorial allegiance, and kinship is constantly constructed and deconstructed. Engaging the intersection of race/ethnicity, gender, and empire, I focus on collective memories of the mothers' resolute mourning of their lost children in constructing ethnicity in Matthew, which illumines my reading in the present context where I encounter sufferings of the displaced, particularly of innocent children and their mothers.

RACE/ETHNICITY IN GRECO-ROMAN ANTIQUITY

Race and Ethnicity in Antiquity

Race began as the biological notion of dividing humankind, usually based on physical traits such as skin color.[5] Yet the idea of distinct and discrete "races" is no longer sustained due to the acknowledgement that scientific theories used to support the ideology of race have been proven and rejected as false. Thus, the theory of race is treated as pseudo-science or "a quasi-biological construct invented to establish a hierarchy of human groups and to delineate differences between them."[6] While sociologically discredited, however, the idea of race remains ideologically preeminent, especially in the U.S. context.[7] When such an idea is activated in belief, attitude, or practice, it lends itself to racism. The construction of race and racism attributes collective traits—physical, mental, and moral—which are "caused by hereditary factors or external influences, such as climate or geography," to establish the "superiority of one group over another."[8]

Because of the negative connotations of "race," scholars often use an alternative term, "ethnicity," as a politically correct term for "race." "Ethnicity" denotes group characteristic based on cultural characteristics such as national origin, ancestry, and language.[9] Ethnicity is mobilized when social and national disputes over the protection and advancement of culture occur.[10]

Now the question is whether the concepts of race and ethnicity are applicable to Greco-Roman antiquity, the milieu of Second Temple Judaism and early Christianity. Benjamin Isaac argues that the idea of race, as a modern construct, did not exist, but racism did in the form of proto-racism. If one finds arguments on the presumed superiority or inferiority of specific groups based on heredity or immutable exterior influences in classical literature, such a phenomenon can be regarded as proto-racism.[11] On the other hand, the concept of ethnicity existed in antiquity, as people determined group membership by distinguishing the group from other social collectivities. Ethnicity is often constructed through a "putative subscription to a myth of common descent and kinship, an association with a specific territory, and a sense of shared history."[12] As this "fictive" quality of origin, descent, and kinship determines an ethnic group, ethnicity is considered a relevant concept for understanding Jews and Christians in antiquity.[13] Ethnicity is a lens through which a group of people constructs the Self and the Other.

Josephus's illustration of the Jews is instructive in this regard. When Caesar made a decree approving Hyrcanus and his children as high priests (*ethnarchs*) who would rule the Jews (*Ioudaioi*) in Judea, the Jews are depicted as an *ethnos*—a people, who follow their ancestors' customs and the Jewish way of life.[14] As an *ethnos,* the Jews in Rome were also tolerated and even had the privilege to follow their ancestral customs.[15] Being allowed to practice their religion, therefore, their Jewish identity as a people (Lat. *gens*) was "inherited." Whether a religion is legitimate or not was "determined by birth and descent."[16] Therefore, by contrast, the Christians were viewed as not fully "a people," but as a sect whose cult was an "acquired religion," deserting the customs of their fathers.[17] Thus, "being" a Christian without any ethnic association was regarded as a crime and caused misunderstanding, hatred, and sometimes persecution. This is the context in which early Christians began to reason themselves a people or nation, using terms such as *genos* and *ethnos* and describing their distinct customs or cultures in relation or opposition to other groups of people.

Diversity of Ancient *Ioudaioi* in the Diaspora and in Palestine

As such, early Christians are depicted as a new nation (*ethnos*) that includes Jews and Greeks or Gentiles or as the "third race" that transcends racial/ethnic boundaries. This universal character of Christianity has functioned to fortify the antithetical perception of Judaism as an ethnoracially particular religion. However, Cynthia M. Baker argues that the identification of ancient *Ioudaioi* and *Yehudim* as an ethnic group was not exclusive, but rather they embodied multiple—often dual—lineages of birth, land, history, and culture.[18] Baker uses passages from Philo's *Flaccus* and *Embassy* to show that Jews living in colonies identified themselves as descendants of those locale's "founding fathers."[19] They shared the same ancestral and territorial identification with other local peoples. Thus, having "dual ethnicity" (e.g., a Syrian and Jew) was generally "over and against a singularly Jewish/Judean ethnicity."[20] "Jewish ethnicity" was no more particular or monolithic than "Hellenic ethnicity."

A discussion of the identification of *Ioudaioi* in Palestine could be more complicated. The majority of scholars translate *Ioudaioi* as "Jews" and also view Galileans (*Galilaioi*) as "Jews" since Jews had moved from Judea to Galilee since the Hasmonean expansion to the north.[21] On the other hand, scholars such as Richard A. Horsley hold a minority position that whereas *Ioudaioi* ("Judeans") "had lived under Jerusalem rule for centuries and under the laws of the temple-state since it was established under the Persian empire," Galileans as descendants of the northern Israelites had been "under separate rulers for centuries until they were brought under Jerusalem rule and subjected to 'the laws of the Judeans' in 104 BCE."[22] Therefore, Horsley does not consider the Galileans to have the same ethnic identity as the Judeans.

While Josephus distinguishes "the Galileans" as a separate *ethnos* from "the Judeans" and the "Idumeans,"[23] the claim of the common ethnic identity and culture of Judeans and Galileans as "Jews" overrides the argument of the distinctive identity of Galileans.[24] Moreover, when modern biblical scholars construct the ethnic identity of Jews in Judea and Galilee as "Jews" or "Jewish," there is a strong connotation of "religion" in this identification.[25] Whether the concept of Jews/Jewish is used to argue for a continuity between the historical past and present forms of Jewish identity, or displays the perception of "Judaism" as a religion over against "Christianity," both perspectives demonstrate contemporary concerns.[26] Scholars of the Bible and religion are particularly interested in the ethnicity of Galilee because of its paramount importance in the formation of Christianity and Rabbinic Judaism.

However, religion is only one aspect of ethnic identity, and other ethnic categories in early Christian expressions need to be explored. For example, Denis Duling discusses the broad semantic range of *"ethnos"* in ancient Greek and constructs a model that explores features of ethnicity in Matthew's gospel, such as name, myths of common ancestry, shared historical memories, kinship, phenotypical features, (home)land, common language, customs, and common religion and religious practices.[27] John Riches focuses on two particular ethnic markers—kinship and place—to illumine the "sense of identity" of the Matthean community.[28] I shall examine how Matthew constructs Jesus's identity also focusing on descent, kinship, and geopolitical notions, which in turn serve to deconstruct his identity, making it fluid and intersectional.

CONSTRUCTION OF JESUS'S ETHNIC IDENTITIES IN MATTHEW

The most pressing question consistently expressed in the gospel narrative is the identity of Jesus: "Who is this?" (*tis estin houtos*, cf. 21:10). Whether historical or literary criticism is employed, or a Jewish or Greco-Roman background is considered, such a question is framed in religious terms, particularly with regard to Christological issues such as the origin and development of understandings of Jesus, as well as various titles of Jesus. [29] While empire-critical scholars, like Warren Carter, interpret the Gospels' presentations of Jesus as challenging or subverting imperial theology, the discussion of imperial politics is also oriented toward religion. Can the portrayals of Jesus such as the son of David, the Son of God, and the Messiah be understood not only as theological or religious claims but also in terms of ethnic identification in the imperial context?

Matthew's gospel begins with Jesus's genealogy from Abraham to David, from David to exile to Babylon, and from the exile to the Messiah (1:1, 17). And the following birth narrative affirms Jesus as the Messiah by highlighting Joseph, Jesus's legal father, as a "son of David" (1:20). Since the Messiah should be of Davidic descent, Matthew also emphasizes Jesus's birth in Bethlehem, King David's hometown, according to the old prophecy (Matt. 2:6; Mich. 5:2; 2 Sam. 5:2). Thus, Jesus is the Messiah whom Israel has long awaited. Jesus's Davidic messiahship, and therefore the fulfillment of Hebrew scriptures, have been interpreted as Matthew's understanding of Jesus in continuity with Judaism. It is reasonable to place Matthew's discourse against the background of Formative Judaism, but I do not limit my argument to religious dynamics within Judaism. Instead, I give attention to such ethnic features in the narrative as birth, descent, kinship, and territorial allegiance. [30]

"Whose Son Is He?"

Matthew's story of Jesus begins with the genealogy (*genesis*, 1:1), an account of descent and birth. The word *gennei* (to beget) is repeatedly used to claim that Jesus is "the son of David" and "the Son of Abraham." [31] However, the pattern of "a father begot (*egennēsen*) a son" is broken in the account of Jesus's birth, "Joseph, husband of Mary from whom Jesus is begotten (*egennēthē*)," in the passive form (v. 16). The answer to "whose son is he" is convoluted. First, Joseph, "son of David" (v. 20), is depicted as more significant than in any other gospels, but he is only the legal father and disappears immediately after the infancy narrative. Even when the people of Jesus's hometown, Nazareth, raise the question of his origin, Joseph's name is not mentioned: "Is not this (*ouch houtos estin*) the carpenter's son?" (13:55; cf. John 6:42).

Second, Jesus is claimed as the son of David and of Abraham at the outset, but soon Jesus asserts, "Do not presume to say to yourselves, 'We have Abraham as our ancestor [*patera*]'." (3:9). Jesus is called "son of David" by people, especially in relation to his healing miracles (9:27; 15:22; 20:30; 21:9, 15): "Can this be the son of David"? (*mēti houtos estin*, 12:23). According to the Israelite tradition, this title is definitely related to the Davidic Messiah. Asking, "Whose son is he [the Messiah]?", however, Jesus argues that the Messiah cannot be the son of David because the latter called the former the Lord (22:42). This statement contradicts his identity as the son of David in the genealogy. The notion of descent—Jesus as the son of David and Israel as the children of Abraham (3:9; 8:11)—is affirmed, decentered, and redefined throughout the narrative.

Finally, it is God who declares Jesus as the Son of God: "This is (*houtos estin*) my Son, the Beloved" (3:17; 17:5). Therefore, it is presented as one of the most reliable statements in the whole narrative. Jesus identifies himself as the "son" of God: "For whoever does the will of my father in heaven is my brother and sister and mother" (12:50).[32] Indeed, Jesus is rejected by his family and kin and negates the established kinship system, and reconstitutes his family.[33] However, Jesus, the Son of God and king of the *Ioudaioi*, is mocked by the bandits, the Judean authorities, and passersby (27:32–43). The Father God does not respond to the Son's cry (v. 46).[34]

Whereas the genealogy and birth narrative show the fictive nature of Jesus's ancestry in order to demonstrate the legitimacy of his Davidic kingship, such invented heredity and kinship are continually decentered. Matthew's Jesus appears to dissociate not only from his family (*oikia*) but also from his country (or "fatherland," *patris*, 13:57). One can see that such ancient kinship language and practice (father, son, brother [meaning family], fatherland, inheritance) are inherently androcentric.

"Where Is the Messiah Born?"

The language of origin (*gennei*) is used to indicate not only the patriarchal lineage but also regional allegiance. The place where Jesus is from would determine whether he is "King of the Jews" and the Messiah (2:2, 4; cf. John 7:42). Jesus is born in Bethlehem of Judea, King David's hometown (*Ioudaia*, 2:1, 5, 22). Yet, as Jesus's identity as the son of David becomes ambiguous, Bethlehem as his geographical origin is quickly decentered in the following episodes.

According to the direction of an angel of the Lord, Jesus and his family escape King Herod's threat to Egypt. Upon Herod's death they return, but not to Bethlehem. Matthew depicts that Jesus "makes his home" (*katōkēsen*) in Nazareth in northern Galilee, knowing that Archelaus rules over Judea (*basileuei tēs Ioudaias*, vv. 19–23). Only when John the Baptist is arrested, does Jesus once again make his home (*katōkēsen*) in Capernaum (4:13). Hence, he is later dubbed "[the prophet] Jesus from Nazareth in Galilee" (21:11), "Jesus the Galilean" (26:69), and "Jesus of Nazareth" (26:71).[35] However, Nazareth, his new "fatherland" (*patris*, 13:54, 57), rejects him, and in response, Jesus repeatedly renounces his kin and hometown (11:23; 12:48–50; 13:57).[36] Despite prevailing notions of Jesus's ethnic identity as a Judean, Nazarene, and Galilean, traditional theological interpretation only highlights the title the King of the Jews as having Christological significance.

Wongi Park critiques this theological interpretation overemphasizing the title "king" of the Jews, which signifies Jesus's religious identity over against the ethnoracial dimensions of "the Judeans." According to Park, such a theological interpretation stresses the use of the title, "the King of the Jews," as to communicate with a Gentile audience the truth that Jesus is the Jewish Messiah—or the narrative effect that Jesus's true identity as King of the Jews is affirmed ironically by mockery (27:11, 29, 37, 42).[37] Park criticizes such an interpretation as a deracializing discourse because, by representing Jesus as ethnoracially unmarked, Matthean scholarship not only perpetuates a "deracializing logic that drives the dominant narrative of a universal Christianity transcending ethnoracial particularity" but also "reveals a strategic alignment between whiteness and Christianness through a politics of invisibility."[38] In other words, Jesus is depicted as non-ethnic/non-racial but ends up whitewashed as white, since to have "no race" is actually to be white, which is normative. Instead, Park constructs Jesus's ethnoracial identity as a marginalized Judean. He asserts that the hailing of Jesus as *ho basileus tōn Ioudaiōn* is not a messianic title but a racial slur that signifies the inferiority of the Jews, especially considering the Roman execution of Jesus on the cross in public is a "minoritizing act of imperial domination."[39]

While for Park Jesus's ethnoracial identity is constructed in light of the oppositional framework of imperial dominance over marginalized Judeans, I further consider the impact of colonial politics in Palestine or among *Ioudaioi*, which causes different territorial alliances between Judeans and Galileans. While scholars provide biblical and archeological evidence of Galilee's settlement history starting from Assyria's conquest, I only highlight the territorial divisions that occurred in Palestine near Jesus's time.[40]

The *ethnos* under the Hasmonean dynasty was divided into five regions governed by each Sanhedrin (*synedrion*) from 57–55 B.C.E.[41] With the support of Rome, Herod as King of the Jews ended the Hasmonean rule in 40 B.C.E. After Herod's death in 4 B.C.E., his kingdom was divided among (and inherited by) his sons in four regions. Herod Antipas ruled Galilee and Perea until 39 C.E.; and Herod Archelaus ruled Judea, Samaria, and Idumea, but when the Roman emperor Augustus removed him from the throne in 6 C.E., his territories were incorporated into a Judean province under direct Roman rule. Although all in Judea, Galilee, and other places would share collectively an experience of the wars against Rome in 66–73 C.E. and 132–36, it can be assumed that Judeans and Galileans had distinct allegiances to their own *patrides* throughout the processes of settlements and imposed divisions by imperial/colonial forces.[42]

"This Is Jesus, the King of the Jews"

Whom is Jesus king of? The Judeans, the Galileans, or all of the Jews? When Jesus's Davidic sonship and his origin in Bethlehem are claimed, it seems that Jesus is legitimately the Messiah for whom Israel has awaited. Yet, after Herod's death, the Galilean Jesus lives under the rule of Herod Antipas and later is tried as the king of the Judeans. It is when Jesus enters Jerusalem that Jesus's place of origin is labeled by others. First, he is recognized by the multitudes as the prophet: "'Who is this *(tis estin houtos)*?' The crowds were saying, 'This is the prophet Jesus from Nazareth in Galilee'" (21:10). In the city of Jerusalem where colonial and local powers are concentrated, his identity as a Galilean prophet or a leader of the popular movement in the village becomes distinct. For the chief priest and the whole Sanhedrin, this seeming leader of Galilean rebels could not be the Messiah, so they browbeat Jesus into admitting that his identity and activities are unsettled: "'[T]ell us if you are the Messiah, the Son of God.' Jesus said to him, 'You have said so'" (26:63–64).[43] I read Jesus's reply as "it is you who have said so," not as a virtual acknowledgement of his own identity as the Messiah. Identifying Jesus's messiahship or kingship is not so simple, as his ethnic identity continues to be challenged.

Peter's association with this ethnicized Jesus endangers Peter. Sitting outside the Judean courtroom, a servant girl recognizes him: "You also were with Jesus the Galilean" (26:69). Another slave girl says to the bystanders, "This man was with Jesus of Nazareth" (v. 71). Peter denies being related to this Galilean "man" both times. The third-time allegation of Peter is poignant: "Clearly you are also *one of them*, for your *accent (lalia)* betrays you" (v. 73). Ethnic markers of geopolitical allegiance and language distinguish Jesus, Peter, and "them."[44] The presence of the Other is loudly visible. It is apparent that the "king of the Judeans" is not just a racial/ethnic slur from the Roman perspective, but also shows that a king from Galilee, not from Bethlehem of Judea, is unacceptable for the Judeans. Jesus appears as an illegitimate king.

I have argued that the identification of Jesus as the Davidic Messiah is ambiguous in Matthew's narrative. Such conflicting identifications not only deconstruct the fixed ethnic identity of Jesus but also challenge the dominant perceptions of ethnicity within and without the *Ioudaioi*. I do not mean that Matthew intends to deconstruct the dominant way of constructing ethnicity. His views accord with how human origin and relationship are conceived and constructed, and how the society is organized and maintained. Ethnic identity is defined by patriarchal lineage (fathers beget sons). A father gives a name to a son (1:21, 25). The sons inherit the father's status and territories (2:22; 21:37–38). A family is represented by brothers (25:40). Ethnicity is attached to a "fatherland" (*patris*). Kings of the earth hold status, wealth, and power, exploiting the conquered (11:8; 17:25; 18:23) and judging *ethnē*.

Although on the surface, Matthew's language and identifications of ethnicity are androcentric, patriarchal, and kyriarchal, our reading can provide an alternative constructive model of ethnicity. Among members of those *ethnē*, there are women listed in Jesus's ancestry: Tamar, Ruth, Rahab, and the wife of Uriah, Bathsheba (1:3, 5, 6). Even commentators notice the significance of the Gentile or problematic women's inclusion in the genealogy; pointing out only one example may be enough for my discussion. Baker contends that, for example, Ruth is transfigured into a Jewish ancestor, still holding her "Moabite" ethnicity.[45] Here is the intersection of gender and (hybrid or multiple) ethnic identity. Furthermore, Joseph does not beget Jesus, but it is Mary who bears (*tiktei*) a son, King of the Jews (1:21, 23, 25; 2:2). Jesus does not inherit his (legal) father's trade and demands renouncing one's family (13:55; 19:28–29). He is rejected by his kin and *patris*, and his home continuously changes.[46] He re-creates his family with no human patriarch except the heavenly Father. Kinship and the right of inheritance are not based on bloodlines but are for those who do God's will (5:5; 12:50; 21:43; 25:32–34, 40). Kingship is represented not by status, wealth, and power, but by meekness and care for the lowly (21:5).

In addition to focusing on Matthew's construction of ethnicity that resists the fixed identification of Jesus's ethnicity, therefore, I propose an intersectional re-reading of the gospel. My reading highlights matriarchal lineage, displacement, and also memory and mourning as a form of historical knowledge of the people's root. As Marianne Bjelland Kartzow argues, given ancient sources, substantial interest in the elite, intersectionality can provide "tools to unpack the rhetoric of the given text" and suggest alternative ways of reading.[47]

READING ETHNICITY IN MATTHEW INTERSECTIONALLY

Halvor Moxnes employs an intersectional approach to the ethnicity of Galilee in which identities are produced, upheld, and contested.[48] For him, locality is an important factor in constructing ethnicity because a place is not just a geographical space but where relations and power structures are challenged and negotiated. In order to destabilize the image of a religiously defined, monolithic Jewish Galilee, he applies David Harvey's distinction between two models of spatial practices—"domination and control of space" and "appropriation and use of space."⁴⁹ While Herod Antipas and the Galilean elites are the model of the former that fosters "multiple and interrelated forms of oppression," Jesus, a different type of lord/master for liberation, presents the latter model "of more egalitarian forms of inclusion/exclusion and boundary making."⁵⁰ While recognizing the invisibility of women, as well as the important role of gender in the gendered space of the Galilean household, Moxnes actually reinscribes women's space in the household by idealizing Jesus's inclusion of distinctive women in that "alternative structure of social identities."⁵¹ A feminist intersectional reading of the Gospel of Matthew is aware of the significance of space where powers are negotiated and contested without being satisfied with pointing out the invisibility of women in the text or confining women in the domestic sphere.

Power Never Dies

In order to see how women, particularly mothers, in Matthew enter the public space, I return to the scene of a power struggle between two kings. What are the political implications of claiming Jesus as King of the Jews before Israel's current ruler, Herod the Great, who bears the title *basileus*?⁵² The king is alerted by the magi's report of the arrival of his rival king. The question is not only about kingship but also about ethnicity: "who is king by right of birth?" (Matt. 2:1–3).⁵³ While the immediate context is the tyrannical reign of Herod the Great rather than the Roman emperor, the contestation between Herod and Jesus is still viewed in the Roman imperial context. Herod the Great was appointed King of the Jews by the Roman Senate in 40 B.C.E.,⁵⁴ and he and his successors were Rome's client rulers. Matthew may not directly challenge or intend to subvert Rome, but he must have been aware of Roman *imperium*—the sovereign power of the empire—even when he portrays Jesus as the Davidic Messiah according to Jewish tradition.⁵⁵

Herod's initial response to the magi's report is agitation, a response shared "with all Jerusalem" (2:3). Herod also immediately calls all the chief priests and scribes of the people, who represent Jerusalem (v. 4). Thus, Jerusalem, the center of political and religious power, appears to be collectively troubled. Herod learns from those scripture specialists that the Messiah, King of the Jews, was born in Bethlehem, but the magi did not comply with Herod's design (vv. 7–12). His attempt to seek and destroy Jesus fails, but not without a cost. Matthew 2:13 and verses 19–20 have almost the same motif, structure, and wording.

> 2:13 Now after they had left,
> an angel of the Lord appeared to Joseph in a dream and said,
> "Get up, take the child and his mother, and flee to Egypt, and remain there until I tell you;
> for Herod is about to search for (*zētein*) the child, to destroy him."

2:19–20 When Herod died,
an angel of the Lord suddenly appeared in a dream to Joseph in Egypt and said,
"Get up, take the child and his mother, and go to the land of Israel,
for those who were seeking (*zēteountes*) the child's life are dead."

Since it is Herod who died, not the chief priests and scribes who colluded with him, the description "those who were seeking the child's life are dead" suggests the collapse of the system. Yet in actuality powers do not die. Since Herod's successor, Archelaus, reigns in Judea, Joseph takes Jesus and Mary to Galilee instead of Bethlehem.

The Lost Ones

The scheme of Herod, the vassal king of the Roman Empire, to "destroy" (*apollymi*) the newborn king Jesus (2:13) is closely connected to the destructiveness of the imperial/colonial rule. The chief priests and the elders, as well as the Pharisees, are not just Jewish religious leaders, but the nation's political elites in collaboration with Rome's client rulers. Later in Matthew, these elites conspire to destroy Jesus and even manipulate the multitudes to kill him (12:14; 27:1, 20). What is striking is that the object of "destroying" is not only Jesus, but also the people of Israel. The people are referred to as "lost" (*ta apolōta*, 10:6; 15:24), and Jesus understands that his mission and that of his disciples is to be sent to the "lost sheep of the house of Israel" (cf. 18:11). If we consider "lost" not merely as meaning "astray" but as "destroyed," the political meaning of this expression is apparent.

Matthew 2:6 said the King of the Jews born in Bethlehem would "shepherd" God's people, Israel, as a ruler, according to the prophecy:

> In Bethlehem of Judea; for so it has been written by the prophet: "And you, Bethlehem, in the land of Judah, are by no means least among the rulers of Judah; for from you shall come a ruler who is to shepherd my people Israel."

Note the contrast between Herod the Great, who is destroying the newborn king, and Jesus, who is expected to shepherd the people who suffer under the destructive power of colonial rule. They are lost/destroyed.

In describing the multitudes (*ochlos*), the sheep of Israel (cf. 15:32), Matthew's primary concern may not be either Israel's failure as the covenant people or the issue of Israel versus the Gentiles in terms of Christian mission, but the destruction of the people by political/religious powers.

> 9:35–36 Then Jesus went about all the cities and villages, teaching in their synagogues, and proclaiming the good news of the kingdom, and curing every disease and every sickness. When he saw *the crowds* (*ochlos*), he had compas-

sion for them, because they were harassed and helpless, like *sheep* without a shepherd.[56]

Jesus also says that it is not the will of God that one of the little ones (*tōn mikrōn*) should be lost or destroyed (18:14). Matthew 18 is known as Jesus's teaching of "welcoming a child" (*paidion*) or the little one that went astray and may be read as community ethics. However, Matthew's use of *paidion*, nine times for Jesus, signals to the audience that he was not welcomed by the political powers.

Having heard Matthew's story, the audience also recognizes that the little ones were lost or destroyed after the magi did not follow Herod's directive to return to him.[57] The child (*paidion*) Jesus is not destroyed, but instead "all of the children (*paidas*) in Bethlehem and in all of its regions" were killed. The word children (*pais/paidas*) here is not gender specific and may include girl babies, as well.[58] They are the least ones among the lost sheep in Matthew's narrative.[59] Hence, the slaughtered infants, the lost sheep, and the unwelcomed baby Jesus are depicted as sharing the same fate.

Yet Jesus fled to Egypt, according to an angel's direction, in fulfillment of Hosea 11:2: "Out of Egypt I have called my son." Sadly, the destruction of so many sons—and daughters—is also the fulfillment of the prophet Jeremiah (2:18):

> A voice was heard in Ramah [in the regions of Bethlehem], wailing and loud lamentation, Rachel weeping for her children [*tekna*]; she refused to be consoled, because they are no more.

Interweaving Stories of Rachels

How could we understand the flipside of the fulfillments—the massive destruction of the innocent infants and the deliverance of the newborn king Jesus? Jesus's escape to Egypt as a political refugee reminds the audience of Pharaoh's decree to kill all the Hebrew male children (Exod. 1:15–22). Just as Moses was rescued from the sacrifice of the Hebrew babies, Jesus is delivered while the infants in Bethlehem were sacrificed. However, instead of fleeing from Egypt like Moses, Jesus finds refuge in Egypt. How is this a fulfillment of the prophecy? Doesn't this salvation story sound oppressive? Rather than solely focusing on the fulfillment of Jewish prophecy itself or continuity between Judaism and Christianity, I read this fulfillment motif as retelling and interweaving stories of the past and the present.[60]

On her journey from Bethel to Ephrath (Bethlehem), as death came upon her through childbirth, Rachel experienced deep sorrow when leaving her son, whom she named *Ben-oni*, meaning "son of my sorrow" (Gen. 35:18), Jeremiah retells her story (Jer. 31:15). In the Genesis story, Rachel was buried in a tomb, but for Jeremiah, her wailing does not cease. He retells the story of Rachel refusing to be consoled because of the loss of the children. Rachel is not the mother of *Ben-oni*, but the mother of the nation of Judah. Rachel, as the mother of many children, sent in exile is given hope by Jeremiah because her children will return to their mother, and their land.

Now Matthew retells the story of Rachel. She weeps because her children have been killed. How can Jesus's escape and survival be good news? Could they, who resist being consoled, finally be comforted? For Jeremiah, the mother should refrain from weeping, because her children will return from exile. However, Matthew ends the Jeremiah citation with Rachel's resolute refusal to be consoled because her children will not return. Instead of the children returning, Jesus returns to his *patris*.

> Jer. 31:17 . . . your children shall come back to their own *country* (38:17, LXX).
> Matt. 2:20 . . . take the child and his mother, and go to the *land* of Israel.

Thus, in Matthew's narrative, the mothers who lost their children keep weeping—collectively but silently—leaving their children behind in sorrow, being separated from their children, and seeing their babies killed. They resist being comforted and no one comforts them. Just as their children "are no more," the mothers are "no more." They became nonexistent. Although Matthew is the gospel of presence—God's Emmanuel in Jesus, God with us—the mothers' sons are absent—as are the mothers.

Empire Cannot Kill the Soul

But Rachel's story is not yet finished. Jesus as a refugee survives the sacrifices of the infants in Bethlehem. He is displaced and re-placed to Nazareth, a town of Galilee. Jesus is relocated one more time to Capernaum, which Matthew depicts as the land of "Galilee of the Gentiles" in 4:14–16 so that what had been spoken through the prophet Isaiah might be fulfilled: "Land of Zebulun, land of Naphtali, on the road by the sea, across the Jordan, Galilee of the Gentiles—the people who sat in darkness have seen a great light, and for those who sat in the region and shadow of death light has dawned."[61]

What implications does Jesus's presence as Emmanuel have in the shadow of death? Just like the Bethlehem mothers, people sit in darkness in Galilee. Death passed over its intended target, Jesus, in Matthew 2. The light has dawned for those who live in the shadow of death through Jesus's ministry. But after his ministry in Galilee of the *ethnē*, Jesus walks into darkness; death will not pass over him again. He is killed on the cross as both a presumed leader of Galilean rebels and the king of Judeans. When the innocent deaths of the children and their mothers' resolute mourning are almost buried in oblivion at the end of the narrative, another mother weeps in silence

over her son's "innocent" death (cf. 27:19). She joins the silent resistance of
the Bethlehem mothers. They may know that there are and will be other
mothers who wail and weep for the losses of their children, as long as the
empire exists. These mothers mourn not in the house, but in the public square
and in the memory of the least and the disposable who do not have a place in
the official history.

Jesus also says, "Do not fear those who kill the body but cannot kill the
soul; rather fear him who can *destroy* both soul and body in hell" (10:28; cf.
v. 39; 16:25).[62] Although the empire can destroy the body of the subjected
people, it cannot kill the soul (*psychē*). The bodies of the subjected people,
including the body of Jesus, are crushed by imperial power, but their souls
and "lives" cannot be killed. Jesus sided with the wretched multitudes living
in the shadow of death in the peripheries of empire to the extent that he was
finally destroyed just like the innocent children. In this respect, Jesus stands
with the punishable or perishable bodies. His resurrection demonstrates that
the soul cannot be killed.

Matthew's Jesus neither speaks about the body/soul dualism nor the re-
suscitation of soul. Rather, I read Jesus's saying about the unquenchable soul
similar to the concept of *han* in Korean minjung theology. Similar to the
multitudes (*ochlos*) in the Gospels, minjung (the "masses of people") is the
politically oppressed, economically exploited, and socially alienated people.
Han is often defined as a collective feeling of unsettled resentment in the
situation of ineffable suffering of minjung, which is often associated with
national calamities.[63]

A second-generation minjung theologian, Jin-Ho Kim, relates *han* to minjung's psychological and linguistic experiences. Minjung are the outsiders of
the social system and thus belong nowhere. They are nonexistent beings.
Since the language of minjung is stolen by the dominant system, they cannot
describe their experiences of exclusion and discrimination. They suffer either
aphasia or speak only the language of the other—the powerful.[64] When they
speak, they internalize the imposed mechanism of exclusion. While deprived
of language, they speak nonverbally or in distorted language. Such *han*-
ridden abnormal utterances of the nameless and the helpless cannot communicate in the society but only to the heavens.[65]

The mothers' voice in Matthew 2 is heard but not actually heard; they
continue to wail loudly in the children's absence. Their unheard cries and
suppressed feelings are similar to minjung's nonverbal language. The cries of
minjung are the wretchedness of *han*, or the soul that cannot be killed by the
empire. In this sense, the mothers' uninterrupted lamenting and refusal to be
consoled exhibit a form of agency. Some ask if there are minjung today. It is
not that minjung are absent, but the social memory of, or witness to, minjung
has waned. Minjung theologians argue that the role of theology is to hear the
suppressed language or *han* of minjung.

SEARCHING FOR MEMORIES OF OUR MOTHERS

Bringing minjung theology and black and womanist theologies together in the global context, Mitzi Smith speaks of a womanist *materology* that says, "I cannot let my neighbor's children starve if I can help it."[66] The black mother embodies this, incarnating a living God in her "body baptized in suffering but anointed by an undying Spirit of love and perseverance, despite and because of living among the masses"—masses of black peoples who "continue to subsist anywhere near the superficial poverty line, are subjected to systemic profiling and racism, do not earn a living wage, have limited or no access to quality education or health care, and are inequitably treated within the justice system."[67] Smith's womanist materology, along with black women's struggle for reproductive justice, shed light on our intersectional reading of ethnicity in Matthew's gospel.

Jesus's shifting identities—his displacement as a refugee, his replacement as a returnee, and his new identity as one from Nazareth—are related to the event of the massacre of infants—boys and girls—in Bethlehem. His identity as King of the Jews is not just a religious claim but is understood in light of these political, diasporic events. He escaped but finally will not escape death. Many share Rachel's mourning in the form of aphasia, in traumas of losing their children throughout history, inviting us to join in collective mourning and resisting the power of death that attempts to kill the souls of minjung. Whereas Matthew cannot be free from the patriarchal and kyriarchal conventions in constructing Galilee of the *ethnē* in relation to *Ioudaioi*, as well as the ethnic identity of Jesus, my intersectional reading is an act of remembering our mothers in the public square. Jesus is the son of Rachel, Tamar, Ruth, Rahab, Bathsheba, and Mary; of the Hebrew mothers and Palestine mothers; and of black mothers, Honduran mothers, and unnamed mothers elsewhere in the globe.[68]

There are mothers who mourn unmourned deaths. Sara Ahmed writes, "The containment of the bodies of others affected by this economy of fear is most violently revealed in the literal deaths of those seeking asylum in containers, deaths that remain *unmourned* by the very nations who embody the promise of a future for those seeking asylum."[69] She continues to argue that it is "the global economies of fear" that construct "those who are 'without home' as sources of 'our fear' and as reasons for new forms of border policing, whereby the future is always a threat posed by others who may pass by and pass their way into our communities."[70] This is the fear that captured King Herod, Herod Antipas, and Pontius Pilate, as well as the Judean political authorities. Jesus without a home walked into the home of the estranged *ethnē*, as well as the lost sheep, in Galilee. And he left Galilee and walked into darkness as the unquenchable soul: "For those who sat in darkness— shadow of death, light has dawned" (4:16). Those who embody and inherit the mothers' resistance in solidarity do not give up the promise of a future for those seeking asylum, seeking light and life.

NOTES

1. See David M. Miller, "Ethnicity Comes of Age: An Overview of Twentieth-Century Terms for *Ioudaios,*" *Currents in Biblical Research* 10, no. 2 (2012): 293–311.
2. David Sim, "Christianity and Ethnicity in the Gospel of Matthew," in *Ethnicity and the Bible*, ed. Mark G. Brett (Leiden, Netherlands: E. J. Brill, 1996), 172–96; John K. Riches, *Conflicting Mythologies: Identity Formation in the Gospels of Mark and Matthew* (Edinburgh, UK: T&T Clark, 2000); Dennis C. Duling, "Ethnicity, Ethnocentrism, and the Matthean *Ethnos,*" *Biblical Theology Bulletin* 35, no. 4 (2005): 125–43. Also see a general discussion of *Ioudaios* in John M. G. Barclay, "Ἰουδαῖος: Ethnicity and Translation," in *Ethnicity, Race, Religion: Identities and Ideologies in Early Jewish and Christian Texts, and in Modern Biblical Interpretation*, ed. Katherine M. Hockey and David G. Horrell (London: T&T Clark, 2019), 46–58.
3. One recent publication is David A. Fiensy and James Riley Strange, eds., *Galilee in the Late Second Temple and Mishnaic Periods, vol. 2: The Archaeological Record from Cities, Towns, and Villages* (Minneapolis: Fortress, 2015).
4. Mark Chancey, "The Ethnicities of Galilee," in *Galilee in the Late Second Temple and Mishnaic Periods, vol. 1: Life, Culture, and Society*, ed. David A. Fiensy and James Riley Strange (Minneapolis: Fortress Press, 2014), 117–18; citing Amy-Jill Levine, *The Misunderstood Jew: The Church and the Scandal of the Jewish Jesus* (New York: HarperCollins, 2006), 159–66.
5. Richard Delgado and Jean Stefancic, *Critical Race Theory: An Introduction* (New York: New York University Press, 2001), 153; Steven Fenton, *Ethnicity*, Key Concepts (Cambridge, UK: Polity), 113.
6. Benjamin Isaac, *The Invention of Racism in Classical Antiquity* (Princeton, NJ: Princeton University Press, 2004), 33.
7. Robert Miles and Malcolm Brown, *Racism*, 2nd ed. (New York: Routledge, 2003), 94; See Jonathan M. Hall's explanation in his *Ethnic Identity in Greek Antiquity* (Cambridge, UK: Cambridge University Press, 2000), 19. "[T]he term 'race' was replaced by another—most often, 'ethnic group'. However, in many cases it was also quite clear that this new use was purely cosmetic, and that the basic conceptual apparatus of 'race' had remained, despite a change in terminology."
8. Isaac, *Invention of Racism*, 23, 37.
9. Miles and Brown, *Racism*, 93; Delgado and Stefancic, *Critical Race Theory*, 146.
10. Fenton, *Ethnicity*, 114. Miles and Brown define "ethnicisation as a dialectical process by which meaning is attributed to socio-cultural signifiers of human beings, as a result of which individuals may be assigned to a general category of persons which reproduces itself biologically, culturally and economically. Where biological and/or somatic features (real or imagined) are signified, we speak of racialisation as a specific modality of ethnicisation" (*Racism*, 99).
11. Unlike proto-racism, ethnic prejudice occurs when the "assumed causes of qualitative differences are human actions or social relations within people's own control." Isaac, *Invention of Racism*, 33–38.
12. Jonathan M. Hall, *Hellenicity: Between Ethnicity and Culture* (Chicago: Chicago University Press, 2000), 9–10.
13. Cynthia M. Baker, "From Every Nation under Heaven," in *Prejudice and Christian Beginnings: Investigating Race, Gender, and Ethnicity in Early Christianity*, ed. Laura Narsrallah and Elisabeth Schüssler Fiorenza (Minneapolis: Fortress, 2009), 82.
14. Josephus, *Jewish Antiquities*, 14.10.2 (194–95): "I will that Hyrcanus, the son of Alexander, and his children, be *ethnarchs* of the Jews, and have the high priesthood of the Jews forever, according to the customs of their forefathers [*kata ta patria ethē*], and that he and his son be our confederates; and . . . reckoned among our particular friends. . . . [I]f at any time

hereafter there arise any questions about the Jewish way of life [*Ioudaiōn agōgēs*], I will that he [Hyrcanus] determine the same."

15. Isaac, *Invention of Racism*, 449. Despite the privilege, there existed ethnic prejudice and stereotypes toward Jewish people.

16. Isaac, *Invention of Racism*, 491.

17. Isaac, *Invention of Racism*, 84–88.

18. Baker, "From Every Nation," 81, quoting Hall, *Hellenicity*, 2. She argues that "the identification of Jews by diverse ethnic-geographic signifiers occurs in all manner of Greek and Semitic (Hebrew and Aramaic) writings by Jews in the Hellenistic and Roman periods" (83).

19. Baker, "From Every Nation," 91.

20. Baker, "From Every Nation," 90.

21. It is argued that the settlers prior to the Hasmonean annexation were the descendants of the pagans who had arrived during the Persian, Ptolemaic, and Seleucid periods, but new settlers from Judea caused demographic changes in Galilee. Chancey, "Ethnicities of Galilee," 116–17.

22. Richard A. Horsley, *Jesus and the Politics of Roman Palestine* (Columbia: University of South Carolina Press, 2014), 136. Also, Horsley develops the same argument elsewhere in *Galilee: History, Politics, People* (Valley Forge, PA: Trinity, 1995), and *Archaeology, History and Society in Galilee: The Social Context of Jesus and the Rabbis* (Valley Forge, PA: Trinity, 1996).

23. Horsley, *Archaeology, History and Society*, 27.

24. Yet the counterargument can be made: "There is no evidence, however, of mass migration of Judeans northward into Galilee during the chaotic last decades of the Hasmoneans and the reign of Herod." Horsley, *Jesus and Politics*, 136. Chancey supports the idea of the same ethnic identity of Judean and Galilean based on the evidence of shared material culture, but does not deny the existence of Gentiles in Galilee as the result of some critical historical events. "Ethnicities of Galilee,"122.

25. Barclay argues that while modern scholarship tends to distinguish ethnic and religious identities, Josephus's understanding of *Ioudaios* and other related terms shows that ethnicity is an "inherently malleable" concept just like that of religion as complex. Likewise, the meanings of "Jews" and "Judeans" overlap and can be used interchangeably. Barclay, "Ἰουδαῖος."

26. Halvor Moxnes, "Identity in Jesus' Galilee—From Ethnicity to Locative Intersectionality," *Biblical Interpretation* 18, no. 4 (2010): 392, 398. Moxnes quotes Sian Jones, *The Archaeology of Ethnicity: Constructing Identities in the Past and Present* (London: Routledge, 1997): "Ethnicity is used to construct cultural identities for groups that are supposed to be 'the same' in history as in the present. . . . [C]ontemporary identity politics are necessarily involved in historical reconstruction of the ethnic origins of the Galileans."

27. Duling takes the example of Herodotus's *Histories* 8.144.2; others such as Eduard Shils and Clifford Geertz use cultural categories of ethnicity: family, territory, language, custom, and religion. Dennis C. Duling, "Ethnicity, Ethnocentrism, and the Matthean Ethnos," *Biblical Theology Bulletin* 35, no. 4 (2005): 127.

28. Riches, *Conflicting Mythologies*.

29. Warren Carter, *Matthew and Empire: Initial Explorations* (Harrisburg, PA: Trinity, 2001), 58.

30. I assume that Matthew, as a diaspora Jewish Christian or Christian Jew living in the Roman Empire, recognizes the Jews as an *ethnos* in relation to other *ethnoi*. All of the uses of the word *ethnos* in Matthew refer to other *ethnoi*, which is translated as "Gentiles" or "nations," except 21:43 in which it points to a people of Jesus's followers distinguished from the Jewish *ethnos*, but not necessarily excluding the Jews. This consciousness of a new *ethnos* may demonstrate what Buell calls "ethnic reasoning"; that is, the Christian identity is speculated in terms of *ethnos* or ethnicity. Denise Kimber Buell, *Why This New Race: Ethnic Reasoning in Early Christianity* (New York: Columbia University Press, 2005).

31. The verb *gennaō* ("beget" or "be father of") is used thirty-nine times in the genealogy (1:1–16). The noun *genesis* is used both 1:1 and verse 18 (cf. *gennēsis*, lineage or birth).

32. The language of inheritance, as well as his status as the heir, is also paid attention to: "This is the heir (*houtos estin ho klēronomos*); come, let us kill him and get his inheritance" (21:38).

33. Also see 25:40: "And the king will answer them, 'Truly I tell you, just as you did it to one of the least of these who are members of my family (*adelphoi*, 'brothers')."

34. The Gentile centurion's statement, "Truly this man was God's Son!" is interpreted in either way of confession or sarcasm (27:54).

35. Instead of using *Nazarēnos* for Jesus (Mark 1:24; 10:47; 14:67; 16:6; Luke 4:34; 24:19), Matthew applies *Nazōraios* (2:23; 26:71). The author of the Gospel of John prefers to use this word, but explicitly displays ethnic prejudice toward Nazareth: "Jesus son of Joseph from Nazareth. . . . 'Can anything good come out of Nazareth?'" (John 1:45–46; cf. 18:5, 7; 19:19).

36. Matthew 13:57 and 26:71 show the strong connection between Jesus's identity as a prophet and Nazareth as the origin of place. Horsley's argument of popular movements of villagers led by "kings/messiahs" or "prophets" would illuminate this relation (Horsley, *Jesus and Politics*, xi). Yet theological commentators pay little attention to the Gospels' presentation of Jesus as the prophet.

37. Wongi Park, *The Politics of Race and Ethnicity in Matthew's Passion Narrative* (New York: Palgrave Macmillan, 2019), 18; quoting R. T. France, *The Gospel of Matthew* (Grand Rapids, MI: Eerdmans, 2007), 1048; and Daniel Harrington, *The Gospel of Matthew* (Collegeville, MN: Liturgical, 1991), 396.

38. Park, *Politics of Race and Ethnicity*, 30, 89. For Park, "this unmarking is essentially a form of privilege for the deracialized-self, eschewing the very category of race/ethnicity as only applicable to the racialized-other."

39. Park, *Politics of Race and Ethnicity*, 107.

40. Chancey, "Ethnicities of Galilee," 113–17. Second Kings 15:29 says, "King Tiglath-pileser of Assyria came and captured . . . Galilee, all the land of Naphtali; and he carried the people captive to Assyria."

41. Josephus, *Antiquities*, 14.5.4 (91): "He brought Hyrcanus to Jerusalem, and committed the care of the temple to him; and when he had ordained five councils, he distributed the nation into the same number of parts: so these councils governed the people; the first was at Jerusalem, the second at Gadara, the third at Amathus, the fourth at Jericho, and the fifth at Sepphoris, in Galilee. So the Jews were now freed from monarchic authority, and were governed by an aristocracy."

42. My reading resonates with the experience of the people of Korea, who share the same ethnic origin but have been divided into two countries—North and South through the interference of foreign powers—the Soviet Union and the United States—at the end of the World War II.

43. Park discusses the four courtrooms in the Passion narrative: the Judean, Roman, popular, and divine. *Politics of Race and Ethnicity*, 115–36.

44. Park, *Politics of Race and Ethnicity*, 116: "These titles ['Jesus the Galilean' and 'Jesus of Nazareth'] are ethnoracial signifiers that mark a minority group (Galileans) from a dominant group (Romans)." Park continues to argue that the manner of Peter's speaking (*lalia*)—"his regional slang, his dialectical peculiarities"—makes his being obvious. Yet Park does not distinguish ethnoracial signifiers between Galileans and Judeans but considers Galileans as Judeans so that Jesus can be the King of Judeans as a Galilean.

45. Baker, "From Every Nation," 85–86. Some scholars speculate that one or two of the women in the genealogy are related to or of Canaanite ethnicity, but when Jesus encounters the Canaanite woman he treats her as an outsider, demonstrating hostile ethnic prejudice (15:21–28). Because of her faith, she and her "daughter" are allowed to be at the table of the "Son of David," just like other Jewish daughters (cf. 9:18–26). Smith argues that the Canaanite woman is a foreigner that illustrates how inclusivity (in the genealogy) does not erase the superiority of Israel or her marginalized status. See Mitzi J. Smith, "Subversive Interpretation in the Context of Racism, Sexism, and White Nationalism," a paper originally presented at the Consultation for Resisting Cultures of Discrimination, Authoritarianism, and Nationalism (RAN) in Bangalore, Thailand, December 7–9, 2018 (upcoming in *Reformed World Journal*).

46. Jesus also appears to be rejected by the Galilean cities (11:20–24) and by Jerusalem (23:37–39). Some scholars argue that Jesus is identified with Woman Wisdom in these passages, as well as in 8:19–22 in which Jesus negates family ties. Although Jesus's strong bond with his heavenly Father is highlighted (11:25–29), Jesus is also portrayed as a mother who desires to shelter her children (23:37). Celia Deutsch, "A Feminist Reading of Matthew's Wisdom Christology," in *Feminist Companion to Matthew*, ed. Amy-Jill Levine (London: T&T Clark International, 2001), 88–113.

47. Marianne Bjelland Kartzow, "Asking the Other Question: An Intersectional Approach to Galatians 3:28 and the Colossian Household," *Biblical Interpretation* 18, no. 4 (2010): 370.

48. Moxnes, "Identity in Jesus' Galilee."

49. David Harvey, *The Condition of Post-Modernity* (Oxford: Blackwell, 1989).

50. Moxnes, "Identity in Jesus' Galilee," 408, 412.

51. Moxnes, "Identity in Jesus' Galilee," 406, 412.

52. Titling Jesus "king" (*basileus*) of the Jews can be seen as anti-imperial, but Keith Dyre contends that the term *basileus* was broadly used for any ruler in the first-century Mediterranean world; instead, other terms such as *kaisar* or *autokrator* were used to designate the emperor. Keith Dyre, "The Empire of God, Postcolonial Jesus, and Postapocalyptic Mark," in *Colonial Contexts and Postcolonial Theologies: Storyweaving in the Asia-Pacific*, ed. Mark G. Brett and Jione Havea (New York: Palgrave Macmillan, 2014), 83–84.

53. Herod, whose father was by descent an Idumean, interprets this king as the Messiah. Daniel Patte, *The Gospel According to Matthew: A Structural Commentary on Matthew's Faith* (Valley Forge, PA: Trinity, 1996), 33.

54. Herod the Great exploited impoverished Jews for the magnificent construction of his palaces and temples and imposed heavy taxation on them.

55. Carter, *Matthew and Empire*.

56. The disciples are also described as sheep. Cf. 10:16; 26:31.

57. In this description, the extensiveness of the massacre is highlighted: "*pantas tous paidas tous en Bēthleem kai en pasin tois horiois autēs.*"

58. Amy-Jill Levine, "Discharging Responsibility: Matthean Jesus, Biblical Law, and Hemorrhaging Woman," in *Feminist Companion to Matthew*, ed. Amy-Jill Levine and Marianne Blickenstaff (Sheffield, UK: Sheffield Academic Press, 2001), 86; Eugene Eung-Chun Park, "Rachel's Cry for Her Children: Matthew's Treatment of the Infanticide by Herod," *Catholic Biblical Quarterly* 75, no. 3 (2013): 478.

59. Park also relates the innocent babies killed on account of Jesus to "the least of these/ these smallest ones (*elachistoi*)" (25:45), as well as "the little ones" (*mikroi*, 10:42). Park, "Rachel's Cry," 483–84. If the slaughtered infants are "the least of these," they are members of his "family"—his brothers and sisters (25:40).

60. While "intertextuality" is a relevant term for this approach, Mark G. Brett and Jione Havea use the term "storyweaving." Mark G. Brett and Jione Havea, eds., *Colonial Contexts and Postcolonial Theologies: Storyweaving in the Asia-Pacific* (New York: Palgrave Macmillan, 2014).

61. Note that "Galilee of the Gentiles" (*Galilaia tōn ethnōn*) has geopolitical, demographical, and linguistic significance and echoes its historical-political implications (Matt. 4:15; Isa. 8:23–9:1; 1 Macc. 5:15 cf. 26:73). 1 Maccabees 5 describes the situation in which the Gentiles (*ta ethnē*), including "all Galilee of Gentiles" (v. 15), surround the territory of Judea to destroy the Judeans led by Judas Maccabeus. Judas sends his brother Simon to Galilee to fight battles against the Gentiles (v. 21).

62. "*Psychē*" translated as "life" is used in 10:39 and 16:25, as well.

63. Yung Suk Kim and Jin-Ho Kim, eds., *Reading Minjung Theology in the Twenty-First Century: Selected Writings by Ahn Byung-Mu and Modern Critical Responses* (Eugene, OR: Wipf and Stock, 2013), 8.

64. For the concept of "social aphasia," refer to Jin-Ho Kim, "*Ochlos* and the Phenomenology of Wretchedness," in Kim and Kim, *Reading Minjung Theology*, 203. Kim cites, Nam-Dong, Suh: "Sin is the name that the powerful gave to the powerless." According to Suh, sin is not the result of minjung's guilt, but the result of exclusion and discrimination. This is one view of the nature of disability: that it is not the disabling condition that disables, but the resultant

exclusion and discrimination. Suh, Nam-Dong, *Research of Minjung Theology* (Seoul, Korea: Hangil, 1983), 44.

65. Kim, "*Ochlos* and Phenomenology," 203.

66. Mitzi J. Smith, "Minjung, the Black Masses, and the Global Imperative: *A Womanist Reading of Luke's Soteriological Hermeneutical Circle*," in Kim and Kim, *Reading Minjung Theology*, 102.

67. Smith redefines minjung in the global terrain: "The minjung are people locally and globally who strive to survive in the rubble and ashes of colonization, deracination and enslavement, Apartheid, holocaust and genocide, Jim Crowism, disenfranchisement, racism, sexism, heterosexism, and unbridled capitalistic greed. The minjung are flesh and blood people cast into the streets and rendered homeless in the midst of a global recovery from a recession caused by Wall Street and disproportionately felt on main street." Smith, "Minjung, the Black Masses," 102, 107, 119. For an appropriation of minjung in the transnational context, see Jin Young Choi, *Postcolonial Discipleship of Embodiment: An Asian and Asian American Feminist Reading of the Gospel of Mark* (New York: Palgrave Macmillan, 2015), 101–5.

68. King Herod's massacre of the innocents can be in the context of international history, considering the magi's involvement, the extensive scale of killing, and the generation of refugees. Cf. Horsley, *Jesus and the Politics*, 12.

69. Sara Ahmed, *The Cultural Politics of Emotion* (Edinburgh, UK: Edinburgh University Press, 2004), 80. Emphasis added.

70. Ahmed, *Cultural Politics*, 80.

WORKS CITED

Ahmed, Sara. *The Cultural Politics of Emotion*. Edinburgh, UK: Edinburgh University Press, 2004.

Baker, Cynthia M. "From Every Nation under Heaven." In *Prejudice and Christian Beginnings: Investigating Race, Gender, and Ethnicity in Early Christianity*, edited by Laura Nasrallah and Elisabeth Schüssler Fiorenza, 79–99. Minneapolis: Fortress, 2009.

Barclay, John M. G. "Ἰουδαῖος: Ethnicity and Translation." In *Ethnicity, Race, Religion: Identities and Ideologies in Early Jewish and Christian Texts, and in Modern Biblical Interpretation*, edited by Katherine M. Hockey and David G. Horrell, 46–58. London: T&T Clark, 2019.

Brett, Mark G., and Jione Havea, eds. *Colonial Contexts and Postcolonial Theologies: Storyweaving in the Asia-Pacific*. New York: Palgrave Macmillan, 2014.

Buell, Denise Kimber. *Why This New Race?: Ethnic Reasoning in Early Christianity*. New York: Columbia University Press, 2005.

Carter, Warren. *John and Empire: Initial Explorations*. New York: T&T Clark, 2008.

———. *Matthew and Empire: Initial Explorations*. Harrisburg, PA: Trinity, 2001.

Chancey, Mark. "The Ethnicities of Galilee." In *Galilee in the Late Second Temple and Mishnaic Periods, Vol 1: Life, Culture, and Society*, edited by David A. Fiensy and James Riley Strange, 112–28. Minneapolis: Fortress, 2014.

Choi, Jin Young. *Postcolonial Discipleship of Embodiment: An Asian and Asian American Feminist Reading of the Gospel of Mark*. New York: Palgrave Macmillan, 2015.

Delgado, Richard, and Jean Stefancic. *Critical Race Theory: An Introduction*. New York: New York University Press, 2001.

Deutsch, Celia. "A Feminist Reading of Matthew's Wisdom Christology." In *Feminist Companion to Matthew*, edited by Amy-Jill Levine, 88–113. London: T&T Clark International, 2001.

Duling, Dennis C. "Ethnicity, Ethnocentrism, and the Matthean *Ethnos*." *Biblical Theology Bulletin* 35, no. 4 (2005): 125–43.

Dyre, Keith. "The Empire of God, Postcolonial Jesus, and Postapocalyptic Mark." In *Colonial Contexts and Postcolonial Theologies: Storyweaving in the Asia-Pacific*, edited by Mark G. Brett and Jione Havea, 81–98. New York: Palgrave Macmillan, 2014.

Fenton, Steven. *Ethnicity*. Cambridge, UK: Polity, 2010.

Fiensy, David A., and James Riley Strange, eds. *Galilee in the Late Second Temple and Mishnaic Periods, Vol. 2: The Archaeological Record from Cities, Towns, and Villages.* Minneapolis: Fortress, 2015.

France, R. T. *The Gospel of Matthew.* Grand Rapids, MN: Eerdmans, 2007.

Hall, Jonathan M. *Ethnic Identity in Greek Antiquity.* Cambridge, UK: Cambridge University Press, 2000.

———. *Hellenicity: Between Ethnicity and Culture.* Chicago: Chicago University Press, 2000.

Harrington, Daniel. *The Gospel of Matthew.* Collegeville, MI: Liturgical, 1991.

Harvey, David. *The Condition of Post-Modernity.* Oxford: Blackwell, 1989.

Horsley, Richard A. *Archaeology, History and Society in Galilee: The Social Context of Jesus and the Rabbis.* Valley Forge, PA: Trinity, 1996.

———. *Galilee: History, Politics, People.* Valley Forge, PA: Trinity, 1995.

———. *Jesus and the Politics of Roman Palestine.* Columbia: University of South Carolina Press, 2014.

Isaac, Benjamin. *The Invention of Racism in Classical Antiquity.* Princeton, NJ: Princeton University Press, 2004.

Jones, Sian. *The Archaeology of Ethnicity: Constructing Identities in the Past and Present.* London: Routledge, 1997.

Josephus, Flavius. *Jewish Antiquities.* Books XII–XIV. The Loeb Classical Library, vol. 7, translated by Ralph Marcus. Cambridge, MA: Harvard University Press, 1943.

Kartzow, Marianne Bjelland. "Asking the Other Question: An Intersectional Approach to Galatians 3:28 and the Colossian Household." *Biblical Interpretation* 18, no. 4 (2010): 364–89.

Kim, Jin-Ho. "*Ochlos* and the Phenomenology of Wretchedness." In *Reading Minjung Theology in the Twenty-First Century: Selected Writings by Ahn Byung-Mu and Modern Critical Responses,* edited by Yung Suk Kim and Jin-Ho Kim, 200–214. Eugene, OR: Wipf and Stock, 2013.

Kim, Yung Suk, and Jin-Ho Kim, eds. *Reading Minjung Theology in the Twenty-First Century: Selected Writings by Ahn Byung-Mu and Modern Critical Responses.* Eugene, OR: Wipf and Stock, 2013.

Levine, Amy-Jill. "Discharing Responsibility: Matthean Jesus, Biblical Law, and Hemorrhaging Woman." In *Feminist Companion to Matthew,* edited by Amy-Jill Levine and Marianne Blickenstaff, 70–87. Sheffield, UK: Sheffield Academic, 2001.

———. *The Misunderstood Jew: The Church and the Scandal of the Jewish Jesus.* New York: HarperCollins, 2006.

Miles, Robert, and Malcolm Brown, eds. *Racism,* 2nd ed. New York: Routledge, 2003.

Miller, David M. "Ethnicity Comes of Age: An Overview of Twentieth-Century Terms for *Ioudaios.*" *Currents in Biblical Research* 10, no. 2 (2012): 293–311.

Moxnes, Halvor. "Identity in Jesus' Galilee—From Ethnicity to Locative Intersectionality." *Biblical Interpretation,* 18, no. 4 (2010): 390–416.

Park, Eugene Eung-Chun. "Rachel's Cry for Her Children: Matthew's Treatment of the Infanticide by Herod." *Catholic Biblical Quarterly* 75, no. 3 (2013): 473–85.

Park, Wongi. *The Politics of Race and Ethnicity in Matthew's Passion Narrative.* New York: Palgrave Macmillan, 2019.

Patte, Daniel. *The Gospel According to Matthew: A Structural Commentary on Matthew's Faith.* Valley Forge, PA: Trinity, 1996.

Riches, John K. *Conflicting Mythologies: Identity Formation in the Gospels of Mark and Matthew.* Edinburgh, UK: T&T Clark, 2000.

Sim, David. "Christianity and Ethnicity in the Gospel of Matthew." In *Ethnicity and the Bible,* edited by Mark G. Brett, 172–96. Leiden, Netherlands: E. J. Brill, 2002.

Smith, Mitzi J. "Minjung, the Black Masses, and the Global Imperative: *A Womanist Reading of Luke's Soteriological Hermeneutical Circle.*" In *Reading Minjung Theology in the Twenty-First Century: Selected Writings by Ahn Byung-Mu and Modern Critical Responses,* edited by Yung Suk Kim and Jin-Ho Kim, 101–19. Eugene, OR: Wipf and Stock, 2013.

———. "Subversive Interpretation in the Context of Racism, Sexism, and White Nationalism." *Reformed World Journal,* upcoming 2020.

Suh, Nam-Dong. *Research of Minjung Theology.* Seoul, Korea: Hangil, 1983.

Chapter Two

In Christ, but Not of Christ

Reading Identity Differences Differently in the Letter to the Galatians

Jennifer T. Kaalund

Difference is always relational, despite the range of possibilities for naming it—for example, subaltern, foreigner, stranger, and Other. There is no conception of a foreigner without a citizen, Orient without the Occident, or Other apart from the Self. And difference always matters. As Toni Morrison notes, there are few, if any, descriptions of difference that are "free of categories of worth or rank."[1] These descriptions represent attempts to construct identities. Identity, a way of being in the world, is informed by sexuality, gender, race/ethnicity, place, religion, and other such categories.

In his letter to the Galatians, Paul creates a religious identity. This nascent Christian identity is constructed in, through, with, and by its environment. Despite its presentation as solely a religious identity, it is nearly impossible to distinguish this identity from its sociopolitical aspects. He constructs an "in Christ" identity over/against his particular understanding of Jewish identity, but in fact, this "in Christ" identity is a Jewish identity. For the distinction to be clear, Paul emphasizes the differences between his understanding of what it means to be a Jesus follower and the interpretation that others are bringing into the community. In the end, Paul wants the Galatian community to choose which teacher they will follow.

Galatians is a discourse concerned with alterity, another way of being in the ancient world. Paul presents a potential way for being a Jesus follower that does not involve circumcision. But how can this difference be read and, perhaps more importantly, understood differently? That is, is it possible to read difference free of rank, worth, or value? Is this what Paul is proposing in

Galatians 3:28? To answer these questions, we must first understand what is to be gained from the creation of the Other. As Morrison instructs, "Because there are such major benefits in creating and sustaining an Other, it is important to 1) identify the benefits and 2) discover what may be the social/ political results of repudiating those benefits."[2] Though Morrison is referring to the various ways in which discourses have constructed African American identity as an outsider identity, I would suggest this tendency can be found in various discourses. In fact, it is instructive to consider the socio-political reasons for creating the Other in Galatians.

To that end, this essay will explore the question of how to read difference differently in four interrelated steps. First, I examine theoretical approaches to discourses of difference according to postcolonial, feminist, and psychoanalytical theorists. Next, I explore an example of the use of scripture to create African American identity as Other. Third, I conduct a womanist postcolonial reading of Galatians 3.[3] Finally, I conclude by examining the potential material implications for being in Christ, but not of Christ in antiquity and in our contemporary moment.[4]

THEORETICAL APPROACHES TO DIFFERENCE

An example of a feminist psychoanalytical approach to alterity can be found in the work of Julia Kristeva. In her book, *Strangers to Ourselves,* Kristeva asserts that the "foreigner lives within us."[5] She reaches this conclusion based upon her analysis of Freud's study of the German adjective *heimlich*, which means inwardly, secretly, or privately. However, the irony is that the German term *heimlich* in the context of the United States is very much associated with the maneuver or procedure for unlodging or expelling whatever is potentially blocking an air passage. For Kristeva, the Other is none other than our repressed familiar fears housed in our unconscious. As such, the struggle against the Other is simply a battle of unconscious fear and desire. The recognition of the Other in the self leads to the realization that if everyone is a stranger, then ultimately no one is a stranger.

In addition to the revelation that the stranger can be located within, Kristeva's analysis of alterity reveals the connection between the stranger and a search for origins. Of the foreigner, Kristeva observes: "His origin certainly haunts him, for better and for worse, but it is indeed elsewhere that he has set his hopes, that his struggles take place, that his life holds together today. Elsewhere versus the origin, and even nowhere verses the roots: the motto for daredevils breeds sterile repressions as well as bold undertakings."[6] Just as, according to Kristeva, origins (specifically "family, blood, and soil") haunt the stranger, origins are similarly pervasive in the discourse of otherness. In search of a beginning, the genesis of the Self is not concerned with inception, but instead seeks a genealogy into which to be grafted. Perhaps what this search uncovers is that such genealogies are about particularities. In this case, the philosophical discourses that inform Kristeva's work point to a very particular origin, specifically a Western one. Mainly, if the genealogy of the discourse of alterity is anchored in Greek roots—or, stated differently, is concerned with Greek self-definition—then the construction of the Other will always be in relation to the Greek or Western self. Place, then, is a significant aspect of otherness.

If the place of the stranger is indeed nowhere or elsewhere as Kristeva purports, then the identity of the Other can be understood as transcending the boundaries of space. It is this transcendent, almost untouchable nature of the Other that challenges the identity of the Self. The contestation of identity is elucidated in the very nature by which identity is constructed—that is, over/against another identity. Identity is built in a place, real or imagined. As such, elsewhere and nowhere are places of otherness where the identity of alterity is constructed. These foundations are unstable and fragile, indeed, not only for those identified as the foreigner, stranger, or Other but perhaps even more for the citizen or the Self. It is this place of difference I wish to continuously underscore throughout this essay.

It is Kristeva's feminist sensibilities, I suggest, that tether her psychoanalytical analysis to the acknowledgement of the existence of *real* foreigners. Mainly, it should be acknowledged that there are material implications for people who are deemed Other. In this projection of the internal to the external that enables one to address this reality, Kristeva proposes an "ethics of psychoanalysis" that would "involve cosmopolitanism of a new sort that, cutting across governments, economies, and markets, might work for a mankind whose solidarity is founded on the consciousness of its unconscious—desiring, destructive, fearful, empty, impossible."[7] Still, this glimpse at the external world points back to an interiority. The sociopolitical context in which strangers are created should be interrogated and ultimately challenged. This can be done alongside the interior work to which Kristeva alludes. Together, the work of addressing how strangers are formed can result in the potential for a different, perhaps even better world.

The world, in its current state, thrives on sustaining the Self through the perpetual formation of the Other. Indeed, strangers are not born; they are made. And yet not all strangers are made equal. Sara Ahmed, a feminist postcolonial theorist, attests to this and presents a challenge to the assessment of the stranger in recent postmodern theory and particularly to its "universalizing" move. In other words, Ahmed cautions against categorizing all strangers as the same; diversity within the category must be further interrogated. She highlights aspects of alterity that must be at the forefront of any assessment concerning otherness: embodiment and epistemology. She writes, "No longer seen as a threat to community, the stranger becomes a reminder of the differences we must celebrate."[8] The celebration of difference is possible when the Other is no longer seen as such. To realize such possibilities, Ahmed argues for an embodied analysis of alterity. She writes: "The stranger is not *any-body* that we have failed to recognize, but *some-body* that we have already recognized *as* a stranger, as a 'body out of place.'"[9] The body, then, becomes a site of differentiation and also a site of learning. Epistemology is important to the construction of alterity. Ahmed argues that strangers are "epistemic communities" and critiques Kristeva's conception of "strangers to ourselves." She suggests, "To conclude simply that we are all strangers to ourselves is to avoid dealing with the political processes whereby some others are designated as *stranger than other others*."[10] Within the community of strangers, there are differences that should be acknowledged. This is what Ahmed wants to remind her reader of. She concludes, "What I am calling for, against either universalism or cultural relativism, is politics that is premised on closer encounters."[11] For Ahmed, it is not enough to acknowledge a body or stranger; an Other must be intimately engaged for an exchange of knowledge to occur, and we must move beyond a simple acknowledgement toward a celebration of difference.

Yet these feminist approaches to difference are limited. Womanist hermeneutics, with an emphasis on embodiment, privileges the experiences of the African American community, and African American woman in particular, in order to establish a richer, deeper, and fuller understanding of the material implication of the process of Othering. Difference is inscribed in/on our flesh. Further, naming this experience is not enough. Womanist analysis of intersections of various systems of oppression (e.g., sexism, classism, and racism) stimulates activism that moves our reading of texts beyond the political act of naming oppression to proposals for the eradication of these systems that will ultimately lead to the creation of a more just world. This vision is undergirded by a dialogical approach that amplifies the voices of those who exist on the margins. In the case of the letter to the Galatians, it is the voice of the Galatians that is lost or ignored when the focus is solely on the words and suggestions of Paul. Though most often read as mandates, Paul's letters are correspondence written from one perspective.

While these theoretical approaches to the creation of the Other are instructive, a more contemporary example of this process can further illumine both how and why the construction of alterity is problematic. The survival of hegemonic systems depend on the perpetuation of otherness, an otherness that is always in danger. The encounter between enslaved Africans and colonists in the United States provides a poignant example of how strangers are made, how sacred text can be used to justify actions, and the material implication of being the Other.

ALTERITY AND THE AFRICAN AMERICAN IDENTITY

He said, "Cursed be Canaan; lowest of slaves shall he be to his brothers." He also said, "Blessed by the LORD my God be Shem; and let Canaan be his slave. May God make space for Japheth, and let him live in the tents of Shem; and let Canaan be his slave." (Gen. 9:25–27)

Since the arrival of enslaved Africans on the shores of the Americas, African American identity has been formed through the lens of alterity. A nation within a nation and considered second-class citizens, not only was the making of this Other codified, but sacred texts were also used to justify the treatment of African Americans, first as enslaved people, and later as free men and women.[12] The myth of Ham is an example of such use of scripture.

This text in Genesis 9 is complicated.[13] The most widely held misconception concerning this text is that Noah curses Ham. The curse is not on Ham; it is on his son Canaan. Despite the fact that race is never explicitly mentioned in the text, how do we come to think of Ham as being black or dark skinned? The troubled relationship between the Israelites and Canaanites that likely informs the text particularly is rarely considered in this interpretation of the text in a liturgical setting. There are a number of queries the text creates and does not answer. This ambiguity allows for a variety of interpretations, most of which cannot be supported by what is actually found in the text—perhaps most importantly, even if the text is employed to explain racial differences among humanity, how does one overlook the fact that the individuals in the text are close relatives? Noah, Ham, Canaan—they are fathers, sons, and brothers.

Noah's curse on Canaan functioned as a way for white colonialists in America to justify African slavery. David Whitford observes, "The Ham myth, as a sacred story, provided a context for legitimizing the white's racial attitudes and slavery in terms of a divine purpose."[14] Not only would Noah's curse function as a justification of slavery, but it also provided characteristics by which enslaved people could be stereotyped. Like their ancestor Ham, the enslaved people were construed as a lewd people, who had no dignity, lacked proper respect and honor, and, importantly, were sorely in need of redemption. How does one understand the need for redemption and enslave concomitantly? As Paul Harvey concludes, "the son-of-Ham thesis served well in the sense that it seemed to explain how black people could be free Christians and unfree slaves at the same time. But the curse on Ham was at best a shaky foundation for religioracial mythologizing."[15] The shaky foundation did not hinder attempts to support this faulty African American identity constructed based upon this text.

Despite the numerous problems with the interpretation of the text, it remained an appealing solution for explaining the very nature of black

Americans. The conundrum it creates, however, is that enslaved Christians could be free in the spiritual sense. At the same time, there is a denial or lack of a critical examination of a text that seems to be used to explain the diversity of human existence despite a common ancestry. This assertion overlooks the very fact that the many come from the one; that is, although diversity or difference may be the emphasis, alongside this exists the fact that the enslaved are family. "According to historian Winthrop Jordan, the 'curse' on Canaan, son of Ham . . . persisted through [the] centuries in spite of 'incessant refutation,' and was 'probably sustained by a feeling that black-ness could scarcely be anything *but* a curse and by the common need to confirm the facts of nature by specific reference to Scripture."[16] This use of scripture sacralized a construction of African American identity that associat-ed their blackness and personhood with a curse. In 1857, James A. Sloan, a Presbyterian minister, provided an example of how the earlier interpretation of the text not only persisted, but became even more degrading and insidious toward African Americans over time. Sloan writes:

> Ham deserved death for his unfilial and impious conduct. But the Great Law-giver saw fit, in his good pleasure, not to destroy Ham with immediate death, but to set a mark of degradation on him. . . . All Ham's posterity are either black or dark colored, and thus bear upon their countenance the mark of inferiority which God put upon the progenitor. . . . Black, restrained, despised, bowed down are the words used to express the condition and place of Ham's children. Bearing the mark of degradation on their skin.[17]

The curse had taken on a life of its own, one that extended far beyond what could be found in the biblical text. African American responses to such constructions varied. If Ham were black, then African Americans could trace their lineage to an ancient past. The irony of being told/taught that African Americans do not have a culture while at the same time inserting them into the lineage of Noah elucidates the fact that logic was not necessary in con-structing this identity. In fact, the instability of this identity formation ena-bled the interpretation of the text to continue to morph over time.

Genesis 9:18–27 illustrates the damage that can be done when a text is interpreted to justify the actions of hegemonic systems; it inflicts irreparable harm. This interpretation of Noah's curse persists to this day. African American identity continues to be constructed through the lens of otherness. The desire to create an Other, whether as an economic endeavor, a religious understanding, or a personal act, is an act of violence. This example high-lights how emphasizing difference (real or imagined) can perpetuate hate, fear, and death.

METHODOLOGY: TOWARD A WOMANIST POSTCOLONIAL HERMENEUTIC

In summary, Kristeva reminds us of the internalized fears that construct the stranger. She informs that a search for origins haunts such a construction. Ahmed, emphasizing the embodiment of otherness, alerts us to the ever-present knowledge being created in the development of Others and warns us against the universalizing tendency that accompanies this formation. Finally, centering African American experience, particularly the use of sacred scripture to justify the treatment of enslaved and later freed blacks, can prove instructive for approaching the ancient text. Mainly, this experience makes real the implications of being viewed as a perpetual outsider.

Postcolonial theory provides another critical lens through which to assess alterity and the systems of power that create and sustain it. While the United States was divided into black and white; postcolonial theorist Edward Said would argue that the world has been divided into two unequal halves. One of Said's contributions to the discourse of alterity is found in his exposition of orientalism. Said defines orientalism as follows: "Orientalism is a distribution of geopolitical awareness into aesthetic, scholarly, economic, sociological, historical, and philological texts. . . . It is, above all, a discourse that is by no means in direct, corresponding relationship with political power in the raw, but rather is produced and exists in uneven exchanges with various kinds of power."[18] Orientalism reveals an unbalanced perception of one group through the lens of another, and as such the power dynamics inherent in this discourse must be interrogated. The empowered group determines the identity of another group, typically in relation to its own identity.

As a result, biases are created by orientalism. These stereotypes are not limited to the construction of racial/ethnic identities but also create discriminatory frameworks through which gender is formed. Said reminds us that "latent orientalism also encouraged a peculiarly (not to say invidiously) male conception of the world."[19] Despite Said's acute awareness of the power dynamics within the discourse he calls orientalism, both latent and manifest, he pays little attention to the precarious nature inherent to the process of othering. The caricature of the Other developed in the discourse lives outside the text and the imagination. Naming or interpellation, being called into being, is the beginning of the violence that accompanies orientalism. The words of this discourse become ideas and the ideas become reality. The epistemological influence of discourse should not be underestimated. Creating boundaries and making distinctions are dangerous endeavors. Being deemed an Other marks a people as perpetual outsiders, in constant need of control and discipline.

Foreigners and strangers are ambivalent identities. The postcolonial theorist Homi Bhabha indicates that the discourse of mimicry is constructed around such an *ambivalence*. The formation of an "almost the same but not quite" identity in colonial discourses is an example of mimicry. Bhabha defines colonial mimicry as "the desire for a reformed, recognizable Other, *as a subject of a difference that is almost the same, but not quite.* Which is to say, that the discourse of mimicry is constructed around an *ambivalence*; in order to be effective, mimicry must continually produce its slippage, its excess, its difference."[20] Bhabha further explicates this concept by describing mimicry as "the sign of a double articulation; a complex strategy of reform, regulation and discipline."[21] In this assessment of colonial discourse, the Other is instructed to be like the Self, when in fact the Other can never be completely or fully the Self. As a result, the Other needs constant reform and discipline. For a people under colonial or imperial rule, difference is seen as a rebellion and a threat to order. The response to being seen as a threat is often violence. The making of the Other is ever attended by the potential for violence.

In summary, Said underscores the ways in which the world has been divided. Being attentive to these power dynamics reveals the biases and stereotypes that accompany the formation of an Other. Bhabha, who is similarly attuned to the power dynamics of colonial discourses, instructs that mimicry is a strategic attempt to create a palatable Other who, despite his or her best attempts, will never become the Self. As a result of this shortcoming, the Other must be under the careful watch of those in power who stand at the ready to provide discipline when necessary.

It is instructive here to understand the relationship between imperialism and colonization. In his book, *Colonization: A Global History*, Marc Ferro defines the relationship between colonization and imperialism as follows: "These then are the primary impulses of imperialism: to colonize, to civilize, to spread one's culture, to expand. And colonization was the 'power' of a people to 'reproduce' itself in a different space."[22] If we understand that the impulse of imperialism is to colonize and spread one's culture, then colonization is simply a form of imperialism. As such, postcolonial theory can prove useful for exploring how "texts are central means in both the imposition of and resistance to imperialism."[23] Muse Dube asserts that "biblical literature was shaped by a constant struggle with imperial phenomena; that is, it was born from the relationships of endorsing, resisting, or living with imperial powers."[24] As such, postcolonial theories can also provide a framework for interrogating these texts, particularly when exploring relationships of power.

Furthermore, the dialogical emphasis of womanist biblical hermeneutics enables the text of African American experience and that of Paul to be in conversation. For example, Galatians and its concern with male flesh (circumcision) excludes a way in which women can be part of this Jesus-following community, but at the same time gender is a part of the in Christ identity construction. Empowering the Galatian audience with the ability to "talk back"[25] and challenge the system that may seek to limit their self-expression and assert their full humanity is informed by a womanist sensibility. Lastly, an emphasis on embodiment and wholeness of the community alongside a postcolonial hermeneutic results in a potentially liberating reading of the text that can in turn support a liberative praxis.

Together these theoretical approaches to otherness provide hermeneutical tools with which to read Galatians, and specifically chapter 3, as a discourse of otherness. Paul attempts to persuade his audience to embrace an identity (an "in Christ" identity) that is seemingly different from their current one (Gauls/Galatians) and he does so by using sacred texts. Using this framework, I will employ a womanist postcolonial hermeneutic. The questions that arise from this approach abound, but I will consider three: (1) What does it mean to be a Galatian, particularly within their context? (2) What are the power dynamics at work in this text? And (3) how does a universalizing identity, such as the "in Christ" one that Paul is proposing, benefit and/or harm this community? With this, we turn to the letter to the Galatians.

THE LETTER TO THE GALATIANS: IDENTITY AND POWER

Galatians is Paul's most combative letter. The tone is harsh and the mood impatient. How could the Galatians be persuaded by a gospel other than the one Paul taught? This letter provides Paul the occasion to rearticulate his argument—to clarify the nascent Christian identity he attempts to form and perhaps to solidify Paul's position of authority over the community.

The first matter to be settled between Paul and the churches in Galatia is Paul's authority. Paul begins this letter with his credentials: "an apostle sent neither by human commission nor human authorities but through Jesus Christ and God the Father who raised him from the dead—and all (*pantes*) of the brothers and sisters with me" (Gal. 1:1 1–2a). Paul is sent by God, the ultimate authority.[26] Paul's biographical sketch serves to portray him as God's messenger in opposition to the "supposed to be acknowledged leaders—those who contributed nothing" to Paul (2:6). Paul is one among many leaders and yet is suggesting he is the *true* leader, the one preaching the truth of the gospel.

Paul as God's appointed apostle is an important criterion he uses to underscore his authority, and he also clearly emphasizes his Jewish identity. He writes: "By nature we are Judean and not of the sinning nations (*ethnē*)."[27] Why is Paul's own ethnic/religious identity important? Paul is concerned that the Galatian churches are being persuaded to become Jewish through the ritual of circumcision. *This* is the concern of the letter. Is it necessary to become Jewish to be "in Christ"? On the surface, it seems that Paul's response is a resounding "absolutely not!" However, Paul uses his position within Judaism and, more specifically, as a leader in this Jesus-following community to argue for a new understanding of Jewishness.

Paul's desire to assert his authority demonstrates the power dynamics that are working in this text. In his book, *Domination and the Arts of Resistance*, James Scott examines the stratification of power both within and outside subjugated groups in terms of public and hidden transcripts. Building on the work of Michel Foucault, Scott asserts, "Power relations are ubiquitous. They are surely different at opposite ends of the continuum, but they are never absent."[28] Scott suggests that subjugated groups operate within public and hidden transcripts; that is, there are distinctive ways in which they interact with those in power both publicly and privately. Moreover, Scott is attentive to power dynamics *within* subjugated groups. Using the example of prisoners, Scott purports, "The difference in power relations toward the hidden transcript segment of the continuum is that they are generated among those who are mutually subject, often as peers, to a larger system of domination."[29] Scott's analysis acknowledges the multiple ways in which the stratification of power within groups must be examined. Paul assumes authority over the audience of his letter. Paul's position(ing) requires further investigation.

Paul's own identity plays an important role in how we can understand his correspondence with the churches of Galatia. Sze-kar Wan, reading the letter to the Galatians through a postcolonial lens, suggests that Paul's "diasporic identity" means he is straddling two worlds, occupying a space of ambivalence.[30] He describes Paul's hybridity as

> simultaneously attracted to the discourse of the Jesus-movement of the metropolis and repulsed by its binarism; simultaneously drawn to his "home" discourse, according to which he occupied the periphery, and to the "native" discourse endemic to his place of exile, by the logic which he was the honoured apostolic founder. Among his folk he was reviled and marginalized as a law-breaker; in the diaspora, among Gentiles, he was a representative carrying the weight of authority that befits an ambassador or viceroy from the centre.[31]

More recently, Ronald Charles has similarly reminded us to take seriously Paul's own social positioning and the influence it had on his thinking. He asserts: "Paul's diasporic identities are constantly in the process of crafting novel ways of being and evolving; his movements across boundaries require him to engage in ever-expanding improvisations susceptible to creating new and complex tapestries of continuity and rupture, similarity and difference."[32] Indeed, Paul's own hybridity is an important consideration. He is both a Jewish leader of this Christ movement and, at the same time, a member of a conquered people within the empire, occupying space at the margins as well as at the center of a very particular marginalized group. These nuances do not seem to exist in Paul's discourse. He constructs a discourse replete with binaries—he presents an either/or scenario for the Galatians. Paul wants the Galatians to understand that their identity "in Christ" does not require them to change who they are. The only requirement is faith. One must either believe and join the community or one makes the work of Christ null and void.

Another important context within which to situate this letter is the first-century Mediterranean world. This world, too, was divided into two unequal halves—the Roman imperial power and their conquered subjects. Paul's letter to the Galatians was written during Roman imperialism. *Pax Romana* (Roman peace) was an imperial prize and promise to the conquered nations. In exchange for peace, the empire expected or, perhaps, demanded loyalty. Although the conquered people typically were able to continue their own worship practices, they were also expected to participate in imperial worship.[33] The ability of the conquered people to participate in and receive the benefits of being part of the empire (waterworks, oil, wheat, etc.) also entailed accepting and understanding their role as a conquered people. What does this mean for the people in Galatia? The Galatians were no longer "Celtic people" with "a notoriously indomitable tendency toward lawlessness."[34] They were the defeated subjects of the empire. These biases and stereotypes, as Said instructs, often accompany the formation of ethnic/racial identity. Brigette Kahl argues that the publicly portrayed image of the Galatians as a conquered people was prominent. She writes, "Whether depicted as enemy invaders or as robbers and plunderers of sacred sites, the perennial pose assigned to the Gauls/Galatians in ancient iconography is the same as Nero saw on that monument: they are failing and falling, dying or dead."[35] These images of vanquished Gauls were part of the propaganda employed to create loyalty to the empire and, as Bhabha describes, a "reformed, recognizable Other."[36] The defeat was not once and for all; the conquered needed a constant reminder of their place. Peace was obtained at a high cost, and the identity of the conquered was constantly being negotiated. As such, choosing to exist outside the identity of a reformed, recognizable Other was seen as a threat to imperial order and was therefore a risk to people's very lives. The ethnicity of the people in the churches in Galatia must be a consideration in fully understanding what Paul is asking them to do when he insists that they reject circumcision. Neil Elliott suggests, "The Galatians may have intended to adopt specific Jewish practices as a sort of *civic camouflage*, hoping to pass off their withdrawal from the civic cults as their newfound interest in an ancient ethnic religion tolerated by the empire, and thus escape harassment."[37] Jewish identity was a known and acceptable identity in the ancient world. To be clear, despite the camouflage, known and acceptable identities did not necessarily mean the absence of violence or retribution for subjects of the empire.

A number of power dynamics are at work in this text. The Roman Empire's presence looms largely, though silently, over the text. As subjects of the empire, Paul, Cephas, James, John, and other leaders of the Jesus movement seem to have different understandings of what it means to be a Christ follower—particularly as it pertains to circumcision. And finally, there is Paul's relationship to the Galatians; not only are they repeatedly referred to as his brothers and sisters (*adelphoi*), but they are also his little children (*teknia mou*, 4:19)—and, therefore, he seems himself to have given birth to this community of believers.

"IN CHRIST" IDENTITY: WHOSE FOOL ARE YOU?

The "in Christ" identity that Paul constructs in Galatians is a communal identity. Paul came into the community and preached the gospel. Based on the letter, others have come into the community and preached another gospel. Paul is trying to persuade his audience that his gospel is the true gospel. We should not presume that the audience has been persuaded, only that they have been presented with this option for how to live together peaceably, how to be in community with one another, and how to make sense of what it means to be a follower of Christ according to Paul.

The third chapter of Galatians, which begins with Paul's rebuke, is the essence of Paul's proposal. Paul, chastising the community, writes: "You foolish Galatians! Who has bewitched you? It was before your very eyes that Christ was publicly portrayed as crucified! The only thing I want to learn from you is this: Did you receive the Spirit by doing the works of the law or by believing what you heard? Are you so foolish? Having started with the Spirit, are you now ending with the flesh?" (3:1–3). Paul wants to know how the Galatians could have allowed themselves to be deceived after having received the truth and the Spirit. Although this chapter begins with a scathing assertion, it ends with the baptismal formula declaring a form of unity that can be found in Christ Jesus. He concludes: "As many of you as were baptized into Christ have clothed yourselves with Christ. There is no longer Jew or Greek, there is no longer slave or free, there is no longer male or female; for all are one in Christ Jesus" (3:27, 28). How does one go from being a bewitched fool to being a child of God? Paul's answer is simply, "For in Christ Jesus you are all children of God through faith" (3:26). What is found between verses 1 and 26 is Paul's argument for why faith is the only necessary condition to be grafted into God's family.

The qualifications for being part of God's family, according to Paul, have been expanded to include the nations. Abraham, the quintessential Gentile, is invoked because he "believed God and it was reckoned to him as righteous" (3:6). That is, Abraham's faith resulted in his being in right relationship with

God. Paul continues: "Those who believe are descendants of Abraham. And the scripture, foreseeing that God would justify the nations by faith, declared the gospel beforehand to Abraham, saying, 'All the nations shall be blessed in you'" (3:7–8). These scriptures also indicate that the sign of this covenant is circumcision, and Abraham, too, was circumcised (Gen. 17:11). Paul apparently makes a case for identifying the Galatians as descendants of Abraham, indicating that faith is the only requirement for participation in a particular socio-religious identity. Yet is Paul calling for the Galatian community to be "almost the same, but not quite" Jewish? The community is disparaged from ending "in the flesh," but it seems it is only male flesh that is of concern here as circumcision would not apply to the women in this community. Who is included or excluded in this community?

Paul's exegesis of Genesis is influenced by how he understands the work of Jesus. As we have seen from the example of the interpretations of Noah's curse on the African American community, one's understanding of texts can have severe and long-lasting negative effects on a community. The dichotomy that Paul establishes between the law and the spirit is problematic and similarly has been understood in ways that have resulted in anti-Semitism and anti-Judaism. As Morrison warns, differences rarely (perhaps never?) are free from value assessments. It is important to understand that Paul's interpretation is just that—one interpretation. It is clear that some Galatians had already acted in ways that were not pleasing to Paul. The existence of the correspondence is evidence that different opinions existed as to what the necessary requirements were for becoming part of this Jesus movement.

Despite an attempt to present a unified identity, Paul replicates binaries (flesh and spirit; works of law or believing what was heard) that can be destructive and/or problematic. For example, Paul's query constructs spirit over and against flesh in support of his argument against circumcision. However, spirit and flesh are not oppositional. This binary, in some interpretations, devalues the body, and this understanding has played out in a myriad of ways. The spirit is not "better" than the body; they both are necessary elements of wholeness, but one implication of promoting the importance of spirit over and against the flesh/body can be found in those who propose an "in this world, but not of this world mentality."[38] This understanding of existence can have adverse effects on our relationship to the earth and all living things. It can result in the promotion of a particular political position or view that is animated by an otherworldly perspective. It can also lead to a lack of empathy or action toward the social injustices that plague this world. Does the identity that Paul proposes for the Galatians similarly place them in a precarious situation? Is he suggesting they be *in* Christ (take on this new identity), but not *of* Christ (not fully participating in all aspects of Jewishness)?

IN CHRIST: ONENESS, UNITY, OR UNIVERSALISM

The oneness of God and the oneness of the community are important points that Paul makes in the third chapter. He writes, "But God is *one*" (3:21) and "All of you are *one* in Christ Jesus" (3:28), in an attempt to build communities that are united around their belief in Jesus. But is this unity also uniformity; is harmony also homogeneity? Daniel Boyarin, reading Paul through the lens of this baptismal formula, claims: "Paul was motivated by a Hellenistic desire for the One, which among other things produced an ideal of a universal human essence, beyond difference and hierarchy."[39] He contextualizes Paul's universal claims within a particular Greco-Roman Judaism. Oneness in Christ gives Paul a mechanism for creating a way of being in the first-century Mediterranean world that enabled him to bring together his Jewishness and his faith in Jesus Christ. Universalism is associated with (strategic) essentialism, both containing inherent dangers.

The unity Paul proposes is understood by many as transcending differences in ethnicity, social class, and gender-—that is, the "in Christ" identity is a universal one, open and available for all who simply believe. Kahl argues that Paul is proposing a oneness that is a "transformative process of co-dying and co-living with the collective body of the conquered that challenges colonial and imperial law in all its variations."[40] Although I do not read this identity as necessarily resistant to imperial power(s), I can see how the potential for a collective identity that stands against such oppressive structures could prove beneficial for organizing a diverse people around a common goal. However, how does this model exclude? What do we make of Romans (soldiers, citizens, etc.) and others who hold positions of power and may also want to be a part of the Jesus movement? Transformation of the soul and spirit are important aspects of the socioreligious identity Paul is proposing. In fact, Love Sechrest argues that the "in Christ" identity is a social identity, one that Paul understands to be a third race. Sechrest writes: "Yet the scandal of Paul's gospel is that it preaches a transformed identity, unapologetically demanding that Christians give preference to the Christian race over their birth race."[41] The creation of a third race enables Paul to expand the borders of Jewishness to include the nations based on their common faith in Christ. Wan similarly surmises: "Paul constructed the Galatians into a 'new' ethnos around a new symbol: inChristness. This new ethnos was not thought of as a new people but really the renewal of an old, since it was built on Jewish and Gentile particularities."[42] However, what particularities are occluded in the creation of this new race? Caroline Johnson Hodge concludes her examination of Pauline epistles with a similar observation: "Ethnicity is not removed from this *universal* goal; it lies at the core of his mission."[43] That is, Paul's universal goal of including the nations in the story of his people, the Jewish people, is conducted in a very particular manner. Universalism in Paul's writing provides the appearance of a unified identity that is beyond individual differences, yet universality is entangled with particularity. This identity isn't "come one, come all"; there are requirements, and as simple as belief in Jesus Christ may sound, the letter to the Galatians makes clear that faith in Jesus already meant various things to different people. This entanglement elucidates a complicated web of relations that exists in any community attempting to bring diverse people together under the rubric of one category.

"Putting on Christ" does not conceal the very distinctions highlighted in the baptismal creed. Paul makes an argument for how distinctive the Galatian converts are to live as believers. (They are to be distinctive from those who are outside the community of believers and to be the same as everyone that is within.) Neil Elliott, in his book, *The Arrogance of the Nation*, suggests that "this ideal of universalism and transcendence as it is understood in a Western context marks the limits of discourse as constrained by capitalist ideology."[44] For Elliott, universalism eclipses the important issues of class and power. Significantly, Elliott also cautions us to be mindful of the lens we are using when reading this text; reading from a Western context will bring to the fore different issues and concerns. For example, Brad Braxton argues that Paul, in fact, is suggesting that the salvific work of Jesus enables the Galatians to embrace what makes them distinctive. Braxton, asserting that in chapter 3 Paul focuses primarily on ethnic relationships, writes: "If Paul's declaration in 3:28 was meant to depict the abolishing of social distinctions, he would have effectively undercut the force of his whole argument. Paul's entire evangelistic campaign was designed to bring the Gentiles into the Church as Gentiles."[45] To be clear, a transformation of sorts was still necessary. However, Braxton suggests that Paul is "not asserting the obliteration of difference, but rather the obliteration of *dominance*."[46] If Paul, in fact, is proposing accepting differences (particularly embodied differences) in a different but equal model, then what we find in this epistle is potentially a way of reading difference differently.

(IM)PERFECT HARMONY: READING DIFFERENCES DIFFERENTLY

Christian identity formation, like all identities, often depends on the creation of an Other to more clearly see the Christian Self. In the text of Galatians, the identity Paul attempts to create is an "in Christ" identity. It is formed over and against a particular Jewish and a Galatian identity. For Paul, if the Galatians are circumcised, they are nullifying the work of Jesus. They do not need to change their physical appearance to be accepted into this community. According to Paul, the work of Jesus concerns the heart, and it is manifested in the spirit. All else is subsumed, but not erased, by an act of faith. However, not conforming in this particular case could potentially have been dangerous for the Galatians. If viewed by the Roman imperial system as a Jewish sect, Jesus followers who could and would be circumcised would likely find themselves in a less precarious situation.

Like Paul, I am concerned with flesh and bodies. The bodies of African Americans that continue to be abused and destroyed by a hegemonic system in the United States necessitates an embodied faith. The belief that spirits and souls are more important than bodies has material implications, and the damaging effects are more likely to affect those with bodies that are always already deemed as disposable, as Others. Thus, I am suspicious of Paul's desire to control Galatian bodies. Despite how liberating "not changing" oneself may sound to our contemporary ears, I am concerned about a people whose own understanding of their conversion is seen as "foolish." Paul asks for the community to imitate him: "Friends, I beg you, become as I am, for I also have become as you are. You have done me no harm" (4:12). However, they cannot become like him in all things, an indication that the community can be "almost but not quite the same" as Paul. The "do as I say but not as I do" argument is never convincing. Paul continues, "For in Christ Jesus neither circumcision nor uncircumcision counts for anything; the only thing that counts is faith working through love" (5:6). Either it matters or it doesn't. Despite these words, it seems to matter a great deal what choice the Galatians make.

Nonetheless, I do think Paul's letter to the Galatians can prove helpful for thinking about how we construct identity today, particularly racial and religious identities. How does one create community and more specifically unity in a community that is diverse? This appears to be Paul's goal. Erasing differences is clearly not the objective. Braxton critiques the promotion of such ideas like that of a "melting pot" and/or "raceless society" as "naïve and misguided" in the United States. He affirms that "genuine unity will emerge from a dialogue among culturally distinct groups. Like textual meaning, racial unity is not discovered; it is created or birthed into existence."[47] Highlighting the difficulty of racial unity, Braxton importantly purports that to achieve unity, it is necessary to do the painful work of acknowledging, celebrating, and understanding the importance of difference. Too often, we begin to think of differences from a place of deficiency—what one lacks or is missing. What if the starting point is how one's presence is beneficial to the community? Angela Parker similarly reads the possibility for racial reconciliation in the letter to the Galatians. She concludes, "As communities seek solidarity across particularities and differences, what might be the basis for our shared dialogue and praxis? I suggest we forgo disembodied readings of scripture that lead to disembodied theological constructions."[48] Understanding the beauty and value and necessity of *all* bodies can be a starting point of reading difference differently.

Paul has suggestions for existing in harmony. He describes the fruits of the spirit as "love, joy, peace, patience, kindness, generosity, faithfulness, gentleness, and self-control. There is no law against such things" (5:22). Paul further admonishes the community by stating, "So then, whenever we have an opportunity, let us work for the good of all, especially for those of the family of faith" (6:10). Paul has a vision for a community of believers and what it would take for them to live peaceably together. I believe his vision was valuable then and is worthwhile in our contemporary moment. Braxton's example of a choral group proves instructive as well. He writes, "Harmony is cooperative union of different voices. The various vocal parts must maintain their distinctiveness, even as they unite, if harmony is to exist."[49] On the other hand, cacophony is the result of the same voices not working cooperatively, but individually. Understanding vocal harmony can very well be the beginning of understanding difference differently.

For a dialogue about diversity in the United States to be productive, it must begin in a place from which difference is understood differently. An emphasis on equity and equality and honest assessments of power that ultimately challenge the ways the Other is demeaned and belittled is a place to start. Diversity of thought, voices, and visions is necessary for change to be real and sustaining. Talking about harmony is not the same as creating harmony.

In some ways, Paul's letter to the Galatians is a cautionary tale—one in which he calls the community to be in Christ, but not of Christ, which has resulted in a universalism in Christianity that subsumes difference (despite whether that was Paul's intent). This is analogous to the platitude that declares one can be in this world but not of this world. Paul does not want the Galatians to participate in a Christ identity in some ways (circumcision and works of the flesh) while participating in this same community in other prescribed ways (faith and works of the spirit). The reality is one cannot divorce themselves from their immediate context. Context informs who one is. This platitude, often employed in some forms of contemporary Christianity, is not only an attempt to stake a claim of a particular kind of otherness (we are spiritual, focused on things from above, concerned solely with an otherworldly future), but also intended to value the otherworldly over this world. As I have suggested to be "in Christ" as Paul describes it could similarly ignore the material implications of the Galatians participating in the Jesus movement. The early Christians could have been seeking a more just world, here and now, and instead were being taught to focus on the justice that had already been achieved in an otherworldly realm. Paul's proposal is just that, a suggestion. It is not clear how the Galatians chose to live out their in-Christ identity.

The implications of an "in this world but not of it" identity construction are wide reaching—from environmental degradation to lack of involvement in the political system. In short, this affirmation is a denial of reality. We are all in this world and of this world. The Galatians are both in Christ and of Christ, both spirit and flesh. As Paul teaches, "for neither circumcision nor uncircumcision is anything; but a new creation is everything" (6:15). It is possible that this community responded to Paul that they are both in Christ and of Christ. Those who could may have participated in the act of circumcision. They could have responded by celebrating an identity that affirms their entire being. Reading difference differently means acknowledging the equal significance of all aspects of identity while at the same time working together to make the vision of community, of the new creation, a reality.

NOTES

1. Toni Morrison, *The Origin of Others* (Cambridge, MA: Harvard University Press, 2017), 3.
2. Morrison, *Origin of Offers*, 19.
3. Shanell T. Smith provides an outline for this approach in her book, *The Woman Babylon and the Marks of Empire: Reading Revelation with a Postcolonial Womanist Hermeneutics of Ambiveilence* (Minneapolis: Fortress, 2014). Here, she suggests the lens of a postcolonial womanist hermeneutic of ambi*veil*ence, combining Bhabha's concept of ambivalence, with W.E.B. DuBois's notion of the veil, alongside womanist biblical interpretation. Of these analytical categories, she writes: "[Postcolonial womanist biblical hermeneutics] enables me to get past the impasse whereby one part of the biblical text appears to be purely anti-imperialistic literature, and the other . . . part is like holding up a mirror in which the text reflects empire" (66). The analytical categories in this essay similarly help me analyze the both/and aspects I identify in Galatians.
4. The genitive most often is translated "of," for example *Iēsou Christou* can be rendered of Jesus Christ and therefore could mean belonging to Jesus Christ or that Jesus Christ is the origin/creator of this new identity. At times, however, the genitive can be rendered "in." In this case, the genitive meaning would be the object of the action: for instance in "faith in Jesus Christ," Jesus is the object of one's faith. For the purposes of this paper, I suggest that to be "of Jesus Christ" may have multiple meanings, one of which may include belonging to the family of Jesus in the sense of kinship, perhaps biological, as opposed to being "in Jesus Christ" whereby Jesus is the object of the identity. One can consider the distinction that Paul could have been attempting to make between Jewish followers of Jesus (of Jesus Christ) versus the other ethnicities that would come to follow Jesus (in Jesus Christ). Ultimately, I suggest the possibility of assuming both identities or eliminating any such distinctions.
5. Julia Kristeva, *Strangers to Ourselves*, trans. Leon S. Roudiez (New York: Columbia University Press, 1991), 1.
6. Kristeva, *Strangers to Ourselves*, 29–30.
7. Kristeva, *Strangers to Ourselves*, 192.
8. Ahmed, *Strange Encounters: Embodied Others in Post-Coloniality* (London: Routledge, 2000), 4.
9. Ahmed, *Strange Encounters*, 55.
10. Ahmed, *Strange Encounters*, 6.
11. Ahmed, *Strange Encounters*, 180.
12. The three-fifths clause is found in Art. I, Sec. 2, of the U.S. Constitution of 1787. Although the clause pertains to representation in Congress, it nonetheless is an indictment of racial views in the United States at this time.
13. The text in Genesis appears to combine different traditions, the Yahwist (J) and Priestly (P) traditions. These sources often tell the same story with different emphases. Though, the present essay is not concerned with source criticism and will only address the text in the

manner in which we have it today, it is important to note the complexity of the text even at its most basic level.

14. David M. Whitford, *The Curse of Ham in the Early Modern Era: The Bible and the Justifications for Slavery* (Burlington, VT: Ashgate, 2009), 169. Whitford provides alternative ways in which Ham was understood. He writes: "As identity became an important factor of interpretation, the characteristics of Ham were modeled on the predetermined descendent of Ham." In the Middle Ages, Ham was a serf. "Annius took the etiological task back to the origins of the postdiluvian sin rather than slavery. For Annius, Ham's importance was founded on his role as Zoroaster and his identity as Saturn. He was important because he explained the origins of magic and sin" (169–70).

15. Paul Harvey, "'A Servant of Servants Shall He Be': The Construction of Race in American Religious Mythologies," in *Religion and the Creation of Race and Ethnicity: An Introduction*, ed. Craig Prentiss (London and New York: New York University Press, 2003), 19.

16. Harvey, "A Servant of Servants," 19.

17. David M. Goldenberg. *The Curse of Ham: Race and Slavery in Early Judaism, Christianity, and Islam* (Princeton, NJ: Princeton University Press, 2003), 176.

18. Edward Said, *Orientalism* (New York: Vintage, 1979), 12.

19. Said, *Orientalism*, 207.

20. Homi K. Bhabha, *The Location of Culture* (London: Routledge, 1994), 122.

21. Bhabha, *The Location of Culture*, 123.

22. Marc Ferro, *Colonization: A Global History* (London: Routledge, 1997), 11.

23. Musa W. Dube, *Postcolonial Feminist Interpretation of the Bible* (St. Louis: Chalice Press, 2000), 47.

24. Dube, *Postcolonial Feminist Interpretation,* 48.

25. Here, my use of "talk back" is informed by Mitzi Smith in her book, *Womanist Sass and Talk Back: Social (In)Justice, Intersectionality, and Biblical Interpretation* (Eugene, OR: Cascade, 2018). Smith defines "sass" and "talk back" thusly: "That is what sass does; it challenges those systems, traditions, and people that are neither just nor moral, but deleterious and deadly to one's self, one's people, and to the human race" (41).

26. Paul reiterates this in 1:11–12: "For I want you to know, brothers and sisters that the gospel that was proclaimed by me is not of human origin for I did not receive it from a human source nor was I taught it, but I received it through a revelation of Jesus." NRSV translations, unless otherwise indicated.

27. Galatians 2:15, my translation.

28. James C. Scott, *Domination and the Arts of Resistance: Hidden Transcripts* (New Haven, CT: Yale University Press, 1990), 26.

29. Scott, *Domination and the Arts of Resistance*, 26.

30. Sze-kar Wan, "The Letter to the Galatians," in *A Postcolonial Commentary on the New Testament Writings*, eds. Fernando F. Segovia and R. S. Sugirtharajah (London: T&T Clark, 2009), 248.

31. Wan, "The Letter to the Galatians," 256–57.

32. Ronald Charles, *Paul and the Politics of Diaspora* (Minneapolis: Fortress, 2014), 88.

33. Stephen Mitchell, *Anatolia: Land, Men, and Gods in Asia Minor, vol. 1: The Celts and the Impact of Roman Rule* (Oxford: Clarendon, 1993). There were a variety of ways in which unity was promoted in the conquered nations of imperial Rome. One example was imperial religion—that is, emperor worship. Mitchell asserts the following:

[E]mperor worship was arguably the most significant way in which provincial subjects were made aware of and came to terms with imperial power within the framework of their communities. Religious activity in the cities of the empire was, with rare exceptions, explicit and public, often involving the whole community in unified celebration of the gods. Its significance lay in rituals which all could observe and in which many citizens participated. These ranged from prayer, sacrifice, solemn ceremony, and religious processions to feasts, games, and festivals. Emperor worship in essence conformed to this familiar pattern, but imperial festivals and rituals in provincial cities frequently outnumbered and outweighed those of the other gods. (113)

34. Brigette Kahl, *Galatians Re-Imagined: Reading with the Eyes of the Vanquished* (Minneapolis: Fortress, 2010), 3.
35. Kahl, *Galatians Re-Imagined*, 31.
36. Bhabha, *The Location of Culture*, 123.
37. Neil Elliott, "The Apostle Paul and Empire" in *The Shadow of Empire: Reclaiming the Bible as a History of Faithful Resistance*, ed. Richard A. Horsley (Louisville, KY: Westminster John Knox Press, 2008), 105–6.
38. In Christ, but not of Christ is a platitude found in some Christian circles. It often indicates a separation from the secular world in some way. It often mitigates any involvement in conflict and particularly any struggle for justice here and now, always pointing to an otherworldly utopian vision.
39. Daniel Boyarin, *A Radical Jew: Paul and the Politics of Identity* (Berkeley: University of California, 1991), 7.
40. Kahl, *Galatians Re-Imagined*, 31.
41. Love Sechrest, *A Former Jew: Paul and the Dialectics of Race* (London: T&T Clark, 2009), 228.
42. Wan, "The Letter to the Galatians," 260.
43. Caroline Johnson Hodge, *If Sons, Then Heirs: A Study of Kinship and Ethnicity in the Letters of Paul* (Oxford: Oxford University Press, 2007), 152.
44. Neil Elliott, *The Arrogance of Nations: Reading in the Shadow of Empire* (Minneapolis: Fortress, 2008), 134.
45. Brad Braxton, *No Longer Slaves: Galatians and African American Experience* (Collegeville, MN: Liturgical, 2002), 93.
46. Braxton, *No Longer Slaves*, 94.
47. Braxton, *No Longer Slaves*, 95–96.
48. Angela Parker, "One Womanist's View of Racial Reconciliation in Galatians," *Journal of Feminist Studies in Religion* 34, no. 2 (2018): 39.
49. Braxton, *No Longer Slaves*, 95.

WORKS CITED

Ahmed, Sara. *Strange Encounters: Embodied Others in Post-Coloniality*. London: Routledge, 2000.
Bhabha, Homi K. *The Location of Culture*. London: Routledge, 1994.
Boyarin, Daniel. *A Radical Jew: Paul and the Politics of Identity.* Berkeley: University of California, 1991.
Braxton, Brad R. *No Longer Slaves: Galatians and the African American Experience*. Collegeville, MN: Liturgical, 2002.
Charles, Ronald. *Paul and the Politics of Diaspora*. Minneapolis: Fortress, 2014.
Dube, Musa W. *Postcolonial Feminist Interpretation of the Bible*. St. Louis: Chalice, 2000.
Elliott, Neil. "The Apostle Paul and Empire." In *In the Shadow of Empire: Reclaiming the Bible as a History of Faithful Resistance*, edited by Richard A. Horsley, 97–116. Louisville, KY: Westminster John Knox, 2008.
———. *The Arrogance of Nations: Reading in the Shadow of Empire*. Minneapolis: Fortress, 2008.
Ferro, Marc. *Colonization: A Global History*. London: Routledge, 1997.
Goldenberg, David M. *The Curse of Ham: Race and Slavery in Early Judaism, Christianity, and Islam*. Princeton, NJ: Princeton University Press, 2003.
Harvey, Paul. "'A Servant of Servants Shall He Be': The Construction of Race in American Religious Mythologies." In *Religion and the Creation of Race and Ethnicity: An Introduction*, edited by Craig Prentiss, 13–27. New York: New York University Press, 2003.

Johnson Hodge, Caroline. *If Sons, Then Heirs: A Study of Kinship and Ethnicity in the Letters of Paul*. Oxford: Oxford University Press, 2007.

Kahl, Brigitte. *Galatians Re-Imagined: Reading with the Eyes of the Vanquished*. Minneapolis: Fortress, 2010.

Kristeva, Julia. *Strangers to Ourselves*, translated by Leon S. Roudiez. New York: Columbia University Press, 1991.

Mitchell, Stephen. *Anatolia: Land, Men, and Gods in Asia Minor, vol. 1: The Celts and the Impact of Roman Rule*. Oxford: Clarendon, 1993.

Morrison, Toni. *The Origin of Others*. Cambridge, MA: Harvard University Press, 2017.

Parker, Angela N. "One Womanist's View of Racial Reconciliation in Galatians." *Journal of Feminist Studies in Religion* 34, no. 2 (2018): 23–40.

Said, Edward. *Orientalism*. New York: Vintage, 1979.

Scott, James C. *Domination and the Arts of Resistance: Hidden Transcripts*. New Haven, CT: Yale University Pres, 1990.

Sechrest, Love. *A Former Jew: Paul and the Dialectics of Race*. London: T&T Clark, 2009.

Smith, Mitzi J. *Womanist Sass and Talk Back: Social (In)Justice, Intersectionality, and Biblical Interpretation*. Eugene, OR: Cascade, 2018.

Smith, Shanell T. *The Woman Babylon and the Marks of Empire: Reading Revelation with a Postcolonial Womanist Hermeneutics of Ambiveilence*. Minneapolis: Fortress, 2014.

Wan, Sze-kar. "The Letter to the Galatians." In *A Postcolonial Commentary on the New Testament Writings*, edited by Fernando F. Segovia and R. S. Sugirtharajah, 246–64. London: T&T Clark, 2007.

Whitford, David M. *The Curse of Ham in the Early Modern Era: The Bible and the Justifications for Slavery*. Burlington, VT: Ashgate, 2009.

Chapter Three

Hagar's Children Still *Ain't* Free

*Paul's Counterterror Rhetoric, Constructed Identity,
Enslavement, and Galatians 3:28*

Mitzi J. Smith

Why is slavery an appropriate moral framework for Christians? In all slave societies, the threat of being enslaved and enslavement terrorized its (potential) victims. Under the Roman Empire, any people or nation that Rome conquered could expect to be enslaved; war was the source of the vast majority of Rome's slaves. Because the Apostle Paul deploys enslavement and the threat of enslavement as a framework for his rhetorical strategy in his letter to the Galatians, I read Galatians as counterterror discourse about those whom Paul characterizes as a terror to the Galatian believers. According to Paul, by demanding that the Galatians submit to circumcision, proponents of circumcision for Gentile believers are a threat to their freedom *in Christ.* The Galatians who are abandoning the gospel of Christ, as Paul preached it, are being (re)enslaved. Paul's counterterror rhetoric strategically deploys slavery/enslavement in defense of the gospel he preached and his apostolic authority. Enough Galatian believers were deserting Paul's gospel to draw his rage. Having heard another/different gospel (*heteron euangelion*), some Galatians made decisions concerning their bodies with which Paul vehemently disagrees.

In this conflict, contested truth/gospel and the Galatian male believers' bodies—specifically their uncircumcised penises as a site of struggle—intersect. Similarly, in the U.S. during the antebellum period and in the later nineteenth to early twentieth centuries, black men and women (and a few whites) were lynched because white people asserted that black men, particularly their penises, threatened white women's virtue and thus white male dominance. The lynching of black men was designed to create a "culture of fear predicated on a fabricated dichotomy of blackness that is antithetical to an imagined whiteness."[1] In contemporary American society, black and brown bodies are constructed as dangerous and the perennial potential domestic terrorists that threaten democratic freedoms connected with or understood primarily as the dominance of white male authority, power, and privilege. Reading from an African American and a womanist perspective, I create an inter(con)textual dialogue between ancient and contemporary (con)texts. Both reading approaches privilege truth telling and epistemologies about black lives, suffering, and enslavement. As a womanist biblical scholar, I talk back to Paul's letter to the Galatians and his rhetorical construction of identity. Talk-back is a subversive mother tongue and language of resistance that is relentless in the pursuit of freedom.[2] A womanist hermeneutics of liberation, Renita Weems asserts, recognizes that even the "Bible cannot go unchallenged in so far as the role it has played in legitimating the dehumanization of people of African ancestry in general and the sexual exploitation of women of African ancestry in particular."[3] Paul exploits slavery and the enslaved woman known as Hagar, while championing his unique freeing gospel. Our failure to challenge Paul as contemporary readers will result in the uncritical adoption of a duplicitous understanding of freedom and slavery or a slaveholder religion.[4]

Just as Paul's opponents are represented as a threat to the Galatians' freedom *in Christ*, nonwhite bodies are viewed as the enemy of or impediment to white liberties, the latter of which have been ideologically and aesthetically secured by the whitewashing of Jesus/Christ, the construction of God as the ultimate slave master, and Jesus as God's overseer.[5] Internal debates and ideas about freedom among the dominant group have an impact on the bodies of minoritized "others," while the voices of the latter are silenced. Generally, as Jennifer T. Kaalund states in her essay in this volume, "In Christ, but Not of Christ: Reading Identity Differences Differently in the Letter to the Galatians," the Galatian believers' voices are ignored or lost when Paul's rhetoric is the focus.[6] When Paul's rhetoric goes unchallenged, and the Galatian believers' experience is neither imaginatively reconstructed nor privileged, the Galatians' perspective about what constitutes freedom is absent. We do not know what about the *heteron euangelion* compelled the Galatians to abandon Paul's *euangelion*, but in Paul's view their desertion constitutes a re-enslavement.

This essay proposes that Paul rhetorically constructs an identity for the Galatian believers on the "back" of slavery/enslavement and with insensitivity to the material conditions of enslavement and manumission/emancipation, which was the lived reality of many in the diaspora and of some who joined the *ekklēsiai*, even in Galatia, Asia Minor.[7] Paul's argument against *heteron euangelion* and in defense of his *euangelion* depends on convincing the *ekklēsiai* in Galatia that the *heteron euangelion* effectively (re)enslaves them. He evokes the traumatic experience of enslavement to supposedly prevent the same trauma. In this way Paul revictimizes or retraumatizes any Galatian believers currently or formerly enslaved. At the least, I imagine they would be confused. Whether or not Paul successfully convinced the Galatians of his argument would have depended on the authority they attributed to Paul, the impact of empire, their current social status (i.e., enslaved, freed, freeborn, poor, wealthy, and so on), and their "religious" worldview (e.g., polytheistic or monotheistic).

As a colonized but freeborn man and likely a Roman citizen, Paul's use of enslavement, metaphorically, metaphysically, or allegorically, constitutes both a desensitization and normalization of the material conditions of enslavement. [8] Although Paul himself has no personal experience of enslavement, having perhaps never been enslaved, his privileged status does not hinder him from attempting to establish his authority among the Galatia *ekklēsiai* rhetorically, using slavery which might very well have been more than common knowledge for them but a lived reality. Slavery was a pervasive, cruel, and terrorizing material reality in the Roman Empire. [9] This chapter first examines how Paul vehemently constructs his fellow preachers as enemies of *the* truth and a terror to the Galatians. Second, I demonstrate how Paul responds to intragroup conflict using the enslaved/enslavement-free/freeborn dichotomy as the framework for constructing an *in Christ* identity. As such, Paul rhetorically employs a counterterror strategy complicit with empire building, namely re-establishing his apostleship among the Galatian *ekklēsiai* on the back of slavery. Similarly, the entanglement of U.S. theological and education institutions with African enslavement allowed them to survive, thrive, and remain competitive. Those institutions like Paul assumed a moderate position regarding slavery, being in practice and theologically both antislavery and proslavery, never holistically liberating the enslaved. Third, I address how Paul mobilizes Galatians 3:28 in the service of his counterterror strategy to support his moderate anti/proslavery stance and to reinforce social binaries. No evidence exists to show that members of the early Jesus Christ movement freed enslaved persons who joined it with their owners or independently of them. In the antebellum South, slave narratives testify that Christian enslavers were the cruelest. The Hagar/Sarah allegory demonstrates that Paul's freedom in Christ is only spiritual, offering no relief from the material conditions of enslavement, particularly for the enslaved who are *in Christ*.

PAUL'S RHETORICAL CONSTRUCTION OF THE TROUBLEMAKERS

Galatians is a letter written by an angry Paul. As far as he is concerned his is a just indignation. Paul wastes no time with the niceties of a thanksgiving or commendation that we find in other Pauline letters (e.g., 1 Cor. 1:4–9; Rom. 1:8–15). First, Paul distinguishes his opponents from himself with his claim to revelatory autonomy and superiority. Paul's claim to special revelation from God is about autonomy or freedom from human authority and author-ities (at least those in Jerusalem, not so much from Rome). Paul begins his letter with an implicit declaration of special revelation explicitly asserting that he neither received it from a human being nor was taught it but received it through the revelation of Jesus Christ (*di' apokalupseos Iesou Christou*; 1:1, 13). Further, Paul implicitly describes himself as free or autonomous in that he was not answerable to the authority of any human being or group of human beings *prior* to explicitly calling himself an enslaved man of Christ (*Christou doulos*) and not a pleaser of people (1:10). In support of his argu-ment, Paul shares his history of persecuting the *ekklēsiai* of God, that God called him while in his mother's womb, and his travel itinerary from the time God revealed his son to him until his visit to Jerusalem of his own accord and in his own time. Any communication and physical contact he had with the Jerusalem leaders and elites occurred after he received God's direct revela-tion and only then as a show of cooperation or collegiality (1:12–2:10). God's revelation and commissioning of Paul as an apostle to the Gentiles (*tois ethnesin*) occurred later than that of the other apostles; nevertheless, it is special revelation (1:15–17). The same God who commissioned Peter with the gospel for the circumcised also entrusted Paul with the gospel for the Gentiles (2:8).

Paul's autonomy from other preachers of the gospel results from God's direct revelation to him and his lack of dependence on Jerusalem for second-hand information or epistemologies filtered through anyone among the Jeru-salem leadership and/or elites, the *hoi dokountes* (1:1, 11–2:10). Cain Hope Felder asserts that "Paul gives notice that he is not motivated to curry the favor of a higher class of Christian leaders. Rather Paul only seeks the favor of an impartial God who has made the Christ-event possible."[10] Yet, Felder argues, according to Galatians 2:6, "Paul does not recognize any higher class of Christian leader with a more authentic call than his own apostolic office, [encouraging] the Galatians to join him in opposing such oppressive external 'authority' by repudiating class distinctions."[11] Paul puts himself in a class by himself, and the Galatians are his subordinates (whether the oppression is only external is another matter). In this constructed hierarchy, Paul is *the* apostle to the Gentiles, and the preacher of the only legitimate and superior gospel proclaimed to the Galatians. Paul expects the Galatians to take his word about what happened in his private meeting with the elites: it was only to ensure that he was not running and had not run in vain (*eis kenon*) (2:2). With this Paul infers that, unlike him, his opponents are dependent on the Jerusalem leaders and elites.

Second, Paul asserts that his "opponents" are perverters of the gospel he preached; they are peddling fake good news. In fact, the others are causing confusion, and they pervert (*metastrepsai*) the good news of Christ, the anointed of God. Thus, they are enemies of God and Paul (1:8). Indeed, they are troublemaker(s) (*ho tarassōn*; *hoi tarassontes*) (1:7; 5:10). Twice Paul pronounces a curse upon these troublemakers and perverters of his gospel (1: 8, 9), which is what Paul himself, an angel from God, or Paul's co-workers would deserve for perverting the gospel of Christ (1:8). To be cursed is the opposite of being blessed; it is the ultimate condemnation and othering: "Let them be anathema (cursed) because they do not preach the gospel of Christ." Such are the enemy of God, of Christ, of the Gospel, of Paul, and of the freedom of the Galatian *ekklēsiai*. Despite recounting his own reign of terror against the *ekklēsiai* in Judea in his former life, Paul demonstrates no mercy toward the troublemakers (1:13–14). According to Paul, those whom he terrorized did not retaliate but instead saw his new life in Christ as an occasion to glorify God (1:24). But the fact that many other preachers are teaching and proclaiming among the Galatian *ekklēsiai* their understanding of what God did in Christ Jesus is not an occasion for praising God in Paul's view.

The troublemakers are like the spying false brothers (*pseudadelphoi*) that attempted to compel Paul to circumcise Titus in Jerusalem; to submit to them would have resulted in enslavement in exchange for freedom in Christ (2:3–5). In his rage, Paul hopes those of the circumcision castrate themselves, presumably as they seek to physically circumcise others (5:12). Do Paul's words represent the neighbor love that Paul encourages the Galatians to practice toward one another—be slaves for one another—or does Paul not see the troublemakers as his neighbors (5:14)? The troublemakers are excluded from the neighbor love Paul commands the Galatians to practice. Ironically, Paul states that anger will forfeit one's inheritance of the kingdom of God (5:20–21). God's kingdom, as implied, is not of the present *kosmos* (world). The Lord Jesus Christ (*kyriou Iesou Christou*) gave himself for "our sins" so that "we might be delivered from the present evil age according to God's will" (1:3–4). Paul argues that the troublemakers are enslaved to the present evil world, and misery is in pursuit of company.

Paul's naming of his "opponents" as "troublemakers" (*hoi tarassontes*) under the gaze of the Roman Empire would have raised the suspicions of Rome toward those who preached a *heteron euangelion*, and perhaps toward the Galatians, if word leaked out. The incitement of the crowds by troublemakers or agitators was a perennial threat within the Roman Empire because unchecked it could lead to rebellion. Rome's identity as a keeper of the peace (*Pax Romana)* depended on its ability to prevent and violently quash revolts.

The roads Rome built allowed for the travel of Paul and his companions to and from Asia Minor *and* the movement of the so-called troublemakers in and out of the region of Galatia to preach. Frequent visits to the region of Galatia placed a burden of hospitality on those who received the many visitors, including the Galatian believers who were expected to demonstrate hospitality toward both "those of the circumcision" and Paul and his co-workers.[12] The relative ease of movement on the roads Rome built is also a reminder of the reach of the Roman Empire and its ability, as the master of the *oikumenē*, to have eyes everywhere, ensuring safe transport of human cargo as well as material goods.[13] Under the Roman Empire a freed person could be returned to enslavement, if his master charged him with the crime of ingratitude and he was found guilty.[14]

Perhaps the ease of travel, the kinds of travelers from around the empire, contributed to the Galatian believers' acceptance of a gospel different from Paul's. Judaism (minus the complexities of a burgeoning Christ movement) would be considered ancient and thus familiar and easier for Rome to control. The Galatian believers who submitted to circumcision after having accepted Paul's gospel by faith in Christ may have been attempting to avoid the gaze of the empire and harassment that would result from adopting a foreign sect and/or failure to participate in the civic imperial cults.[15] Perhaps the socio-economic status of the Galatian believers, particularly of most enslaved and poor free persons, would not permit them to demonstrate in tangible and monetary ways their loyalty to both the imperial cult and to Paul, particularly given Paul's commitment to collect money for the poor in Jerusalem (and not the diaspora?) and the hospitality required of them when any of the preachers visited (Gal. 2:10; Rom. 15:26).

Paul constructs the identity of his "opponents," who are not so different from himself, over against his own sense of self, using violent rhetoric (cf. 1 Cor. 1:10–2:5). Paul's sense of his own self is in flux, depending on the opponents, the circumstances, and what is at stake. Ronald Charles puts it this way:

> Paul's social positioning in the diaspora allows him to imagine, think through, and wrestle with issues of spaces, identities (social, economic, gender), cultures, and traditions. Paul's diasporic identities are constantly in the process of crafting novel ways of being and evolving; his movements across boundaries require him to engage in ever-expanding improvisations susceptible to creating new and complex tapestries of continuity and rupture, similarity and difference.[16]

Paul's improvisations sometimes conflict with the ethics he proposes for those to whom he writes. But in patriarchal and kyriarchal societies, men who are angry about the loss (or threatened loss) of status, privilege, authority, and power do not think clearly.

Paul also implicitly accuses the troublemakers of bewitching the Galatians (3:1; cf. 5:20). The Galatians have foolishly allowed themselves to be bewitched. They played the fool, resulting in the troublemakers casting an evil spell on them. Instructively, in advancing reasons to convert enslaved Africans to Christianity, the Presbyterian evangelist Charles Colcock Jones, a professor of ecclesiastical history and polity at Columbia Theological Seminary (CTS) in two separate stints and a board member in the nineteenth century, believed that conversion could eliminate the threat that "superstitions brought from Africa" might become weapons in the hands of the enslaved against their enslavers. Jones had in view the Denmark Vesey Conspiracy of 1822 that the conjurer Gullah Jack influenced.[17] Paul took the Galatian's abandonment of the truth of his gospel as a personal attack against his apostolic authority and a blow against their status as enslaved of Christ *and* free in Christ.

THE INTRAGROUP CONFLICT AND THE ENTANGLEMENTS OF FAITH, EMPIRE, AND SLAVERY

Like Paul himself, the spies and the troublemakers or perverters of Paul's gospel are Judeans/Jewish men (*Ioudaioi*) who are insisting that the Galatians who joined the Jesus Christ movement, which is a Judean/Jewish movement, submit to circumcision (2:8–10).[18] But Paul is quite practical. How much success can he realize in the diaspora as the one whom God sent to preach the gospel of Christ to the Gentiles if grown men are compelled to be circumcised? This is an intragroup conflict, and the stakes are high for Paul, as his rhetoric and tone demonstrate. Paul is concerned about his own authority, his unique call to preach the gospel of Christ to the nations/Gentiles, and his vocational success.

Paul is both an insider and an outsider. He spends a great deal of time among Gentiles, but he is Judean/Jewish and desires to be accepted by the latter but on his own terms. Paul "finds solidarity among the mostly non-Judean members of his communities, yet he strives, or seems to crave, to find acceptance from his kinsmen."[19] Paul also struggles to maintain his authority among Gentile believers. We do not know how the Galatian believers ultimately responded to Paul's letter and/or how his competitors fared in Asia Minor; their writings, if any, and proclamation were not canonized. Canonization sacralized and in some sense deified Paul and his truth or perspective, silencing his competitors.

Paul argues that the Gentiles can only be free *in Christ* and that means without circumcision but by faith through grace; faith is the only necessary condition for being included in the family of God (3:29). Faith "makes room for a perception of the Messiah Jesus."[20] But faith in Christ also means a rejection of gospels that are contrary to Paul's, leaving Paul to his own designs, void of internal (or external) critique. Faith is not simply faith, in Paul's view; it is faith based on the acceptance of his gospel or teaching as *the* truth and a rejection of all others. I prefer the Paul that acknowledges that we "see through a glass darkly" (cf. 1 Cor. 13:12). Paul evokes "faith" as if it is objective, neutral, and never political or contingent on human-constructed truths or beliefs, even if inspired/revealed. Faith, in Paul's view, has no room for doubt, dispute, dialogue, or error regarding the "truth" upon which it is based or that evokes it. No human opinion—neither the Galatians' nor that of the leaders in Jerusalem—matters to Paul because in his view God's revelation to him through Jesus Christ is special and unique.[21] Such certainty is hostile to self-critique and to other voices. Elsa Tamez argues that a reading of Galatians demonstrates "that freedom is the experience of liberation from any condition of slavery, be it from the law (*nomos*), from the power of sin, from 'the weak and beggarly elements' of the world (*stoicheia*) or any other type of alienation or subjugation."[22] But what about freedom to reject Paul's singular claim to *the truth* and to use one's God-given freedom to determine what constitutes good news relative to one's own context and circumstances?

It was faith in God that compelled enslaved Africans to ask if (and how) God is a liberator God or a God who enslaves? Is God a liberator who only emancipates people who identify with one group or truth? Slave masters in the antebellum South in collusion with Christian missionaries or sometimes as evangelists themselves agreed to preach to the enslaved that God is a liberator of the soul and not of the body, and that their salvation depended on an acceptance of the gospel as preached and taught to them through evangelists/preachers whom the enslavers authorized and their catechisms, catechisms often prepared especially for teaching the enslaved.[23]

Paul's argument is framed around the explicit and implicit dichotomy of freedom/autonomy versus enslavement. Paul *employs* the Greek masculine noun *doulos* (slave), the verbs *douloō* (to slave for) and *katadouloō* (to re-enslave), the feminine noun *douleia* (slave), and the noun *paidiskē* (slave girl) sixteen times (1:10; 2:4; 3:28; 4:2–3, 8–9, 22–23, 30–31; 5:1, 13). The antithesis of enslavement or to enslave is articulated with the Greek noun *eleutheria* (freedom), the verb *eleutheroō* (to free), and the adjective *eleutheros* (free) eleven times (2:4; 3:28; 4:22–26, 30–31; 5:1,13).[24] The Greek words "slave/to slave" and "freedom/free/to free" usually appear together. Instructively, the Greek noun *charis* (grace) only appears seven times; two instances are in the opening and closing greeting as in all Paul's letters (1:3, 6, 15; 2:9, 21; 5:4; 6:18).

Paul's argument against the troublemakers and their *heteron euangelion* is framed by and grounded on the dichotomous social reality of enslavement and freed/freeborn status. Paul's counterterror discourse is directed against the (re)enslavement and enslavers of the Galatian believers. Enslavement was a terrible and imminent or potential threat that many nations desperately fought to avoid, but one that Paul conjures here. The deployment of enslavement and freedom is a reminder of the oppressive power and pervasive presence of Rome—a slave society that terrorized peoples and lands, conquering and enslaving them. Both Jews/Judeans and Gentiles were colonized peoples under the Roman Empire, but not all were enslaved. Paul "is both a Jewish leader of this Christ movement and a member of a conquered people within the empire, occupying space at the periphery as well as at the center of a very particular marginalized group. These nuances do not seem to exist in Paul's discourse.[25]

It is not unreasonable to presume that many enslaved persons and some freed persons resided in rural Galatia and some of them became members of the *ekklēsiai*. In the rural areas ofGalatia, or the empire generally, one would find the greater numbers of enslaved persons, called *rustici* or agricultural slaves with little hope of social mobility.[26] Perhaps, therefore when Paul leverages (re)enslavement to support his argument in defense of his apostolic authority, he imagined that the Galatian believers would want to avoid the double jeopardy of being physically and metaphysically enslaved.

Paul Is Both Antislavery and Proslavery

The propagation of spiritual emancipation among enslaved Africans enabled antebellum enslavers to sleep well at night believing they had satiated the enslaved with the promise of spiritual freedom in the hereafter where God or Jesus was the ultimate slave master. Thus, enslaved Africans would not expect liberation when they became *in Christ*. In this way, enslavers in the antebellum South were both antislavery and proslavery.

Not a few U.S. educational institutions demonstrated ambivalence regarding the enslavement of Africans during the antebellum period. The Civil War between the South and the North was about the enslavement of Africans, the desire of the South to continue uninhibited its trafficking in human cargo. The American South did not want to abandon the slavocracy and emancipate the Africans they had enslaved; they had more to plant, harvest, and build, and had become accustomed to the pampering and comforts they enjoyed from the enslavement of Africans. Many American institutions were built using enslaved Africans, including Ivy League schools like Harvard, Princeton, Brown, and Yale, and theological schools like Princeton Theological Seminary and Columbia Theological Seminary (CTS), where I now teach.[27] Erskine Clarke recently documented CTS's entanglement with slavery in *To Count Our Days*. It was through its entanglement in the enslavement of Africans with all the economic gains and comforts it brought that CTS survived and amassed huge endowments. CTS professors, board members, executives, students, and donors were among the large plantation owners of the South, as at other schools. Slave owners could secure loans from CTS for planting, mortgages, and human property/enslaved persons; the latter would be held as collateral despite the chance that the seminary itself could become slave owners. Clarke writes that "financial entanglements of the seminary with slavery were not incidental but fundamental to the seminary's life. The Telfair Scholarship was a gift from a family whose firm had, in one decade alone, 'handled and disposed of fifteen cargoes' of slaves"; the seminary's endowment increased through the sale of enslaved Africans, and owners of large slave plantations contributed to CTS's endowment.[28] During the antebellum period, CTS's board and faculty were embroiled in an intragroup conflict about the abolition and morality of enslavement. In the wake of the Civil War, CTS's "unionists" attempted to achieve a "middle way" between enslavement and emancipation and between the worldviews of the South and the North. In 1860, Columbia, South Carolina, where CTS was first established, voted to secede from the Union. The antislavery/proslavery "common ground" that CTS's leadership reached among themselves did not consider the voice of the enslaved and their cry for freedom.[29] Nor did it prioritize the biblical characterization of God as a liberator. As Elsa Tamez argues, "society tied to the market has no more to give; it is exhausted, despite all the money that has been injected. We have not been born for buying and selling or to be objects of the ups and downs of the market. We have been created to continue becoming better human beings."[30] We have never been created to be enslaved/slaves, even to the deity.

Paul, a colonized man, exhibits both antislavery and proslavery fidelities. "Paul" is a Roman name. The Apostle Paul's Jewish name is Saul; we know this from Acts and not from Paul's authentic letters (Acts 13:9).[31] We do not know how Paul came by his Roman name. At the least, that a Jewish/Judean man is named "Paul" signifies an identity marked by hybridity and ambivalence. According to postcolonial cultural and literary critic Homi Bhabha, ambivalence signifies the presence of dualities, which engenders hybridity; the colonized (and colonizer) are hybrid beings; the cultural identity of the colonized and colonizer are not mutually exclusive. Colonial mimicry is a product of and produces ambivalence and hybridity. "Mimicry . . . 'appropriates' the Other as it visualizes power."[32] We can view Paul's rhetorical use of enslavement, metaphorically, metaphysically, or allegorically, in terms of colonial mimicry. Paul identifies himself both as a *doulos Christou* (slave of Christ) and as the apostle who proclaimed the gospel of Jesus Christ resulting in liberation for the Gentiles (1:10).[33] Implicitly, Paul expects the Galatians to see themselves as he views himself, as slaves of Christ. As noted, the Galatian believers are exhorted to slave for each other through love (5:13).[34] Enslavement is emblematic of empire; "the holiest of books—the bible—

bearing both the standard of the cross and the standard of empire finds itself strangely dismembered."[35] As Frederick Douglass wrote, "the morality of *free* society can have no application to *slave* society. . . . Make a man a slave, and you rob him of moral responsibility. Freedom of choice is the essence of all accountability."[36]

Paul deploys enslavement, metaphorically and metaphysically, to characterize his own relationship to Christ *and* the Galatian believers' association with the *stoicheia* (basic components of their pre-Christ lives) in the world (*kosmos*) and their being "in the flesh" (*sarki*) (3:3).[37] Further, Paul argues that "Christ bought us from the condemnation of the *nomos* (*exagorazō ek tēs kataras tou nomou*), having become condemnation for us" (3:13; also 4:5). The verb *exagorazō* signifies the material reality of enslavement, namely, the purchase of human property by one slave owner from another. When Paul likens the *nomos* to a *paidagōgos*, he again invokes the lived reality of enslaved persons who were often the *paidagōgoi* charged with accompanying a young boy to and from school as his tutor or instructor.[38] Given the rhetorical context, that the threat of (re)enslavement is the framework of his argument, and that many of Paul's readers would envision a *paidagōgos* as an enslaved person who supervisors a child's education, it stands to reason that Paul's use of *paidagōgos* strategically invokes enslavement. Children who were under the authority of a *paidagōgos* were subject to same, but in Christ the Galatian believers have become children (*huioi theou*) through their faith in Christ (and of course, as noted, a slave to Christ who has removed the condemnation of the *nomos/paidagōgos*) (3:26; cf. 1:10). This argument further deploys the material reality of enslavement by using the word *paidagōgos* immediately before Galatians 3:28 where Paul asserts that there is neither slave nor free in Christ Jesus. Paul's argument rhetorically replicates an understanding of the dominant social hierarchy and also sacralizes and normalizes the cruelty of enslavement. It is a violent, trauma-inducing rhetorical strategy that Paul employs.

In *Ebony and Ivy*, Craig Wilder asserts that the Christian ministers who were also trustees and administrators at U.S. colleges and universities controlled their enslaved Africans with violence:

> In 1698 the Reverend Samuel Gray, a founding trustee of the College of William and Mary, murdered an enslaved child for running away. Rev. Gray struck the boy on the head, drawing blood, and then put a hot iron to the child's flesh. The minister had the boy tied to a tree, and then ordered another slave to whip him. The boy later died. Gray argued that "such accidents" were inevitable, a position that seems to have succeeded, as a court declined to convict him. The congregation at Christ Church in Middlesex County gave him a considerable quantity of tobacco to resign. The following year, Gray settled at a parish in Westmoreland. He later became the pastor of St. Peter's Church in New Kent . . . Benjamin Wadsworth ministered the First Church in

Boston [where he told his parishioners to] give their slaves time for prayer and
private contemplation, give them to God and pray for them, and let them read
the Bible and other books that would enhance their faith. . . . Leaning on
biblical references, the future Harvard president also instructed his congre-
gants to beat their slaves. Corporal punishments were needed to chastise and
deter wrong, for "a servant will not be corrected by words." Preferring the
biblical term "correction," the pastor warned his audience to avoid "rage and
passion" and "cruel unmerciful" acts, instead always choosing the mildest
penalty that would effectively cure the fault, remember that a good master
needed neither tyranny nor terror. Rev. Wadsworth instructed the slaves sitting
in his church to willfully submit to every godly act and demand made by their
masters including physical punishments. A servant's life should be consumed
in work and prayer, interrupted by brief moments of rest for sustenance. . . .
Neither church nor academy moderated the horrors of slavery.[39]

A slave master's view of terror differs from that of the terrorized enslaved
person.

Paul's metaphorical mobilization of enslavement, particularly in a slave
society where enslaved and freed persons (former enslaved persons) are pervasive, is problematic because it asks the Galatians to continue to view
themselves through the social framework of enslavement when many of them
are likely enslaved, freed persons, and/or enslavers. Paul is a moderate like
many of the Christian board members, professors, students, and donors of
U.S. seminaries, colleges, and universities that built their institutions, reputa-
tions, wealth, well-being, and endowments on the backs of enslaved
Africans.[40] Differently, Amos Jones views Paul as a "militant opponent of
slavery," but Felder rejects Jones's argument as an effort to "contemporize
Paul."[41] As Felder further asserts, Paul "was shrewd and practical enough not
to advance ideas of social revolution, which would not only bring him into
disfavor with the Jerusalem church but cause the Roman obliteration of the
very churches he worked so hard to establish."[42] Dale Martin understands
Paul's metaphorical use of slavery as positive; he argues that Paul summons
"Christians" to abandon "their own interests and to identify themselves with
the interests of those Christians of lower status"; he is no revolutionary in
Martin's view, but Paul "deconstructs the presuppositions that make hierarchical structure unassailable."[43] I argue that Paul's deployment of slavery/
enslavement demonstrates insensitivity, at the least, on Paul's part toward
those among the Galatians who might be enslaved. As Angela Parker asserts,
Paul does not share habitus or a similar decreased body capital as the enslaved persons of the Roman Empire.[44] Also by placing his status as a *doulos
Christou* in apposition to "people pleasers," Paul trivializes the enslaved
person's predicament; the enslaved man or woman *must* please his or her
enslaver or suffer physical violence or death (e.g., Matt. 24:45–25:30).[45]

Further, by describing the Galatians as formerly enslaved, Paul is asking them to view themselves as freed persons, albeit spiritually, and not freeborn. Freed persons or formerly enslaved and now manumitted persons always carry the stigma of their enslavement in their bodies and remain in an oppressive relationship with their former enslavers. As stated above, a freed person could be re-enslaved for demonstrating ungratefulness toward his former slave master. Paul in his ambivalence and mimicry is both antislavery and proslavery, and like the enslavers in the antebellum South, he cannot face his own duplicity and complicity. It is difficult to do the latter, when one surrounds one's self only with those with whom one agrees and views one's truth as the only truth, as Paul seems to have done.

Former enslaved African, Harriet Jacobs also known as Linda Brent, wrote the following in her slave narrative:

> Are the doctors of divinity blind, or are they hypocrites? I suppose some are the one, and some the other; but I think if they felt the interest in the poor and the lowly, that they ought to feel, they would not be so *easily* blinded. A clergyman who goes to the south, for the first time, has usually some feeling, however, vague, that slavery is wrong. The slaveholder suspects this and plays his game accordingly. He makes himself as agreeable as possible; talks on theology, and other kindred topics. The reverend gentleman is asked to invoke a blessing on a table loaded with luxuries. After dinner he walks around the premises, and sees the beautiful groves and flowering vines, and the comfortable huts of favored household slaves. He asks them if they want to be free, and they say, "o, no, massa." This is sufficient to satisfy him. He comes home to publish a "South-Side View of Slavery," and to complain of the exaggerations of abolitionists. He assures people that he has been to the south, and seen slavery for himself; that it is a beautiful "patriarchal institution"; that the slaves don't want their freedom; that they have hallelujah meetings, and other religious privileges. . . . What does *he* know of the half-starved wretches toiling from dawn till dark on the plantations? Of mothers shrieking for their children, torn from their arms by slave traders? Of young girls dragged down into moral filth? Of pools of blood around the whipping post? Of hounds trained to tear human flesh? Of men screwed into cotton gens to die? The slaveholder showed him none of these things, and the slaves dared not tell of them if he had asked them.[46]

GALATIANS 3:28 AND PAUL'S AMBIVALENT STANCE ON ENSLAVEMENT

Minimally, Paul's counterterror rhetoric idealizes the institution of slavery and presents it as an innocuous phenomenon rather than the oppressive and evil system that it was.[47] Paul's use of enslavement obscures and sacralizes the institution of slavery by depicting Christ as an alternative slave master. To affirm enslavement, even metaphorically and metaphysically, makes Galatians 3:28 doublespeak. Either God and Christ are liberators and antislavery or not. Either God and Christ are abolitionists or not. In the antebellum South, abolitionists, who preached a holistic, nondualistic freedom refusing to separate the enslaved person's body from her soul, were considered troublemakers or agitators by Christian and non-Christian slave masters. Both did not want to emancipate enslaved Africans and were willing to fight a bloody civil war to keep them enslaved until it was no longer economically beneficial.

Social categories like race, gender, sexuality, and class tend to reify socially constructed binaries (e.g., white/nonwhite, female/male, heterosexual/homosexual, rich/poor, and slave/free) and camouflage complex identities, relationships, and oppressions. The pre-Christian, ancient Jewish baptismal formula at Galatians 3:28 consists of a list of binaries: Jewish/Judean and Gentile, male and female, enslaved and free. Galatians 3:28 imagines a world of pure binaries that distinguishes certain bodies from others (i.e., Galatians/Gentiles, perverters of the gospel/those of the circumcision, and Jews/Judeans). It affirms a perspective of the world as consisting of Judeans/Jews and the non-Jewish/Judean Other or Gentiles. Within those categories people are either enslaved or free and male or female. Binaries require people to identify as one thing or another and obstruct the different ways that people self-identify and experience oppression and violence. People have intersectional or overlapping identities; they experience the world as, for example, an enslaved/female/mother/believer in Christ. Any oppressions directed at or based upon one's intersecting social identities are experienced as multiple jeopardies. Black feminists and womanists have argued that intersectional analysis allows readers to critically consider what and how social categories such as gender, race/ethnicity, class, sexuality, religious affiliation, dis/ability, nationality, and so on, co-constitute in human experience.[48] Marianne Kartzow has shown that in NT studies we can demonstrate a more complex social structure and identify other social statuses like Greek-slave-female and Jewish-slave-female, for example.[49] We might consider how age, geographical location, sexuality, socio-economic class, and religious affiliation of an enslaved female's enslaver would impact the life of an enslaved female. Bernadette Brooten discusses the construction of females as virgins or as sexually immoral, and she notes that enslaved women, whose bodies were compelled to be constantly available to enslavers, were viewed as inherently sexually immoral or deviant.[50] Black feminists and womanist scholars and activists have long asserted the significance of intersectional social identity, oppressions, and analysis for and on nonwhite women's lives in contemporary discourse and for enactment of laws, justice, and policymaking.[51] In ancient and modern slave societies, enslaved women were thus forced into prostitution. The idea of encouraging an enslaved female (or male) to treat a freeborn male with *agapē* might very well be traumatizing given the sexual and other violence to which they were already subjected (5:13). Little consideration is given to the sexual abuse and sexuality of freed, freeborn, or enslaved men. Further to declare that there is neither male nor female, metaphysically and/or socio-politically, within the rhetorical framework of a dispute about circumcision and in a patriarchy and kyriarchy privileges the experiences of uncastrated men.

Some interpreters understand the baptismal formula in Galatians 3:28 as evidence of the historical practice of social equality among believers within the early *ekklēsiai* and/or at least of spiritual oneness among them. Thus, it is viewed as an appropriate paradigm for building relationships of equality among contemporary Christians. I argue that the creed normalizes racial-ethnic-religious, gender, and class binaries.[52] Elisabeth Schüssler Fiorenza posits that the immediate literary context of the baptismal formula concerns neither baptism nor social relationships; Paul is concerned *not* with the "cultural-political distinctions" but the "religious relationship between Jews and Gentiles."[53] Of course, the terms "religion" and "religious," like "race," are anachronistic, as we note in the introduction to this volume. I am not certain that ancient Jews/Judeans and Gentiles would have made such a distinction but perhaps viewed their lives more holistically. The larger framework or literary context of Galatians 3:28, I argue, concerns and/or assumes sociopolitical relationships among Paul, the troublemakers, the Galatians, and enslaved persons. Fiorenza further asserts that although Galatians 4 addresses "bondage and slavery," the enslaved woman and the freeborn woman, the terms as used "characterize the religious but not the social situation of the Galatian Christian."[54] Nevertheless, we as readers should be concerned with the material realities signified by the terms "enslaved" and "freeborn." However, Fiorenza understands Paul's use of the baptismal creed differently in First Corinthians. She asserts that it undoubtedly affirms "the equality and charismatic giftedness of women and men in the Christian community," where both serve as prophets and worship leaders, are called to a marriage-free existence, and "have mutual rights and obligations within the sexual relationships of marriage."[55] Agreeing with and quoting Wayne Meeks, Fiorenza argues that the baptismal formula engendered basic behavioral changes that modified social roles "at least with respect to women who exercised leadership roles in the house churches and mission of the early Christian movement."[56] Did this include enslaved females? Brad Braxton asserts that Galatians 3:28 encourages faith communities "to strive for more equitable relationships across ethnic, economic, and gender lines"; ethnic differences are maintained but dominance is obliterated.[57]

But in Galatians Paul rhetorically maintains Gentiles and Jews/Judeans as distinct racial-ethnic groups. As Kang-Yup Na asserts, "even as Paul argues . . . for the meaninglessness of those ethno-religious categories in Christ, declaring that in Christ 'there is no longer Jew or Greek' . . . he reveals, almost in the same breath, his bias against gentiles calling them simply sinners" (Gal. 2:15).[58] All the Gentiles are blessed in Abraham because they have faith in Christ (3:8–9). The Gentiles are included but through one Jewish ancestor and on Paul's terms, who is also a Jewish man. In Paul's argument in Galatians, exclusivity is sacralized as race, class, and gender intersect with socio-political "religious" identity.[59] Ethnoreligiously, the Galatian believers cannot be Jewish/Judean without circumcision. Thus, they are being asked to become liminal peoples, being *in Christ* and by extension members of Abraham's family, but not proselytes in the Jewish Jesus Christ movement (3:29). Love Sechrest argues that the Gentile believers are a new race or ethnic group; she states that "the scandal of Paul's gospel is that it preaches a transformed identity, unapologetically demanding that Christians give preference to the Christian race over their birth race."[60] Actually, Paul implicitly asks them to see themselves as *douloi Christou* (1:10; 5:13). Enslaved persons are stripped of race-ethnicity. Mary Gordon posits that

> [t]he typical slave of the early empire belonged to neither east nor west: he was a product of Graeco-Roman civilization [sic], an example of Rome's strange power of absorbing and assimilating aliens. His name was Greek or Roman; his speech, Latin. . . . He lost the great gifts of nationality, its inheritances and inspirations, its vigorous creativeness, its unique, individual quality . . . but he also escaped the limitations of race and tradition.[61]

Even when familial or fictive language of inclusion is used to describe the relationship between the enslaved and their enslavers, neither the hierarchical social distinction between the two nor the oppressive nature of the relationship is abrogated.[62] When Charles Colcock Jones accepted a call to CTS, he brought several slaves with him; they had lived on the two plantations that Jones owned. Jack, Jones's enslaved butler who accompanied him to CTS and when Jones returned to his plantation, could not forget the difference between white people and the enslaved, no matter how relatively "kind" the slave owners could be; the enslaved had to be strategic when resisting the "harsh oppression of [Christian] whites."[63]

The *heteron euangellion* proclaimed by those of the circumcision is likely more appealing to the Galatians since they will not find themselves in a liminal social status that is virtually foreign to Rome. Paul does not renounce his own racial-ethnic-religious identity in favor of a "Christian race." He does not want to raise the suspicions of the empire, but he does want to reclaim his authority as the apostle to Gentiles among the Galatian believers and on his terms.

Ethnic differences are maintained in the Pauline corpus and not within a framework of equality or equity. The Jesus movement is a Jewish/Judean one and its Jewish/Judean male leaders decide on what ethno-religious grounds others, particularly non-Jews/Judeans, will be accepted and retained, and their conduct is scrutinized and judged. Thus, anyone attempting to upset the identity that Paul constructs for Gentile converts through his gospel, whether they be Jew/Judean or Gentile, is considered an outsider, a threat or terror. And they should be cursed, castrated, and accused of witchcraft. Paul characterizes himself as the antithesis of his opponents.

Since Paul constructs the troublemakers as a common enemy terrorizing the community, he deploys the baptismal formula to promote unity within the community. Patricia Hill Collins and Sirma Bilge argue that "identities mobilized in political struggles of disenfranchised groups are not fundamentally fixed and unchanging but rather are *strategically essentialist . . .* [which] creates space for subordinated groups to use identity politics for political goals."[64] In this case, Paul sees himself as under attack and perhaps outnumbered. Paul's attempts to persuade the Galatians that he is not inferior to the Jerusalem leaders perhaps indicate that he was treated as subordinate to them.

The negated binaries in Galatians 3:28 refer only to Jews and Gentiles, male and female, slave and free who were baptized in Christ Jesus, and only metaphysically or spiritually. Galatians 3:28, as part of Paul's counterterror strategy, is more a statement about boundaries, exclusion, insiders and outsiders; Paul has "circled the wagons." It is deployed as a statement of unity against the agitators. Calls for unity against a common terror threat are neither predicated on nor require that equity exists within the community. In counterterror rhetoric, constructing identity over against a common enemy can divert attention away from internal inequities and inequalities. The U.S. has historically characterized black people as the common enemy of a capitalistic nation, convincing poor white people that it is because of black people that they have not experienced the socioeconomic mobility they deserve. Some authorities in the U.S. constructed immigrant populations (primarily those of African descent, Muslims, and Latinx) as a common threat to America's socio-economic stability and growth, its nationalism and American patriotism (i.e., white nationalism). Such rhetoric deflects from the domestic terror within the U.S., which in terms of mass shootings has been overwhelmingly white and male.

Hagar's Children Still Ain't Free

Hagar's children continue to be constructed as the offspring of an enslaved woman forced to be the surrogate of Abram's deferred promise.[65] Hagar continues to be identified and stigmatized as an enslaved woman who births only slave children and the perennial outside threat, despite God's promise that the descendants of Hagar's child Ishmael would also become a great nation (Gen. 21:11–13).

In Galatians 4:21–5:1 the racial-ethnic boundaries are drawn, exclusivity is sacralized, and truth is truncated and recontextualized.[66] And the good news for Hagar's children is lost in translation, when, as a counterterror strategy, Paul invokes Hagar to support his argument: those *in Christ* are Abraham and Sarah's freeborn children. As in all slave societies, the children born to an enslaved woman are born "slaves" and belong to their mother's slave master. Thus, Paul asserts that Hagar's children are born slaves/enslaved; the Galatian believers are not children of the *paidiskē* (enslaved girl) Hagar (4:31). Contrary to Galatians 3:28, there *is* slave *and* free after all.

In Paul's mind, slavery and the Hagar/Ishmael/Abram "slave" narrative are appropriate paradigms to deploy in his rhetorical strategy against his fellow preachers. N. T. Wright argues that in Galatians, the story of Israel is creatively recounted beginning with Abraham backward and ending with *Christos* (in an incorporative and participatory sense signifying the "church"), and this retelling is strategic on Paul's part, demonstrating that *Christos* is Messianic and not just a title (4:1–7).[67] Wright further states that the political sense of Christos can be understood in the letter's warning against *heteron euangelion*, signifying the gospel of Caesar and Rome.[68] Bill Richards names Paul's allegory "the competing wives-and-sons, Hagar-and-Ishmael / Sarah-and-Isaac" allegory. Paul, Richards asserts, is saying that those of the circumcision "are only offering [the Galatian believers] slave-status in the household of faith." [69] Further, considering the Christological hymn in chapter 2 of Philippians, which asserts that Jesus emptied himself and assumed the form of a *doulos*, Richards writes, "But what if that god had himself taken the form of a slave? A god who knew the slave experience first-hand? Had known the lash of human masters? Had even been crucified like so many of them? And had risen above it? Now there was a god worth slaving to."[70] It is much easier for those who have never been enslaved, and never expect to be, like Paul and Richards, to celebrate a god depicted as a slave master. Unfortunately, Richards begins his essay by describing the material conditions of enslavement in the Roman Empire and slides into a partial metaphysical understanding of slavery.

I propose that Paul's mobilization of enslavement and freedom is geopolitical; it is about regaining apostolic authority among the Galatian *ekklēsiai* in Asia Minor, which Paul lost to so-called agitators who infringed upon the territory where Paul preached his gospel to the Galatians as the apostle to the Gentiles. But Paul is neither anti-Caesar or anti-Rome. On the contrary, he reinscribes the dichotomy of enslaved/freeborn in order to draw boundaries between the circumcisers/troublemakers and those *in Christ*, while the material conditions of enslavement remain unchallenged.

Nonwhite peoples are Hagar's contemporary enslaved children. A religion that attempts to eliminate inequality and inequity only within a community of believers and only metaphysically does not practice equality and equity but exclusivity and a false gospel. Such a community ultimately condones and is complicit in the use of terror as a counterterror strategy against the Other who is constructed as outsider and against those who challenge dualistic ideas of freedom that leave bodies enslaved and oppressed. Additionally, Paul's use of the Sarah/Hagar allegory demonstrates he does not reject enslavement of the material body and that enslavement is a useful and appropriate image for describing what the Galatian believers are *not* called to be, namely Hagar or her slave children. Hagar's children are constructed as the antithesis of Abraham and Sarah's children. The Galatians can become Abraham and Sarah's children without submitting to circumcision, since Abram responded to God's call and promise prior to the covenant symbolized by circumcision (4:5–7; 5:21–31). If the Gentile believers reject Paul's construction of their identity as both enslaved *and* free in Christ, they are Hagar's progeny, and they are condemned to the fate of being the enslaved children of a *paidiskē*. Hagar's children still *ain't* free. For Hagar's children to be free, they must reject a Christology and theology of enslavement. Unlike Paul, God is not a moderate. God is a liberator.

NOTES

1. See Angela D. Sims, *Lynched: The Power of Memory in a Culture of Terror* (Waco, TX: Baylor University Press), 22.

2. See Mitzi J. Smith, *Womanist Sass and Talk Back: Social (In)Justice, Intersectionality, and Biblical Interpretation* (Eugene, OR: Cascade Press, 2018), 29–30.

3. Renita J. Weems, "Re-Reading for Liberation: African American Women and the Bible," in *I Found God in Me: A Womanist Biblical Hermeneutics Reader*, ed. Mitzi J. Smith, 42–55 (Eugene, OR: Cascade, 2015), 47.

4. See Jonathan Hartgrove-Wilson, *Reconstructing the Gospel: Finding Freedom from Slaveholder Religion* (Downers Grove, IL: InterVarsity, 2018) for a discussion about how Christians have inherited a slaveholder religion.

5. See Shelia F. Winborne, "Images of Jesus in Advancing the Great Commission," in *Teaching All Nations: Interrogating the Matthean Great Commission*, eds. Mitzi J. Smith and Lalitha Jayachitra, 159–74 (Minneapolis: Fortress, 2014).

6. Jennifer T. Kaalund, "In Christ, but Not of Christ: Reading Identity Differences Differently in the Letter to the Galatians," in *Minoritized Women Reading Race/Ethnicity.*

7. See Mitzi J. Smith, "Roman Slavery in Antiquity," in *The African American Jubilee Bible*, 157–84 (New York: American Bible Society, 1999); Mitzi J. Smith, "Slavery in the Early Church," in *True to Our Native Land: An African American New Testament Commentary*, eds. Brian L. Blount, Cain Hope Felder, Clarice J. Martin, and Emerson B. Powery, 11–22 (Minneapolis: Fortress, 2007); and Jennifer A. Glancy, *Slavery in the Early Church* (Oxford: Oxford University Press, 2002).

8. I take the position that although Paul does not claim Roman citizenship in his letters, he probably does not do so because it serves no purpose to do so. Yet we do not have to argue *de silentio* (from silence) given Paul's Roman citizenship is central to the narrative plot of the Acts of the Apostles.

9. In dialogue with pertinent ancient literature and archaeology, Sandra R. Joshel and Lauren Hackworth Petersen (*The Material Life of Roman Slaves* [Cambridge, UK: Cambridge University Press, 2014]) imaginatively reconstruct the pervasive material existence of enslaved persons in Pompeii.

10. Cain Hope Felder, *Troubling Biblical Waters: Race, Class, and Family* (Maryknoll, NY: Orbis, 1989), 111.

11. Felder, *Troubling Biblical Waters*, 112.

12. Laura Salah Nasrallah, *Archaeology and the Letters of Paul* (Oxford: Oxford University Press, 2019).

13. Nasrallah, *Archaeology and the Letters of Paul*. Nasrallah asserts that a bilingual (Latin and Greek) inscription from Sagalassos dated in the first half of the first century C.E., in which Galatians was written, "refocuses the lens away from the traveler and toward the majority on whose shoulders the burdens of travel fell: in the case of the Letter to the Galatians, not the apostles who wandered, but the locals of the ekklēsiai who received them" (99).

14. Orlando Patterson, *Slavery and Social Death: A Comparative Study* (Cambridge, MA: Harvard University Press, 1982), 241.

15. Neil Elliott, "The Apostle Paul and Empire," in *In the Shadow of Empire: Reclaiming the Bible as a History of Faithful Resistance*, edited by Richard A. Horsley (Louisville, KY: Westminster John Knox, 2008), 97–116.

16. Ronald Charles, *Paul and the Politics of Diaspora* (Minneapolis: Fortress, 2014), 87–88. See also William E. Arnal, *The Symbolic Jesus: Historical Scholarship, Judaism and the Construction of Contemporary Identity* (London: Equinox, 2005), 80.

17. Albert J. Raboteau, *Slave Religion: The "Invisible Institution" in the Antebellum South* (Oxford: Oxford University Press, 1978), 283.

18. For a discussion of *Ioudaios* as an ethnicity and ethnic label, see John M. G. Barclay, Ἰουδαῖος': Ethnicity and Translation," in *Ethnicity, Race, and Religion: Identities and Ideologies in Early Jewish and Christian Texts and in Modern Biblical Interpretation* (London: T&T Clark, 2019), 46–58. See Pamela Eisenbaum, *Paul Was Not a Christian: The Original Message of a Misunderstood Apostle* (New York: HarperOne, 2010).

19. Charles, *Paul and the Politics of Diaspora*, 101.

20. Mark W. Elliott, "Judaism, Reformation Theology, and Justification," in *Galatians and Christian Theology: Justification, the Gospel, and Ethics in Paul's Letter*, eds. Mark W. Elliott, Scott J. Hafeman, N. T. Wright, and John Frederick (Grand Rapids, MI: Baker, 2014), 143.

21. See Mitzi Smith, "'Unbossed and Unbought': Zilpha Elaw and Old Elizabeth and a Political Discourse of Origins," *Black Theology: An International Journal* 9, no. 3 (2011): 287–311. Nineteenth-century black preaching women claimed their calls came from a special revelation, but all other women should obey Paul's imperative that women remain silent in public.

22. Elsa Tamez, "Pauline Freedom and Market Freedom," *Trinity Seminary Review* 30, no. 1 (2010): 17–25 (19).

23. Mitzi J. Smith, "US Colonial Missions to African Slaves: Catechizing Black Souls, Traumatizing the Black *Psyche*," in *Teaching All Nations: Interrogating the Matthean Great Commission*, eds. Mitzi J. Smith and Lalitha Jayachitra, 57–88 (Minneapolis: Fortress 2014).

24. At 1:4 the Greek verb *exelētai* from *exaireō* can be translated "to deliver or rescue" and perhaps may be understood as a synonym of "free" and a prelude to the theme of freedom taken up explicitly with the Greek noun *eleutheria*.

25. Kaalund, "In Christ, but Not of Christ."

26. Keith Bradley, *Slavery and Society at Rome* (Cambridge, UK: Cambridge University Press, 1994), 71.

27. Craig Steven Wilder, *Ebony and Ivy: Race, Slavery, and the Troubled History of America's Universities* (New York: Bloomsbury, 2014), and Erskine Clarke, *To Count Our Days: A History of Columbia Theological Seminary* (Columbia: University of South Carolina Press, 2019).

28. Clarke, *To Count Our Days*, 18, 19.

29. On October 20, 2019, Princeton Theological Seminary's board announced an action plan to make reparations for its involvement with the enslavement of Africans and the wealth that resulted from it. On a blog post entitled "'Princeton Seminary Repents of Its Ties to Slavery'—A Flawed Process," Professor Mark Lewis Taylor accuses PTS of ignoring the voices of its black students and their allies who challenged PTS. Taylor asserts, "It appears that the new report only wants to foreground a drama of its own piety of repentance, without admitting that

it needed the pressure and resistance of those in its midst who most feel the impact of slavery's legacy."

30. Tamez, "Pauline Freedom and Market Freedom," 24.

31. Of course, the Acts of the Apostles claims that Saul was his Jewish/Judean name and Paul his Roman name and that he had Roman citizenship. Paul's letters are silent on the matter and it is not the objective of any of his letters to highlight his citizenship if he possesses it; perhaps to do so would be helpful in his letter to the Romans. Acts does not have to be false.

32. Homi Bhabha, *The Location of Culture* (New York: Routledge, 1994), 122.

33. See John Byron, *Slavery Metaphors in Early Judaism and Pauline Christianity: A Traditio-Historical and Exegetical Examination* (Tübingen, Germany: Mohr Siebeck, 2003), 200.

34. The Greek noun translated *love* at Galatians 5:13 is *agapē*; however, I do not understand *agapē* as signifying only divine love in the NT nor do I believe that God only chose to express God's love in human language with the invention of the Greek language (see, e.g., John 3:19; 15:12–15).

35. Bhabha, *Location of Culture*, 131.

36. Frederick Douglass, *My Bondage and My Freedom* (New York: Dover, 1969), 191.

37. Neil Martin, "Returning to the *stoicheia tou kosmou*: Enslavement to the Physical Elements in Galatians 4.3 and 9?" *Journal for the Study of the New Testament* 40, no. 4 (2018): 434–52.

38. *Paidagōgos, Greek-English Lexicon. Abridged from Liddell and Scott's Greek-English Lexicon* (Oxford: Clarendon, 1998), 511.

39. Wilder, *Ebony and Ivy*, 129–30. See also Thomas A. Foster (*Rethinking Rufus: Sexual Violations of Enslaved Men* [Athens: University of Georgia, 2019]), who addresses the gender gap with respect to the sexual violation of enslaved men in the antebellum American South.

40. Wilder, *Ebony and Ivy*; Clarke, *To Count Our Days.*

41. Amos N. Jones, Jr., *Paul's Message of Freedom: What Does It Mean for the Black Church?* (Valley Forge, PA: Judson, 1984), 64–66; Felder, *Troubling Biblical Waters*, 108.

42. Felder, *Troubling Biblical Waters*, 108.

43. Dale Martin, *Slavery as Salvation: The Metaphor of Slavery in Pauline Christianity* (New Haven, CT: Yale University Press, 1990), 148.

44. See Angela N. Parker, "One Womanist's View of Racial Reconciliation in Galatians," *Journal of Feminist Studies in Religion* 34, no. 2 (2018): 23–40.

45. See Mitzi J. Smith, *Insights from African American Interpretation* (Minneapolis: Fortress, 2017), 77–98.

46. Harriet Jacobs, "Incidents in the Life of a Slave Girl, Seven Years Concealed," in *Slave Narratives,* eds. William L. Andrews and Henry Louis Gates, Jr., 743–948 (New York: Library of America, 2000), 820–21.

47. Anders Martinsen ("Was There New Life for the Social Dead in Early Christian Communities? An Ideological-Critical Interpretation of Slavery in the Household Codes," *Journal of Early Christian History* 2, no. 1 [2012]: 55–69) argues that the use of the idealized slave-master relationship in Colossians 3:22–4:1, Ephesians 6:5–9, 1 Timothy 6:1–2, and Titus 2:9–10 failed to represent or engender significant changes to slavery as practiced but instead continued the necessary loyalty and submission to maintain the institution of slavery.

48. See Kimberlé Crenshaw, "Mapping the Margins: Intersectionality, Identity Politics, and Violence against Women of Color," *Stanford Law Review* 43 (1991): 1241–99; Patricia Hill Collins, *Black Feminist Thought: Knowledge, Consciousness, and the Politics of Empowerment*, 2nd ed. (New York: Routledge, 1991); Patricia Hill Collins and Sirma Bilge, *Intersectionality* (Malden, MA: Polity, 2016); Jennifer Jihye Chun, George Lipsitz, and Young Shin, "Intersectionality as a Social Movement Strategy: Asian Immigrant Women Advocates," *Signs* 38 (2013): 917–40.

49. Marianne Bjelland Kartzow, "'Asking the Other Question': An Intersectional Approach to Galatians 3:28 and the Colossian Household Codes," *Biblical Interpretation* 18 (2010): 364–89.

50. Bernadette J. Brooten, "Enslaved Women in Basil of Caesarea's Canonical Letters: An Intersectional Analysis," in *Doing Gender—Doing Religion*, eds. Ute E. Eisen, Christine Gerber, and Angela Standhartinger, 325–55 (Tübingen, Germany: Mohr Siebeck, 2013).

51. See Crenshaw, "Mapping the Margins."
52. See the introduction to this book for a discussion of "race" and "ethnicity" and the hyphenated term "race-ethnicity."
53. Elisabeth Schüssler Fiorenza, *In Memory of Her* (New York: Crossroad, 1983), 208.
54. Fiorenza, *In Memory of Her*, 208.
55. Fiorenza, *In Memory of Her*, 235.
56. Fiorenza, *In Memory of Her*, 209. She quotes W. A. Meeks, "The Image of the Androgyne: Some Uses of a Symbol in Earliest Christian," *History of Religions* 13 (1974): 165–208 (182).
57. Brad R. Braxton, "Galatians," in *True to Our Native Land: An African American Commentary of the New Testament*, gen ed. Brian L. Blount (Minneapolis: Fortress, 2007), 340; Brad R. Braxton, *No Longer Slaves: Galatians and African American Experience* (Collegeville, MN: Liturgical, 2002), 94. See also Cain Hope Felder, "Race, Racism, and the Biblical Narratives," in *Stony the Road We Trod: African American Biblical Interpretation*, ed. Cain Hope Felder, 127–45 (Minneapolis: Fortress, 1991), esp. 139.
58. Kang-Yup Na, "Of Great Walls, DMZs, and Other Lines in the Sand: The Truth (of the Gospel) about Borders and Barriers—And Crossing Them in Galatians," in *Landscapes of Korean and Korean American Biblical Interpretation*, ed. John Ahn, 217–40 (Atlanta: Society of Biblical Literature, 2019), 232. Na reads Galatians 2:11–14 and 3:25–29 with insights from the perspective of *dao* and anthropology. A *dao*-inspired translation of Galatians 3:28 is "In the beginning, there was no Jew or Greek, no slave or free, no male and female" (234).
59. On the other hand, Jae-won Lee (*Paul and the Politics of Difference. A Contextual Study of Jewish-Gentile Difference in Galatians and Romans* [Eugene, OR: Pickwick, 2014]) argues that Paul opposed an "exclusivist logic of identity," but he articulated an "inclusive hermeneutics of faith" within the framework of table fellowship between Jews and Gentiles (96).
60. Sechrest, *A Former Jew*, 228.
61. Mary L. Gordon, "The Nationality of Slaves under the Early Roman Empire," in *Slavery in Class Antiquity*, ed. M. I. Finley, 171–211 (Cambridge, UK: W. Heffer and Sons, 1964), 188.
62. Mitzi J. Smith, "Utility, Fraternity, and Reconciliation: Ancient Slavery as a Context for the Return of Onesimus," in *Onesimus Our Brother: Reading Religion, Race, and Culture in Philemon*, eds. Matthew J. Johnson, James A. Noel, and Demetrius K. Williams, 47–58 (Minneapolis: Fortress, 2012).
63. Clarke, *To Count Our Days,* 21, 22
64. Collins and Bilge, *Intersectionality*, 133.
65. See Delores Williams, *Sisters in Wilderness*: *The Challenge of Womanist God-Talk* (Maryknoll, NY: Orbis, 1993) for a womanist reading of Hagar that compares her story with African American women's history of surrogacy.
66. See David I. Starling, "Justifying Allegory: Scripture, Rhetoric, and Reason in Galatians 4:21–5:1," *Journal of Theological Interpretation* 9, no. 2 (2015): 227–45.
67. N. T. Wright, "Messiahship in Galatians?," in *Galatians and Christian Theology: Justification, the Gospel, and Ethics in Paul's Letter*, eds. Mark W. Elliott, Scott J. Hofemann, N. T. Wright, and John Frederick, 3–23 (Grand Rapids, MI: Baker, 2014).
68. Wright, "Messiahship in Galatians?" 3.
69. Bill Richards, "Bought with a Price: Slavery and Freedom in the Pauline Circle," *Touchstone* 37, no. 1 (2019): 4–15 (12).
70. Richards, "Bought with a Price," 15. Geoffrey Turner ("The Christian Life as Slavery: Paul's Subversive Metaphor," *Heythrop Journal* 54 [2013]: 1–12) argues that Paul makes a remarkable shift when he asserts that slavery to God engenders freedom. Thus, he subverts conventional understandings of slavery.

WORKS CITED

Arnal, William E. *The Symbolic Jesus: Historical Scholarship, Judaism and the Construction of Contemporary Identity.* London: Equinox, 2005.
Bhabha, Homi. *The Location of Culture.* New York: Routledge, 1994.

Bradley, Keith R. *Slavery and Society at Rome*. Cambridge, UK: Cambridge University Press, 1994.

Braxton, Brad R. "Galatians." In *True to Our Native Land: An African American Commentary of the New Testament*, edited by Brian L. Blount, Cain Hope Felder, Clarice J. Martin, and Emerson B. Powery, 333–47. Minneapolis: Fortress, 2007.

———. *No Longer Slaves. Galatians and African American Experience*. Collegeville, MN: Liturgical, 2002.

Brooten, Bernadette J. "Enslaved Women in Basil of Caesarea's Canonical Letters: An Intersectional Analysis." In *Doing Gender—Doing Religion*, edited by Ute E. Eisen, Christine Gerber, and Angela Standhartinger, 325–55. Tübingen, Germany: Mohr Siebeck, 2013.

Byron, John. *Slavery Metaphors in Early Judaism and Pauline Christianity: A Traditio-Historical and Exegetical Examination*. Tübingen, Germany: Mohr Siebeck, 2003.

Charles, Ronald. *Paul and the Politics of Diaspora*. Minneapolis: Fortress, 2014.

Chun, Jennifer Jihye Chun, George Lipsitz, and Young Shin. "Intersectionality as a Social Movement Strategy: Asian Immigrant Women Advocates." *Signs* 38 (2013): 917–40.

Clarke, Erskine. *To Count Our Days: A History of Columbia Theological Seminary*. Columbia: University of South Carolina Press, 2019.

Collins, Patricia Hill, and Sirma Bilge. *Black Feminist Thought: Knowledge, Consciousness, and the Politics of Empowerment*, 2nd ed. New York: Routledge, 1991.

———. *Intersectionality*. Cambridge, UK: Polity, 2016.

Crenshaw, Kimberlé. "Mapping the Margins: Intersectionality, Identity Politics, and Violence against Women of Color." *Stanford Law Review* 43 (1991): 1241–99.

Douglass, Frederick. *My Bondage and My Freedom*. New York: Dover, 1969.

Eisenbaum, Pamela. *Paul Was Not a Christian: The Original Message of a Misunderstood Apostle*. New York: HarperOne, 2010.

Elliott, Mark W. "Judaism, Reformation Theology, and Justification." In *Galatians and Christian Theology: Justification, the Gospel, and Ethics in Paul's Letter*, edited by Mark W. Elliott, Scott J. Hatemann, N. T. Wright, and John Frederick, 143–58. Grand Rapids, MI: Baker, 2014.

Elliott, Neil. "The Apostle Paul and Empire." In *In the Shadow of Empire: Reclaiming the Bible as a History of Faithful Resistance*, edited by Richard A. Horsley (Louisville, KY: Westminster John Knox, 2008), 97–116.

Felder, Cain Hope. "Race, Racism, and the Biblical Narratives." In *Stony the Road We Trod: African American Biblical Interpretation*, edited by Cain Hope Felder, 127–45. Minneapolis: Fortress, 1991.

———. *Troubling Biblical Waters: Race, Class, and Family*. Maryknoll, NY: Orbis, 1989.

Fiorenza, Elisabeth Schüssler. *In Memory of Her*. New York: Crossroad, 1983.

Foster, Thomas A. *Rethinking Rufus: Sexual Violations of Enslaved Men*. Athens: University of Georgia, 2019.

Glancy, Jennifer A. *Slavery in the Early Church*. Oxford: Oxford University Press, 2002.

Gordon, Mary L. "The Nationality of Slaves under the Early Roman Empire." In *Slavery in Class Antiquity*, edited by M. I. Finley, 171–211. Cambridge, UK: W. Heffer and Sons, 1964.

Hartgrove-Wilson, Jonathan. *Reconstructing the Gospel: Finding Freedom from Slaveholder Religion*. Downers Grove, IL: InterVarsity, 2018.

Jacobs, Harriet. "Incidents in the Life of a Slave Girl, Seven Years Concealed." In *Slave Narratives*, edited by William L. Andrews and Henry Louis Gates, Jr., 743–948. New York: Library of America, 2000.

Jones, Amos N., Jr. *Paul's Message of Freedom: What Does It Mean for the Black Church?* Valley Forge, PA: Judson, 1984.

Joshel, Sandra R., and Lauren Hackworth Petersen. *The Material Life of Roman Slaves*. Cambridge, UK: Cambridge University Press, 2014.

Kaalund, Jennifer T. "In Christ, but Not of Christ: Reading Identity Differences Differently in the Letter to the Galatians." In *Minoritized Women Reading Race/Ethnicity*, eds. Mitzi J. Smith and Jin Young Choi, ____. Lanham, MD: Rowman & Littlefield, 2020.

Kartzow, Marianne Bjelland. "'Asking the Other Question': An Intersectional Approach to Galatians 3:28 and the Colossian Household Codes." *Biblical Interpretation* 18 (2010): 364–89.

Lee, Jae-won. *Paul and the Politics of Difference: A Contextual Study of Jewish-Gentile Difference in Galatians and Romans*. Eugene, OR: Pickwick, 2014.

Liddell and Scott. *Greek-English Lexicon.* Oxford: Oxford University Press, 1998.

Martin, Dale. *Slavery as Salvation: The Metaphor of Slavery in Pauline Christianity.* New Haven, CT: Yale University Press, 1990.

Martin, Neil. "Returning to the *stoicheia tou kosmou*: Enslavement to the Physical Elements in Galatians 4.3 and 9?" *Journal for the Study of the New Testament* 40, no. 4 (2018): 434–52.

Martinsen, Anders. "Was There New Life for the Social Dead in Early Christian Communities? An Ideological-Critical Interpretation of Slavery in the Household Codes." *Journal of Early Christian History* 2, no. 1 (2012): 55–69.

Na, Kang-Yup. "Of Great Walls, DMZs, and Other Lines in the Sand: The Truth (of the Gospel) about Borders and Barriers—And Crossing Them in Galatians." In *Landscapes of Korean and Korean American Biblical Interpretation*, edited by John Ahn, 217–40. Atlanta: Society of Biblical Literature, 2019.

Nasrallah, Laura Salah. *Archaeology and the Letters of Paul*. Oxford: Oxford University Press, 2019.

Parker, Angela N. "One Womanist's View of Racial Reconciliation in Galatians." *Journal of Feminist Studies in Religion* 34, no. 2 (2018): 23–40.

Patterson, Orlando. *Slavery and Social Death: A Comparative Study*. Cambridge, MA: Harvard University Press, 1982.

Raboteau, Albert J. *Slave Religion: The "Invisible Institution" in the Antebellum South*. Oxford: Oxford University Press, 1978.

Richards, Bill. "Bought with a Price: Slavery and Freedom in the Pauline Circle." *Touchstone* 37, no 1 (2019): 4–15.

Sims, Angela D. *Lynched: The Power of Memory in a Culture of Terror*. Waco, TX: Baylor University Press, 2017.

Smith, Mitzi J. *Insights from African American Interpretation*. Minneapolis: Fortress, 2017.

———. "Roman Slavery in Antiquity." In *The African American Jubilee Bible*, 157–84. New York: American Bible Society, 1999.

———. "Slavery in the Early Church." In *True to Our Native Land: An African American Commentary of the New Testament*, edited by Brian L. Blount, Cain Hope Felder, Clarice J. Martin, and Emerson B. Powery, 11–22 Minneapolis: Fortress, 2007.

———. "'Unbossed and Unbought': Zilpha Elaw and Old Elizabeth and a Political Discourse of Origins." *Black Theology: An International Journal* 9, no. 3 (2011): 287–311.

———. "US Colonial Missions to African Slaves: Catechizing Black Souls, Traumatizing the Black *Psyche*." In *Teaching All Nations: Interrogating the Matthean Great Commission*, edited by Mitzi J. Smith and Lalitha Jayachitra, 57–88, Minneapolis: Fortress, 2014.

———. "Utility, Fraternity, and Reconciliation: Ancient Slavery as a Context for the Return of Onesimus." In *Onesimus Our Brother: Reading Religion, Race, and Culture in Philemon*, edited by Matthew J. Johnson, James A. Noel, and Demetrius K. Williams, 47–58. Minneapolis: Fortress, 2012.

———. *Womanist Sass and Talk Back. Social (In)Justice, Intersectionality, and Biblical Interpretation*. Eugene, OR: Cascade, 2018.

Starling, David I. "Justifying Allegory: Scripture, Rhetoric, and Reason in Galatians 4:21–5:1." *Journal of Theological Interpretation* 9, no. 2 (2015): 227–45.

Tamez, Elsa. "Pauline Freedom and Market Freedom." *Trinity Seminary Review* 31, no. 1 (2010): 17–25.

Taylor, Mark Lewis. "'Princeton Seminary Repents of Its Ties to Slavery'—A Flawed Process." October 20, 2019, blog post. http://marklewistaylor.net/blog/princeton-seminary-repents-for-its-ties-to-slavery-a-flawed-process/.

Turner, Geoffrey. "The Christian Life as Slavery: Paul's Subversive Metaphor." *Heythrop Journal* 54 (2013): 1–12.

Weems, Renita J. "Re-Reading for Liberation: African American Women and the Bible." In *I Found God in Me: A Womanist Biblical Hermeneutics Reader*, edited by Mitzi J. Smith, 42–55. Eugene, OR: Cascade, 2015.

Wilder, Craig Steven. *Ebony and Ivy: Race, Slavery, and the Troubled History of America's Universities*. New York: Bloomsbury, 2014.

Williams, Delores. *Sisters in Wilderness. The Challenge of Womanist God-Talk*. Maryknoll, NY: Orbis, 1993.

Winborne, Shelia F. "Images of Jesus in Advancing the Great Commission." In *Teaching All Nations: Interrogating the Matthean Great Commission*, edited by Mitzi J. Smith and Lalitha Jayachitra, 159–74. Minneapolis: Fortress, 2014.

Chapter Four

Feminized-Minoritized Paul?

A Womanist Reading of Paul's Body in the Corinthian Context

Angela N. Parker

To this day, my father will not admit that he often told my mother to keep me in the kitchen because he did not want my future husband bringing me back home if I could not cook. My father, who has been married to my mother for over fifty years, is a wonderful man and excellent father. However, for a young girl to think that her future husband could "return her" if she does not know how to cook was an issue of socialization that influenced my relationships with black men.[1] For many years, I have often thought about how I became complicit in my own domination within my marital, professional, and even ecclesial relationships. If my husband, male colleague, or my male senior pastor exhibited domination over me, then I was bound by God and my patriarchal upbringing to submit to the domination.

I do not mention my father's "kitchen sayings" in the context of this essay to disparage my upbringing but to contextualize the following reading of 1 Corinthians. Arguments surrounding Paul's mimetic power toward paternal authoritarianism in 1 Corinthians and Paul's "Europeanization" in general have persisted in Pauline exegetical thought.[2] However, what happens when a minoritized (i.e., a person experiencing differential and unequal treatment because of the fluid nature of both her physical [i.e., race] and cultural characteristics [e.g., ethnicity]) reader engages mimetic power and "Europeanization" while recognizing that interpretations resulting from skewed Pauline identity have resulted in cultural and ideological readings that produce a Paul who is the "patron saint" for patriarchal and white supremacist thought? This essay will engage that question from a minoritized womanist

(African American and female) view. Critiquing the aforementioned dominant epistemological viewpoint in Pauline studies, this essay engages a womanist approach to Paul's rhetorical construction of his masculine body as
feminine according to his racial/ethnic identity as a member of Judaism.

Specifically, this essay argues that we should interpret Paul's rhetorical
construction of his body in 1 Corinthians 4:6–21 as both minoritized and
feminized over against the Corinthian women prophets in 1 Corinthians 11.
By problematizing Paul's rhetorical construction of his own racial/ethnic/
masculine identity in relationship to the Corinthian women prophets, I argue
that Paul rhetorically feminizes his Jewish masculine body as an enslaved
female body over against the liberating stance of the Corinthian women
prophets.[3] Moreover, as I read 1 Corinthians 4:6–21 in conjunction with 1
Corinthians 11, I argue that Paul emphasizes his minoritized Jewish racial
and ethnic identity over against the predominant Gentile membership of the
Corinthian church, thus underscoring his decreased racial and ethnic power
in Corinth even as he seemingly exerts patriarchal power with mimetic language.

A WOMANIST VIEW FOR INTERPRETING
PAUL'S POWER IN 1 CORINTHIANS

I opened this essay with a personal anecdote pertaining to patriarchal and
ecclesial power and its use in my own life. As a way to begin to theorize
around issues of power and my own womanist identity, I will develop a
womanist lens for interpretation by engaging black feminist and womanist
thinkers Patricia Hill Collins and Marcia Riggs.[4]

Reading Collins aids my womanist ideas of power and power relations in
a number of ways. As she theorizes a politics of empowerment, Collins
questions the dialectical relationship that seemingly does not link oppression
and activism.[5] More specifically, I read Collins contra Michel Foucault (and
Castelli) since Collins notes that, for black women, thinking through power
is not simply an intellectual activity but is representative of real life. Hence,
activism and resistance are inherent in the power relations. I would argue that
the Corinthian women share in activism and resistance against Paul, especially when I engage the work of Antoinette Clark Wire. How would women
engage Paul's use of power in their real lives? Further, since power is not
something that a group possesses but is, in fact, an intangible entity that
operates and circulates within a matrix of domination wherein people stand
in varying relationships, Collins prompts me to ask where the Corinthian
woman prophets engage and push back against Paul's matrix of domination.[6]

Turning to the ideas of socialization, gender, and power, Riggs's work
specifically engages my opening anecdote. As a womanist ethicist, she delin-

eates two issues: (1) how socialization occurs around African American sexual-gender relations, and (2) the ways in which the African American church is a site of sexual-gender oppression that can be transformed through church members acting as moral agents who move the "moral agency axis" from complicity to accountability. Riggs provides a framework for me to ask how the Corinthian women prophets may have attempted to move the "moral agency axis" even as Paul slides his own "moral agency axis." Paul uses language that oscillates between high status masculine language to low status feminine language and language surrounding his low status as Jewish to high status mimetic language around Jesus as messiah. Moreover, while Riggs identifies that the African American church lives under white racist-capitalist-patriarchal oppression, she finds that there is a paradoxical coexistence of women's traditions of resistance coupled with male gatekeeper-ship that stand at the heart of complicity and duplicity of sexual-gender relations in the church.[7] In her all too brief reading of Paul, Riggs puts forth the idea of relational power that addresses the issue of the "power of the cross" and its relationship to unity and mutual service.[8]

Thinking through Collins and Riggs, relational power/interpersonal power occur through courage, partnership, and dialogue. Since the power of the cross is a prevalent idea in Pauline literature, I engage Collins and Riggs as conversation partners in constructing a womanist view of power for reading Paul's epistles. Just as Pauline literature can be used to silence women in ecclesial settings, oppressive leaders continue to use hierarchical power against women to compel them to be the "bearers of the cross" for the good of the church. Accordingly, my developing womanist view of power engaging the theories of Collins and Riggs will perform an exegetical analysis that places the *relational power of the cross* within the context of the Corinthian women's freedom as opposed to Paul's hierarchical view of the cross that places God-Jesus-Paul-man-woman as the proper hierarchal order. Moreover, my womanist view of power as I read 1 Corinthians will allow a nuanced reading of Paul that problematizes his argumentation for his specified power and order.

In summary, interweaving the work of Collins and Riggs allows me to construct a reader response strategy that takes into account the black feminist and womanist ideas of power while also theorizing and asking questions around relational power in the ecclesial settings for women who often "bear" the cross at higher rates than the men in the ecclesial setting.[9] More specifically, my womanist re-reading of Paul will probe the relational power that the Corinthian women would most likely want to espouse in their relationship with Paul as they read and hear Paul's rhetoric concerning his own body.

A WORD ON THE CORINTHIAN WOMEN PROPHETS

Scholarship is divided on the existence of the Corinthian women prophets. Two scholars who have written exhaustively on the Corinthian women prophets are Elisabeth Schüssler Fiorenza and Antoinette Clark Wire.

In her work, Fiorenza argues for taking the exegetical focus off of Paul and placing it within the Corinthian community.[10] Fiorenza essentially attends to the actual world of the Corinthian community as opposed to said world as constructed and told through Paul's rhetoric. Arguing that Paul's rhetoric in 1–4 is not an apology but actually a re-establishment of his apostolic authority, Fiorenza states that Paul argues his point in a rhetorically deliberative manner that seeks a future decision from the affluent male members of the Corinthian church who are of higher social and educational status.[11] For Fiorenza, the entire Corinthian community was trying to understand itself according to the language of the baptismal formula of Galatians 3:28 since the status divisions between Greeks and Jews, slave and free, men and women, rich and poor, wise and educated where no longer constitutive for the new creation in the Spirit.[12] Fiorenza argues that Paul had to set up a line of authority between God, Christ, Paul, Apollos, Timothy, Stephanas, and other local co-workers to which the Corinthians should subordinate themselves instead of living in their freedom in the new creation.[13] Some scholars later argue that Paul's hierarchical chain of power occurs by giving Paul a share of Christ's authority and power through the language of imitation thus implicitly generating a God-Christ-Paul-man-woman chain in his argumentation of chapter 11.[14] Pace Fiorenza, if Paul rhetorically argues for the establishment of his authority in chapters 1–4, then I am arguing that 1 Corinthians 4:6–21 is where Paul uses his body in a minoritized and feminized way but, in actuality, undermines his further argumentation in 1 Corinthians 11 where Paul exerts authority with all Corinthian men over all Corinthian women (and, by virtue of his argument, all Corinthian women prophets as well). Thus, Paul stops any argument by the Corinthian women prophets for a sexually ascetic lifestyle and compels them in his rhetoric to return to their marital relationships.[15] Apparently, Paul would worry that the community would be vulnerable to sin while also lacking order.

Wire's work is the only full-length social-historical reconstruction on the subject of the Corinthian women prophets that seeks to hear the voices of these women through Paul's rhetoric in the text of 1 Corinthians. Wire's goal is to reconstruct as accurate a picture of the women prophets in the church of first-century Corinth as possible.[16] Employing the approach of "the New Rhetoric," Wire essentially argues that many of the Corinthian women prophets have withdrawn from sexual relations (7:1–40) with their men because they now claim new freedom (i.e., not wearing head veiling. 11:2–16) in Christ. Moreover, the Corinthian women prophets show new authority in

Christ since they now proclaim God's wisdom to the community while also demonstrating life in the Spirit through their ecstatic speech (1 Cor. 12–14).

While essentially granting what the Corinthian women prophets affirm (7:1, 8:1, 4: 10:23), Paul does criticize how they exercise their new life in Christ. Paul does not want their freedom to be at the expense of the entire community. In essence, in 1 Corinthians 7–15, Paul discourages the married women from leaving their sexual relations with their men while also encouraging unmarried women to marry if it is necessary to preserve the morality of the men (not the women) in the community. The whole community runs the risk of being polluted by the immorality of many men who want to marry but have been denied the marital relationship because the women are refusing to marry. Essentially, Wire's argument helps us realize that the Corinthian women prophets must sacrifice themselves to marriage and sexuality for the greater "good" of the Corinthian community rather than live in an existence that withdraws them from marriage and sexuality.[17]

A WOMANIST EXEGETICAL ANALYSIS OF
1 CORINTHIANS 4:6–21

Reading with the Corinthian Women Prophets

"Feminized Paul"

As stated above, I am taking the position that 1 Corinthians 1–4 is Paul's re-establishment of his power and authority. What I find interesting as I read 4:6–21 with 11:2–16 in mind is that I find similar tropes occurring in the passages which prompt me to argue Paul's rhetorical feminization of his Jewish masculine body as an enslaved body over against the claimed freed-woman status of the Corinthian women prophets.

At the beginning of verse 6, Paul makes a statement about applying "all this" to Apollos and himself for the benefit of the Corinthian community. Many scholars are uncertain about what "all this" includes. However, most want to argue that Paul and Apollos have no quarrel with each other but that Paul is setting up the Corinthian community to see that their own boasting is heavily mistaken. As Paul proceeds to verses 8 and 9, he begins a series of antitheses between them and himself to which shame is the only suitable response (despite the demurrer of verse 14). However, before I get to most scholars' belief that "shaming" is a good thing for the Corinthian community, I must address Paul's catalog of afflictions and its rhetoric in 8–13 as a "theology" or as an "ethic of the cross."[18] While I do not deny that Paul is alluding back to his language of the wisdom of the cross in chapter 1, I do question how the interpretation and use of his catalogue impacts the Corinthian women prophets and women today in contemporary ecclesial settings.

Most interpreters of Paul understand his catalogue of afflictions to be related to a plethora of sources. Paul may be engaging Stoic-Cynic tradition, Jewish apocalyptic tradition, Hellenistic Jewish writings, or even pharisaic-rabbinic material in the Mishnah. However, most commentators land on the definitive idea that Paul speaks through the Jewish apocalyptic tradition to begin speaking about a theology of the cross.[19] The Stoic-Cynic and Hellenistic traditions appear to be less persuasive for some scholars. Again, for me, the Jewish apocalyptic tradition may be the background for Paul's argumentation. However, I question if that is the only way that Paul's original audience, namely the Corinthian women prophets, would have interpreted Paul's rhetoric.

The catalog of afflictions serves a number of purposes for interpreters of 1 Corinthians.[20] First, it may act as a connection to the *dynamis* power of Jesus the Christ as opposed to the weakness and foolishness of Paul as an apostle. For the sage, "power" manifests itself in adversity. Others argue that Paul shows his "power" in his weakness because his power does not come by authoritarian self-assertion but by the efficacy of his word. Still others, such as Michael Gorman, argue that the catalog of afflictions actually shows Paul's connection to the cross and that cruciformity comes by nature of being a slave for Jesus. In each of these renditions power is connected to some form of enslaved weakness.[21]

While the circumcised penis served as a marker of shame over against the "manly" uncircumcised Greco-Roman man, I would argue that Paul's "feminized" penis is not the only source of his feminization.[22] Aside from the ways that others have argued for Paul's feminization resulting from his feminized penis due to circumcision, I argue that Paul's enslaved status also serves as a tool of feminization.[23] Even if scholars believe that Paul's source for the catalog comes from Jewish, Stoic-Cynic, or even Hellenistic sources, the fact remains that Paul is "weak" and probably enslaved as well.

As I have argued in another context, Paul does not share habitus or a similar decreased body capital as the enslaved persons of the Roman Empire.[24] While Paul mentions beatings during his ministry, those beatings would not have been the same as those suffered by Roman slaves. Furthermore, I argue that the difference (or problem) with Paul's characterization as a slave by contemporary interpreters is the lack of nuance in understanding a man describing his experience as a slave. I argued that female readers of Paul's Letters would have known the difference between the bodily experiences of a female slave over against a male slave. As a womanist reader, while I understand Paul's use of the identity of a slave and a slave's body, I believe that Paul's characterization is problematic.

Moreover, if Paul is, in fact, a feminized enslaved person, I argue that Paul rhetorically feminizes his body in the catalog of afflictions by talking about being "exhibited" before the world and "angels" as the "scum" of society. Why is this exhibition before "angels" important? I would argue that Paul rhetorically links his exhibition before "angels" to the idea that the woman should be covered "on account of the angels" in 11:10. Scholars have long puzzled over Paul's cryptic use of "angels" in 11:10 but have not linked 11:10 to 4:9. Apparently, Paul recognizes that the apostles' act of being displayed (*apodeiknymi*) during a triumphal procession renders them "booty" of war. [25] In this sense, Greco-Roman studies in masculinities help us to understand that Paul, as displayed as a "booty" of war, becomes "un-man" and essentially feminine. [26] Coupling this with the "angel" language and scholarship surrounding the women being sexual provocation to the angels according to Genesis 6:1–4, Paul, in essence, feminizes himself. Paul exhibits shame in both his "feminized" penis and in his enslaved body, which may be sexual shame akin to the Corinthian women prophets "on account of the angels."

As I have already alluded to Paul's feminized shaming in relation to his penis and his exhibition as an enslaved person, I now move to the issue of "shame" (*entrepō*) (4:14) unto "imitation" (*mimētēs*) (4:16) as Paul's major rhetorical tool in 4:6–21. Some scholars argue that Paul's shaming techniques are not for "low self-esteem" but for "realism" in order to bring about good "Christian sanity."[27] While such an interpretation may be accurate, I would argue that interpreters must ask if that is what the Corinthian women prophets would have experienced as opposed to what we think they should have experienced from our twenty-first-century vantage point.

In its colloquial context the Greek word *entrepō* connotes someone hanging their head in shame. Further, Paul moves on to address the Corinthians as his "dear children" (v. 15). He accomplishes two tasks in verses 14–15. First, he makes the Corinthian community feel a sense of shame and hanging of their heads while also infantilizing them in the process. Paul, even in his feminized body, takes on the patriarchal role of father and supreme power by calling the other instructors of the Corinthians mere "guardians" (*paidagōgos*). That means that even as Paul states that there is no quarrel between Paul and Apollos as identified in verse 6, Apollos (and others) have been relegated to "guardian" status while Paul has become the supreme father. Again, I wonder if Paul can have it both ways. I also wonder if the Corinthian women prophets thought the same?

How did Corinthian women prophets receive such language? I would argue that while theological interpreters of Paul would not engage theoretical frameworks on shame and womanist thought, these frameworks are ripe for expanding our knowledge. In her work, Melissa Harris-Perry identifies how black women are conditioned to attempt to "stand straight in a crooked room" by holding on to shame in the context of American society. [28] Cognitive psychologists understand that people try to find the "upright" in their surroundings. However, socialization, power dynamics, and racism make black women's rooms so crooked that it is nearly impossible to "stand straight in a crooked room." Internalized shame develops when others see you lacking the ability to stand straight even though their room may not be crooked (e.g., as a result of privilege). However, before continuing this line of argumentation, Harris-Perry's definition of "shame" is helpful.

> The emotion of shame has three important elements. The first is social. Individuals feel ashamed in response to a real or imagined audience. We do not feel shame in isolation, only when we transgress a social boundary or break a community expectation. Our internal moral guide may lead us to feel guilt, but shame comes when we fear exposure and evaluation by others. This may be especially true for girls and women, who draw a larger sense of self-identity from their friendly, familial, and romantic relationships. Second, shame is global. It causes us not only to evaluate our actions but to make a judgment about our whole selves. A person may feel guilty about a specific incident but still feel that she is a good person. Shame is more divisive; it extends beyond a single incident and becomes an evaluation of the self. Psychologists commonly refer to shame as a belief in the malignant self: the idea that your entire person is infected by something inherently bad and potentially contagious. Finally, shame brings a psychological and physical urge to withdraw, submit, or appease others. When we feel ashamed, we tend to *drop our heads*, avert our eyes, and fold into ourselves . . . [because] shame makes us want to be smaller, timid, and more closed. Shame transforms our identity. We experience ourselves as being small and worthless and as being exposed. (emphasis added) [29]

I would argue that when the original auditors of the letter heard Paul's language in 1 Corinthians 4, they may have assumed that Paul was addressing both men and women: men for visiting prostitutes and being puffed up about it while the women rightfully assumed a posture toward ascetic living and being puffed up about it. However, the lengthy dialogue of 1 Corinthians 7 and 11 would actually reify the injury of shaming to the women according to my reading of this text. Specifically, Paul reinstitutes a hierarchy that shames the women and places the blame of their men's morality squarely on women's shoulders. No matter how we read Paul's language of shaming today, we must read it with this nuanced view on how the original auditors would have heard the text and then carefully nuance any interpretations ethically into our contemporary contexts.

Scholars note that they often suffer whiplash while reading Paul's rhetorical argumentation since, as I argue, he rhetorically transforms his identity from masculine to feminine and then back to hyper-masculine with his father language. Instead of whiplash, I hold that Paul is actually trying to use his power to shift the room of the Corinthian women prophets so that they will have to attempt to stand "upright" in a "crooked room." They will have to marry, bear children, and "bear" the shaming for the good of the Corinthian community. The Corinthian women prophets would begin to see the inequities that Paul attempts to force them back into. The Corinthian women prophets would be considered a constant problem in their community that must be analyzed and solved (or purged from the Corinthian body). The Corinthian women prophets would hear in Paul's language the intent of shaming to correction for which "father" Paul argues. Their freedom in Jesus is now crooked.

In this reading, I agree with Dale Martin's observation that Paul uses "patriarchal rhetoric" but I disagree with Martin's conclusion that Paul uses said rhetoric to "make an anti-patriarchal point."[30] I believe that Paul is still making his patriarchal "power" point from the context of shaming unto imitation "for some" and not all (i.e., Corinthian women prophets).

"Minoritized Paul"

Even though my last point in the "Feminized Paul" section is that Paul is making his patriarchal "power" point, I do not believe patriarchy is his only point. In this section, I argue that Paul is making his "imperial" point by calling on the Corinthian community to imitate his minoritized Jewish racial and ethnic identity. Comparing the Greek words *logos* and *dynamis* in conversation with Paul's use of the term *basileia tou theou*, I argue that Paul's rhetoric highlights his minoritized Jewish racial and ethnic identity over against the predominant Gentile membership of the Corinthian church, thus emphasizing his decreased racial and ethnic power in Corinth (and in the Roman Empire) even as he seemingly exerts racial and ethnic power with mimetic language connected to the exalted body of Jesus.

At 4:19, Paul writes that he will come to the Corinthians quickly, if the Lord wills. Additionally, Paul wants to know what the "talk" (or speech/ reasoning even though most translations render *logos* as "talk") of the puffed-up people entails and if that talk has any power/*dynamis*. Paul continues that line of thought in verse 20 when he states that the *basileia* of God is not a matter of talk but rather in power/*dynamis*.

I have chosen to provide several translations for *logos* and *basileia* in order to begin my argument. Again, assuming that Paul is legitimizing his apostolic authority through rhetorical practices, I am not convinced that the "best" translation for *logos* is "talk" or "speech." If the Corinthians are skilled in their own rhetorical forms, then they may believe that their high status in Greco-Roman rhetoric is better than average. If that is the case, I would argue that translating *logos* as "reasoning" may be a better rendering. However, Paul does not believe that their reasoning is better than his because if that were the case, he would not be arrogant enough to state that he may come to Corinth with a rod as he states in 4:21. Nonetheless, their reasoning is still no match in Paul's mind against the power given to Paul through

Jesus. As Tat-Siong Benny Liew argues, Paul reasons for his continued *dynamis* power as constructed by the rejected and crucified-by-the-Roman-Empire Jewish body of Jesus the Christ. For Liew, Paul's body-building project is on the rejected Jewish body of Jesus.[31] Liew asserts that the Corinthian community experienced a status inversion in joining a racial/ethnic minority within the Roman imperial system.[32]

But how do we know that Paul is even thinking within the Roman imperial system? I now turn to Paul's use of the phrase *basileia tou theou*. Paul does not use this phrasing often in his writings.[33] I would argue that the nuance of translation is helpful again when thinking through the term *basileia*. As I read traditional scholarship on verse 20, most commentators argue that Paul's "casual" use of the term *basileia* means that the term functions in Paul's thinking and teaching as eschatological.[34] Moreover, these scholars note that the kingdom often refers to the active dynamic reigning of God as sovereign, even if this reign is in part veiled until its full revelation. In essence, commentators take a highly spiritualized and theological view of the kingdom of God.

The problem with highly spiritualized and theological views of biblical interpretation is not just that the kingdom becomes spiritualized but Paul becomes highly spiritualized and universal as well. Paul sits at the intersection that brings Jewish and Gentile folks together under the "umbrella" of Christianity thereby allowing the Europeanization of Paul (and eventually, Jesus).[35]

The work of Shawn Kelly will be helpful to expound on my point. Kelly evidences the problem that language centered on the Jesus of history and the glorified Jesus actually conveys. Arguing that nationalism arose in European scholarship and thinking through Hegelian philosophy, Kelly shows that the idea of an authentic, pure, uncontaminated culture rose up in scholarship. The prominence of pure ideas meant that ideas (and people) which Western thought considered alien, foreign, or corrupting had to be expelled. Specifically, the "pure" folk had to expel the racially "alien" (the Jew, the Oriental, the African, the non-European) from multiple areas of knowledge and the narrative of world history.

Moreover, as nationalism arose in European academic thinking, the Hegelian logic of moving from lower consciousness to higher levels of consciousness began to take root in academic thought. Hegel espoused consciousness as developing geographically and racially, as the levels of consciousness are assigned to particular races and particular peoples. For Hegel, lower levels of consciousness are real, albeit backwards and despotic, elements of lesser culture. On the other hand, Europeans, particularly Germans, were capable of higher levels of consciousness. It is the Germanic Europeans who possess the potential for authentic culture and for real freedom. Hegel develops a narrative of history that denies humanity to Africans and denies the consciousness of freedom to Jews and Orientals.

As we fast-forward to the beginning of biblical scholarship, I agree with Kelly's delineation that Jesus (and, I would argue, even more so Paul because of his move toward the West) become Aryan, German, or rational. As Hegelian philosophy encroached on academic scholarship, biblical scholarship, particularly, had to disavow both Jesus and Paul of their Jewish roots to make Christianity universal. Thus, Paul becomes the "hero" of both European and white supremacist thought to the detriment of his own minoritized Jewish identity, thereby, reconstructing race at the level of academic biblical scholarship and within interpretation of the biblical text.

After this summation of how Paul becomes Europeanized, I believe a possible way forward would be to translate *basileia* as "empire" instead of the overused (and over-spiritualized) "kingdom." I argue that tweaking a contemporary reader's ears to hear what the Corinthian women prophets may have heard allows for a critique of the Roman Empire in 1 Corinthians while also providing a better understanding of what the Corinthian women prophets' freedom in Christ means in the empire of God as opposed to the empire of Caesar.

And here is where I think reading Paul with nuance is most important. I would argue that understanding Paul's view against Roman imperial systems may help contemporary readers with their understanding of oppression and hierarchy in nations that observe ethnonationalism today. More specifically, theorists, such as Frantz Fanon, identify a type of nationalism that stems from a return to mythic origins of the land which then leads to an ultra-nationalism, chauvinism, and racism within the nation.[36] In essence, Fanon's nationalism leads to ethnonationalism that echoes much of the chauvinism in Paul's rhetoric. So while Paul leans heavily on his Jewish identity as minoritized in the national and imperial context, he also becomes chauvinistic in his mimetic language around Jesus. I would argue that Fanon, even though writing in the context of Africans fighting against France, is helpful for thinking about the connection between empires and nations and how both share a tendency towards male chauvinistic thinking. As contemporary readers of the Pauline text grapple with the language of empire, I would hope that such a grappling would force laypersons and parishioners to connect properly the language of empire to the oppressive and chauvinistic language of nations today.

Nonetheless, I do not believe that Corinthian women prophets heard a difference between the empire of Caesar, or the empire of God as Paul alludes in verse 20. John Dominic Crossan and Jonathan L. Reed highlight that the Augustan marital laws made the private matters of the *paterfamilias* law.[37] In essence, Caesar Augustus provided tax breaks and accelerated climbs up the political ladder if high class men married and fathered children.

Paul's language of being a father to the Corinthian community simply reinforces the language of empire that is oppressive and chauvinistic to everyone
except high class men. I argue that the Corinthian women prophets may not
necessarily hear a difference between the chauvinistic language of empire
and the chauvinistic language of Paul through the Jewish body of Jesus. The
Corinthian women prophets would have to resist Paul's inability to provide
relational models for being in power.

As I have thought through "feminized Paul" and "minoritized Paul," it
appears that Paul's patriarchal power unto imitation still keeps him in a
hierarchical relationship over all of the Corinthian community even though
his rhetoric is twisted and at times hard to follow. Even still, the Corinthian
women prophets would have heard Paul's demand for them to return to
marriage and full sexuality for the benefit and sake of their husbands. Even
as Paul attempted to get the women back into their proper places, I still
believe that nuancing Paul's rhetorical argument to show the faulty nature of
his "feminization" and utilization of his "minority" status (while still remaining connected to the Jewish body of Jesus as high status because of the nature
of Jesus's kingship), Paul remains in a hierarchal position and contemporary
readers must frame areas of resistance towards relational power as understood by Riggs and Collins.

CONTEMPORARY MEANINGS FOR THE MINORITIZED
WOMANIST PAULINE READER

In the above essay, I have argued that Paul has taken both his status as a
minority and his status as feminine to upend the status of the Corinthian
women prophets by wielding both as powerful battering rams against the
Corinthian community. As a womanist biblical scholar, my critique centers
heavily on the way that Paul becomes feminized and minoritized while ignoring the lived realities of those embodied identities. Essentially, the decreased position of relational and interpersonal power is akin to a hermeneutics of sacrifice for certain members of the body of Christ. It appears that
Paul reinscribes a hermeneutics of sacrifice to the Corinthian women prophets. [38] More disturbingly, I believe that even as scholars recognize Paul's
attempt to argue for the Corinthian community's imitation of him and his
minoritized Jewish identity, the Europeanization of Paul unto white supremacist ideologies latched on to Paul's Jewish identified body for the purpose of
casting Paul's Jewish body with the Europeanized and universal body of
Jesus. These interpretations then resulted in a skewed Pauline identity making Paul the "patron saint" for patriarchal and white supremacist thought.

Even if the Corinthian women prophets were unable to resist Paul to a
lived reality of relational power, I do believe that the enterprise of a woman-

ist reading of Paul's feminized and minoritized body is a helpful venture towards balancing contemporary readings of biblical text for today's ecclesial settings. Since Paul has become the exemplar of normative thought for Eurocentric Christianity, interpreters of Paul often use Pauline text as a bludgeoning tool against minoritized identities, ethnicities, and sexualities within ecclesial systems and society. Just as womanists have questioned black women's forced surrogacy and sacrifice for the benefit of white society to the detriment of black society and family, contemporary readers of Paul must ask whether the ecclesial/leadership power that Paul yields lends itself to an idea of relational or interpersonal power within our ecclesial settings. If not, where are the dissenting voices that push back against patriarchal mimetic power?

Indeed, as of this writing, a number of state legislatures are putting forth and passing strict abortion laws thereby doing what Paul attempted to do with the Corinthian women prophets. One especially egregious example of the strict abortion laws that disproportionately affect black women occurred when an Alabama woman was indicted for manslaughter when she miscarried her unborn fetus after being shot during a fight. Alabama sought to make the pregnant woman culpable for the death of the fetus even though she did not pull the trigger on the gun.[39] While the State of Alabama eventually dismissed the indictment against Marshae Jones, the United States witnessed firsthand the "slippery slope" of strict abortion laws. As Paul wanted to force the Corinthian women prophets into marriage, sexuality, and surrogacy, governmental officials are employing the same tactics against women's bodies now. Many of these laws are denying abortions even in the case of rape and incest. In essence, we are seeing powerful men dictate to women what their bodies must endure for the sake of some misplaced pro-life ideas. Accordingly, reading against the grain of Paul and toward relational power is a much-needed venture for the flourishing of church and society.

NOTES

1. In my upbringing there was also no imagination for a "future wife." I must acknowledge my heteronormative upbringing even as I engage a variety of scholars of Paul including various queer biblical interpreters.

2. See R. S. Sugirtharajah, *Postcolonial Reconfigurations: Alternative Ways of Reading the Bible and Doing Theology* (Nordich, UK: SCM, 2003), 104. Sugirtharajah claims that Paul's missionary journeys were a fabrication of Western exegetes because they are attempting to export their Europeanization of theology through missionary endeavors. Accordingly, Paul had to be reconfigured as a person who turns his back on Asia and looks towards Europe. Since I do not rely only on Sugirtharajah argumentation, I will pair Sugirtharajah's work with European philosophy in order to add more "meat" to the argumentation of Paul's Europeanization.

3. In this essay, I am not engaging a strong distinction between free elite women and freed formerly enslaved women who may have been a part of the Corinthian community and served as Corinthian women prophets as that is beyond the scope of this essay. For an excellent

delineation of those nuances, please see Mitzi J. Smith's forthcoming article, "Chloe, a Freed-woman in Corinth (1 Cor. 1:11): A Womanist Reconstruction."

4. As a term coined by Alice Walker, "womanism" may be defined as a type of thought pertaining to black women in order to set aside mainstream white feminists from feminists of color while also resisting anti-blackness within the feminist movement. By focusing specifically on black women, womanism aims for the transformation of society and liberation of all people in the black community. Some seminal womanist works include Jacquelyn Grant, *White Women's Christ, Black Women's Jesus: Feminist Christology and Womanist Response* (Atlanta: Scholars, 1989); Katie Cannon, *Black Womanist Ethics* (Atlanta: Scholars, 1988); Katie Cannon, *Katie's Canon: Womanism and the Soul of the Black Community* (New York: Continuum, 1995); Cheryl Kirk-Duggan, *Exorcising Evil: Theodicy and African American Spirituals—A Womanist Perspective* (Maryknoll, NY: Orbis, 1993); Emilie Maureen Townes, *Womanist Justice, Womanist Hope* (Atlanta: Scholars, 1993); and Emilie Maureen Townes, *A Troubling in My Soul: Womanist Perspectives on Evil and Suffering* (Maryknoll, NY: Orbis, 1993).

5. See Patricia Hill Collins, *Black Feminist Thought: Knowledge, Consciousness, and the Politics of Empowerment* (New York: Routledge, 2000), 274.

6. Collins, *Black Feminist Thought*, 274.

7. See Marcia Y. Riggs, *Plenty Good Room: Women Church Versus Male Power in the Black Church* (Eugene, OR: Wipf and Stock, 2003), 83.

8. Riggs, *Plenty Good Room*, 100.

9. For excellent discussion on reader response criticism, please see Wolfgang Iser, *The Act of Reading: A Theory of Aesthetic Response* (Baltimore: John Hopkins University Press, 1978), 37, 169, 214. Iser's theory serves the interests of my work because he stresses the idea of the reader's central role in determining meaning. Iser maintains that in the interaction between the reader and the text, "the role prescribed by the text will be stronger but the reader's own disposition will never disappear totally." The reader's disposition will instead form the background and serve as a frame of reference for the act of understanding and comprehending the material of the text.

10. See Elisabeth Schüssler Fiorenza, "Rhetorical Situation and Historical Reconstruction in 1 Corinthians," in *Christianity at Corinth: The Quest for the Pauline Church*, eds. Edward Adams and David G. Horrell, 145–60 (Louisville, KY: Westminster John Knox, 2004).

11. Fiorenza, "Rhetorical Situation," 159.

12. Fiorenza, "Rhetorical Situation," 157.

13. Fiorenza, "Rhetorical Situation," 157.

14. Elizabeth Castelli, *Imitating Paul: A Discourse of Power* (Louisville, KY: Westminster John Knox), 112–13. See also, Joseph Marchal, "Female Masculinity in Corinth? Bodily Citations and the Drag of History," *Neotestamentica* 48, no. 1 (2014): 93–113.

15. See Margaret Y. MacDonald, "Women Holy in Body and Spirit: The Social Setting in 1 Corinthians 7," in *Christianity at Corinth: The Quest for the Pauline Church*, eds. Edward Adams and David G. Horrell, 161–72 (Louisville, KY: Westminster John Knox, 2004). In her work, MacDonald argues that women were the main pushers of sexual ascetic living in terms of child-rearing roles and marriage. Following Fiorenza, MacDonald also argues that the community was interpreting Galatians 3:27–28 in a way that there was no longer male or female in the community. Believing that the ascetic push is why Paul wrote 1 Corinthians 7, MacDonald argues that Paul was worried about the ascetic women gaining power, and, therefore, he wanted to establish that (1) society needs order and (2) he was afraid that the outer world would not think well of the Corinthian Christian community.

16. Antoinette Clark Wire, *The Corinthian Women Prophets: A Reconstruction through Paul's Rhetoric* (Eugene, OR: Wipf and Stock, 2003), 1.

17. I am still shocked at recent scholarship that dismisses Wire or does not engage with her work at all. See Cynthia Long Westfall, *Paul and Gender: Reclaiming the Apostle's Vision for Men and Women in Christ* (Grand Rapids, MI: Baker, 2016), and Roger M. Porter, "Does Paul Really Understand? A Reconstruction of the Life and Issues of Paul's Corinthian Community with an Assessment of His Responsive Effectiveness," *Journal of Biblical Theology* 1, no. 3 (2018): 114–24.

18. One scholar who uses this language is Gordon Fee, *The First Epistle to the Corinthians* (Grand Rapids, MI: Wm. B. Eerdmans, 1987), 166. Others pick up on similar ideas. See Richard Hays, *First Corinthians* (Louisville, KY: John Knox, 1997), 72, and Anthony Thiselton, *The First Epistle to the Corinthians* (Grand Rapids, MI: Wm. B. Eerdmans, 2000), 365–71.

19. See Thiselton, *The First Epistle to the Corinthians*, 368.

20. Thiselton, *The First Epistle to the Corinthians*, 365–71.

21. Michael J. Gorman, "Cruciform or Resurrectiform? Paul's Paradoxical Practice of Participation in Christ," *Ex Auditu* 33 (2017): 60–83.

22. See 1 Macc. 1:41–49, 60–61; 2:42–48; 2 Macc. 6:7–11; Tacitus, *Hist.* 5.5; Suetonius, *Dom.* 12:2; Petronius, *Sat.* 102.

23. Scholars have argued that Paul has a decreased sense of masculinity and passes his abjection onto female and homoerotic bodies. See Daniel Boyarin, *Unheroic Conduct: The Rise of Heterosexuality and the Invention of the Jewish Man*, Contraversions 8 (Berkeley: University of California Press, 1997). In his delineation of Paul's feminization, Tat-Siong Benny Liew picks up on Boyarin's argument. See Tat-Siong Benny Liew, "Redressing Bodies at Corinth: Racial/Ethnic Politics and Religious Difference in the Context of Empire" in *The Colonized Apostle: Paul through Postcolonial Eyes*, ed. Christopher D. Stanley, 127–43 (Minneapolis: Fortress, 2011).

24. See Angela N. Parker, "One Womanist's View of Racial Reconciliation in Galatians," *Journal of Feminist Studies in Religion* 34, no. 2 (2018): 23–40. For an excellent account of slavery in the classics, please see Sandra R. Joshel and Lauren Hackworth Petersen's *The Material Life of Roman Slaves* (Cambridge, UK: Cambridge University Press, 2014).

25. I am specifically trying to evoke the double entendre of Paul being a "spoil" of war and a potential passive male in the context of the Greco-Roman world.

26. See Joseph Marchal's "Female Masculinity in Corinth? Bodily Citations and the Drag of History," *Neotestamentica* 48, no. 1 (2014): 93–113.

27. See Fee, *First Corinthians*, 184, and Thiselton, *First Corinthians*, 368–69.

28. Melissa Harris-Perry, *Sister Citizen: Shame, Stereotypes, and Black Women in America* (New Haven, CT: Yale University Press, 2011), 28–50.

29. See Melissa Harris-Perry, *Sister Citizen*, 104.

30. See Dale Martin, *Slavery as Salvation: The Metaphor of Slavery in Pauline Christianity* (New Haven, CT: Yale University Press, 1990), 142.

31. Liew, "Redressing Bodies," 136–39.

32. Liew, "Redressing Bodies," 133.

33. See Rom. 14:17; 1 Cor. 4:20; 6:9, 10; 15:24, 50; Gal. 5:21; Eph. 5:5; Col. 1:13; 4:11; 1 Thess. 2:12; 2 Thess. 1:5; 2 Tim. 4:1, 18.

34. See Fee, *First Corinthians*, 193; See Hays, *First Corinthians*, 79; and see Thiselton, *First Corinthians*, 377.

35. At the beginning of this essay, I alluded to the work of Sugirtharajah. However, I find Sugirtharajah's work, while fascinating and helpful to my argument, a bit thin since he focuses on missions as a way to speak of the Europeanization of Paul. More specifically, I am placing Shawn Kelly's philosophical thought in conversation with Sugirtharajah. See Shawn Kelly, *Racializing Jesus: Race, Ideology and the Formation of Modern Biblical Scholarship* (New York: Routledge, 2002), 47.

36. Frantz Fanon, *The Wretched of the Earth*, trans. Constance Farrington (New York: Grove, 1963), 156.

37. John Dominic Crossan and Jonathan L. Reed, *In Search of Paul: How Jesus' Apostle Opposed Rome's Empire with God's Kingdom* (New York: HarperCollins, 2004), 69, 123.

38. See JoAnne Marie Terrell, *Power in the Blood?* (Maryknoll, NY: Orbis Books, 1998).

39. See Tamar Lapin, "Alabama Woman Indicted for Manslaughter after Miscarrying When Shot," *NY Post*, June 6, 2019, https://nypost.com/2019/06/26/alabama-woman-indicted-for-manslaughter-after-miscarrying-when-shot/.

WORKS CITED

Boyarin, Daniel. *Unheroic Conduct: The Rise of Heterosexuality and the Invention of the Jewish Man.* Contraversions 8. Berkeley: University of California Press, 1997.

Cannon, Katie. *Black Womanist Ethics.* Atlanta: Scholars, 1988.

———. *Katie's Canon: Womanism and the Soul of the Black Community.* New York: Continuum, 1995.

Castelli, Elizabeth. *Imitating Paul: A Discourse of Power.* Louisville, KY: Westminster John Knox, 1991.

Collins, Patricia Hill. *Black Feminist Thought: Knowledge, Consciousness, and the Politics of Empowerment.* New York: Routledge, 2000.

Crossan, John Dominic, and Jonathan L. Reed. *In Search of Paul: How Jesus' Apostle Opposed Rome's Empire with God's Kingdom .* New York: HarperCollins, 2004.

Gorman, Michael J. "Cruciform or Resurrectiform? Paul's Paradoxical Practice of Participation in Christ." *Ex Auditu* 33 (2017): 60–83.

Grant, Jacquelyn. *White Women's Christ, Black Women's Jesus: Feminist Christology and Womanist Response.* Atlanta: Scholars, 1989.

Fee, Gordon. *The First Epistle to the Corinthians.* Grand Rapids, MI: Wm. B. Eerdmans, 1987.

Fiorenza, Elisabeth Schüssler. "Rhetorical Situation and Historical Reconstruction in 1 Corinthians." In *Christianity at Corinth: The Quest for the Pauline Church*, edited by Edward Adams and David G. Horrell, 145–60. Louisville, KY: Westminster John Knox, 2004.

Hays, Richard. *First Corinthians.* Louisville, KY: John Knox, 1997.

Kirk-Duggan, Cheryl. *Exorcising Evil: Theodicy and African American Spirituals—A Womanist Perspective.* Maryknoll, NY: Orbis, 1993.

Harris-Perry, Melissa. *Sister Citizen: Shame, Stereotypes, and Black Women in America.* New Haven, CT: Yale University Press, 2011.

Iser, Wolfgang. *The Act of Reading: A Theory of Aesthetic Response.* Baltimore: John Hopkins University Press, 1978.

Joshel, Sandra R., and Lauren Hackworth Petersen. *The Material Life of Roman Slaves.* Cambridge, UK: Cambridge University Press, 2014.

Kelly, Shawn. *Racializing Jesus: Race, Ideology and the Formation of Modern Biblical Scholarship.* New York: Routledge, 2002.

Lapin, Tamar. "Alabama Woman Indicted for Manslaughter after Miscarrying When Shot," *NY Post*, June 6, 2019. https://nypost.com/2019/06/26/alabama-woman-indicted-for-manslaughter-after-miscarrying-when-shot/.

Liew, Tat-Siong Benny. "Redressing Bodies at Corinth: Racial/Ethnic Politics and Religious Difference in the Context of Empire." In *The Colonized Apostle: Paul through Postcolonial Eyes*, edited by Christopher D. Stanley, 127–43. Minneapolis: Fortress Press, 2011.

MacDonald, Margaret Y. "Women Holy in Body and Spirit: The Social Setting in 1 Corinthians 7." In *Christianity at Corinth: The Quest for the Pauline Church*, edited by Edward Adams and David G. Horrell, 161–72. Louisville, KY: Westminster John Knox, 2004.

Marchal, Joseph. "Female Masculinity in Corinth? Bodily Citations and the Drag of History." *Neotestamentica* 48, no. 1 (2014): 93–113.

Martin, Dale. *Slavery as Salvation: The Metaphor of Slavery in Pauline Christianity.* New Haven, CT: Yale University Press, 1990.

Parker, Angela N. "One Womanist's View of Racial Reconciliation in Galatians." *Journal of Feminist Studies in Religion* 34, no. 2 (2018): 23–40.

Porter, Roger M. "Does Paul Really Understand? A Reconstruction of the Life and Issues of Paul's Corinthian Community with an Assessment of His Responsive Effectiveness." *Journal of Biblical Theology* 1, no. 3 (2018): 114–24.

Riggs, Marcia Y. *Plenty Good Room: Women Church Versus Male Power in the Black Church.* Eugene, OR: Wipf and Stock, 2003.

Sugirtharajah, R.S. *Postcolonial Reconfigurations: Alternative Ways of Reading the Bible and Doing Theology.* Nordich, UK: SCM, 2003.

Terrell, JoAnne Marie. *Power in the Blood? The Cross in the African American Experience.* Maryknoll, NY: Orbis Books, 1998.

Townes, Emilie Maureen. *A Troubling in My Soul: Womanist Perspectives on Evil and Suffering*. Maryknoll, NY: Orbis, 1993.

————. *Womanist Justice, Womanist Hope*. Atlanta: Scholars, 1993.

Thiselton, Anthony. *The First Epistle to the Corinthians*. Grand Rapids, MI: Wm. B. Eerdmans, 2000.

Westfall, Cynthia Long. *Paul and Gender: Reclaiming the Apostle's Vision for Men and Women in Christ*. Grand Rapids, MI: Baker, 2016.

Wire, Antoinette Clark. *The Corinthian Women Prophets: A Reconstruction through Paul's Rhetoric*. Eugene, OR; Wipf and Stock, 2003.

Chapter Five

Gender, Race, and the Normalization of Prophecy in Early Christianity and Korean and Korean American Christianity

Jung H. Choi

This chapter explores how discussions of race, ethnicity, and gender are intertwined with discourses about prophecy in the NT and other early Christian texts and in contemporary Korean and Korean American Christianity. Discussions of prophecy in early Christianity, I argue, served as a means of constructing identity, negotiating and renegotiating boundaries, and, in doing so, legitimizing or illegitimating certain religious practices. Consequently, they were often inextricably connected to the "three axes of power" (race, gender, and class).[1] And in important ways, the intersection of power with the discussions of prophecy in early Christianity is also reinscribed in contemporary Korean and Korean American Christianity.

As part of the Korean diaspora, I have been a frequent visitor to both Korean and Korean American churches. Having grown up in a Korean church setting, and as a musician and preacher in several Korean and Korean American churches, I have experienced both ecclesiastical worlds, and yet, simultaneously, I do not fully belong to either. As Tat-Siong Benny Liew puts it, I have "an ambivalent feeling" of insider-ness as well as outsider-ness.[2] In these contexts, I witnessed many Korean and Korean American Christian women participate in charismatic practices centering on prophecy, and I became interested in their stories.[3]

My analysis of both early and contemporary Christianity draws on feminist and postcolonial biblical scholarship. I am influenced by the feminist historiography emphasizing that ancient literature should be read not as descriptive but as prescriptive—as engaged in struggling over and contesting practices and ideas. Enacting this feminist historiographical practice, I focus on the processes by which texts authorize, valorize, or erase particular practices.[4] I particularly draw on the theories of rhetoric discussed by Elisabeth Schüssler Fiorenza, and thus I analyze historical texts as rhetorical: that is, I ask how and to what ends the text persuades.[5] The practices discussed in the texts, I argue, are prescribed in order to persuade readers and hearers to draw a legitimate boundary around prophecy.[6] Building on work from other feminist and womanist biblical scholars and historians, I ask both historical and contemporary questions. What are the historical possibilities for women prophets? Do modern Christians still use a similar rhetoric to marginalize prophets, especially women prophets?

I also employ postcolonial biblical criticism, which concerns "politics of inclusion and exclusion," or as Liew asserts, the "issue of community" formation.[7] I ask questions such as: who are the people conceived of as legitimate members of Christian communities? Can only certain people be elected to be messengers of God? How are Korean and Korean American charismatic practices denigrated through the rhetorics of feminization and paganization?[8]

This chapter proceeds as follows: First, I analyze Origen's discussions of 1 Corinthians 11–14, one of the most substantial discussions of prophecy in the NT. I trace how Origen privileges certain practices as prophetic forms over against other formats. Thereby, Origen attempts to constitute a particular prophetic self (i.e., moral/rational and thus masculine). Second, I move to Origen's *Contra Celsum* Book 7, where we can see more explicit polemics against the form of prophecy he criticizes, sexualizing and attributing to paganism rival prophetic practices. Origen associates the female with the passive and polemically argues that the Pythian prophetesses are penetrated by demonic spirits. He strategically deploys his discussions on prophecy and uses the discussions on prophecy to circumscribe acceptable and legitimate religious practices. Thus, we see a process of ethnic reasoning that constructs Christianity as moral and rational, while racializing/ethnicizing the prophetic opponents as pagan. Finally, I address how early Christian strategies regarding prophetic practices resonate in contemporary Korean and Korean American churches.

EARLY CHRISTIAN EXAMPLE: ORIGEN'S *COMMENTARY ON ROMANS* 9.3.8: "STRIVE FOR PROPHECY"

In his *Commentary on Romans* (hereafter *Comm.Rom.*), Origen provides a compelling glimpse of prophecy as a relationship between the divine and the human. Particularly, Origen reinforces his overarching premise that the gifts of God (*charismata*) are located in a complex synthesis of divine-human relationships and, specifically, that prophecy is inextricably connected to the relationship between God and humanity, giving prophecy an *ethical register*.[9] In the absence of a *Commentary on 1 Corinthians*, and given that his *Homilies on 1 Corinthians* now only exist in fragments, Origen's *Comm.Rom.* gives us a crucial lens for understanding his view of 1 Corinthians 11–14, one of the most substantial discussions of prophecy in the NT.

In *Comm.Rom.* 9.3.8, Origen argues that human beings can desire and attain prophecy. Since this passage is so crucial, I cite it in full:

> However, in these things the question is asked whether in us or from us *a certain kind of prophecy can exist that is not entirely from God but derives even in a small measure from human efforts.* This will be viewed as totally impossible to other people, but with Paul it is clearly approved when he says, *"strive for the spiritual gifts, but most of all that you should prophesy."* There the Apostle is showing that, just as one is zealous for ministry and teaching and exhortation, etc., through his exhibiting zeal and effort toward these things, in a similar way this should happen for prophecy. (*Comm.Rom.* 9.3.8, emphasis added)[10]

In this passage, Origen weaves Romans 12:6–8 together with 1 Corinthians 12:31 and 14:1 and argues that prophecy is a phenomenon still current in Christian communities. He maintains that Christians can achieve prophecy by putting forth zealous effort.[11] He also places prophecy on the same plane as other gifts insofar as it is possible to *cultivate* it. In this way, Origen couches spiritual gifts in moralistic terms.[12] Spiritual gifts, like moral qualities, can be and should be intentionally developed.[13] On the one hand, he emphasizes a human responsibility to receive whatever spiritual gifts God gives. On the other, he enjoins his readers or hearers to participate in making themselves worthy to receive spiritual gifts.

Origen considers it utterly necessary that his (Christian) audience/readers be encouraged in self-conscious ethical development. Just as Origen notes that it is imperative for Christians, in general, to engage in scriptural interpretation, so he invites the same Christians to participate in the program of cultivating moral profiles for themselves in order to receive spiritual gifts and prophecy. This theme is evident when he informs his audience that they possess the power to engender their own moral formation.

According to Origen, Paul's epistles are meant to be read by a universal and diachronic Christian community, and Origen interprets them as relevant to this broad context. Focusing on his own audience, Origen constantly invites them (including himself) into Paul's epistles, as signaled by his use of "we" language. In the passage, Origen repeatedly refers to the "we." Indeed, for him, "it is possible *for us* to exhibit zealous effort to attain this kind of prophecy, and it also lies *within our power* that the prophecy that is from God should be added unto us." (*Comm.Rom.* 9.3.8.) Hence Origen takes *zēloute* (strive for, or be zealous for) as Paul's command to a diachronic and universal Christian audience.[14] While the discussions in *Comm.Rom.* 9.1.1–9.3.7 pertain to the cultivation of a proper self-worthiness to receive spiritual gifts, *Comm.Rom.* 9.3.8–14 show that Origen not only is interested in the individual, but also argues for the cultivation of the self in relation to diachronic Christian community (that is, Paul speaking to everyone over time) and in relation to the community of Christians reading Origen's commentaries (a kind of ecclesiastical-scholastic group).

The Normalization of Moral and Rational Prophetic Practices

Origen tries to construct an ideal Christian prophecy over against competing forms of prophecy. What other Christian ideas regarding spiritual gifts is Origen seeking to temper or to exclude? To answer this, I return to the crucial passage of *Comm.Rom.* 9.3.8. where Origen seeks to control the definition of prophecy by citing Luke 16:16.

> This is why this prophecy should be understood as that which Paul teaches, not that through which one says, "Thus says the Lord." For that latter was in effect until John, according to what is written in the Gospel, "The law and the prophets were until John." Rather it is that concerning which the same apostle says, "He who prophesies speaks to people for their edification and exhortation and consolations." So then, for Paul, "prophecy" is mentioned when anyone speaks to people for their edification and when anyone speaks for their exhortation and consolation. (*Comm.Rom.* 9.3.8)

Origen specifies that the prophecy to which Paul refers in 1 Corinthians 12:39 and 14:1 ("strive to prophesy") is to be understood "as that which Paul teaches, not that through which one says, 'Thus says the Lord.'" He argues that Paul's discussion of prophecy refers to "edification," "exhortation," and "consolation," and that this sort of prophecy should be pursued with "zealous effort" even in the present.

Yet there is another kind of prophecy that only existed up to the time of John the Baptist, a kind of prophecy in which one spoke in God's own voice, often marked in scripture by the phrase "Thus says the Lord." Origen differentiates the kind of prophecy in which God speaks directly through a medium/prophet, where the usual format starts with "thus says the Lord," from the kind of prophecy to which Paul refers in 1 Corinthians 12 and 14. Here Origen attempts to control the type of prophecy because he is attempting to control the type of prophecy that is relevant among Christian communities by championing what he takes to be a correct understanding of prophecy. The "correct" kind of prophecy that Origen inscribes is the prophecy which "should be understood as that which Paul teaches."

Two later writers who refer to 1 Corinthians 14:1 shed light on how Origen tries to connect prophecy with teaching. Cyril of Alexandria takes a similar position to Origen, writing in allusion to 1 Corinthians 14:1–5:

> I mean the gift of prophecy, that is, the ability to interpret the words of the prophets. For once the Only Son had become man and suffered and been raised and the plan for our salvation had been accomplished, what sort of prophecy was required or what things still needed to be foretold? In these verses, therefore, prophesying must mean *simply* this: *the ability to interpret the prophecies*. (emphasis added)[15]

Similarly, Ambrosiaster, writing in the fourth century, contends: "Paul urges them to desire prophecy earnestly, so that they might become stronger through constant discussion of the law of God and learn that the preaching of the false prophets is wrong."[16] Origen does not explicitly dichotomize "constant discussion of the law of God" and "the preaching of the false prophet" as Ambrosiaster does. Clearly, however, Origen is on a similar trajectory in tightly connecting prophecy to discussion of the scripture.

We find confirmation of this redefinition of prophecy, likely in relation to other Christians, in a passage in 1 Corinthians 14:6–12:

> Paul refers to teachings of a more theoretical or contemplative nature as a flute and harp since they do not treat the moral life, while *he calls the exhortation to virtue a bugle*. For this reason, one could maintain that the obscure parts of Scripture, for example, the discussions of sacrifices in Leviticus and of the tabernacle in Exodus, should not be read unless *someone interprets and makes their meaning clear*. (*Homilies on 1 Corinthians*, emphasis added)[17]

Here, Origen discusses the trope of a musical instrument as a prophet, albeit briefly. The sounds of musical instruments were often used as metaphors of unintelligible or prophetic language.[18] Contrary to this unintelligible language, Origen privileges someone "who interprets and makes the meaning [of the scripture] clear."

In these passages, Origen does not demarcate the relationship between exhortation, consolation, teaching, and scriptural study. He rather loosely connects all of these to correct forms of prophecy. Obviously, however, Origen tries to craft an ideal prophet as the one who is different from the ecstatic one (described as the one "who speaks in the voice of the divine" or the mouthpiece of the divine). In doing so, he constructs a rational, intelligent, and moral activity as an ideal prophecy. His construction of proper prophecy is a masculine one, for rational, intelligent, and moral are all considered to be masculine virtues.[19] Origen's strategy is more clearly shown in the next section when he polemicizes rhetorical (ecstatic) opponents.

A series of questions ensues here. One strand of questions would be about Origen's correlation between reading and interpreting scripture, teaching, consolation, and so on, and proper forms of prophecy. In this correlation, are only certain people privileged for prophecy? Does the emphasis on moral and rational (read: masculine) elements in prophecy inevitably exclude women?

The crucial point to explore is the reason why Origen works so hard to constitute morality and rationality as ideal prophetic traits. Some may argue that Origen's motive is opposition to the so-called Montanists (or New Prophecy as its adherents called it) and his desire to craft a Christian identity over against this internecine opponent. Yet he does not explicitly denounce this group in his writings, and certainly "Montanists" were not the only Christians of his time who participated in prophetic practices that privileged loss of control and even possession.[20] Thus, I argue that there is no single rhetorical opponent against whom Origen directs his discussions on prophecy in his writings. Reading against the grain of his arguments, there must have been many Christians who were participating in prophetic experiences of which Origen does not approve, a situation that provokes Origen to constitute a masculine prophet as ideal. Likewise, the prescriptive nature of canonization reveals the existence of those who participated in various kinds of prophetic activities. The implicit polemics are the canonization process itself, as one of the main thrusts of canonization is, arguably, to construct an ideal identity of early Christian prophecy in response to contemporary practitioners of prophecy.[21]

Feminization and Paganization of Rival Prophets: Origen's *Contra Celsum* Book 7

In the previous section, we saw one instantiation of constructing Christian prophecy as moral/rational and thus masculine in Origen's discussions on prophecy. In this section, we see another strategy of ethnic reasoning that challenges the rival prophetic practices by deploying the rhetorics of feminization and paganization. In *Contra Celsum* (hereafter *Cels.*) Book 7, Origen polemicizes against the Pythia, positioning her as an emblematic figure of pagan prophecy whose loss of control is problematic. A key emphasis in his understanding of bad prophecy derives from a distrust of losing control of one's consciousness during prophecy. As we saw above, Origen emphasizes that the will of God initiates prophecy, but he equally highlights the will and control of the prophet. He defies the notion that the moment of prophecy is involuntary and involves losing control of one's consciousness. Several of our key texts will show how passivity in prophecy or divination is linked to the feminine and is marked as problematic.

Origen's critique of the Pythia is twofold. First, she lacks the virtue and morality necessary for true prophets. Origen deploys the themes of virtue and control as crucial criteria of the true and worthy prophet. He emphasizes the importance of worthiness, morality, and virtue as necessary prophetic qualities. This theme of the moral character of a prophet is highlighted in several places in *Cels* (2.51; 4.95; 5.42; 7.3). In addition, over against the Pythia, Origen emphasizes "those of the prophets in Judea"—who are "our" prophets—as the champions of virtues, such as strength, courage, and holy life, which makes them "worthy of" (*axios*) God's spirit:

> That is the reason why we reckon of no account the predictions uttered by the Pythian priestess, or by the priestesses of Dodona, or by the oracle of Apollo at Claros, or at Branchiade, or at the shrine of Zeus Ammon, or by countless other alleged prophets; whereas we admire *those of the prophets in Judaea*, seeing that their strong, courageous, and holy life *was worthy of* God's Spirit, whose prophecy was imparted in a new way which had nothing in common with the divination inspired by daemons. (*Cels.* 7.7, emphasis added)[22]

This emphasis on "being worthy of" the Holy Spirit (or seeking "to deserve/ earn" the Spirit) recurs throughout Origen's other works such as *Commentary on Romans* and *De Principiis*.[23]

Origen highlights that the Holy Spirit chooses the prophet "on account of the quality of their lives" (*Cels.* 7.7). In a later passage, he reiterates that the prophets "received the divine Spirit because of purity of life" (*Cels.* 7.18). Furthermore, he continues,"the prophets, according to the will of God, said without any obscurity whatever could be at once understood as beneficial to their hearers and helpful towards *attaining moral reformation*" (*Cels.* 7.10, emphasis added). Morality is considered a crucial element of the Christian prophet over against the Other.

In *Cels.* 7, Origen constructs Christian prophecy over against so-called pagan prophecy and mantic practices, with the Pythia as the main target of his polemic. He employs her as a useful epitome of pagan mantic practices more generally, and through this invective, Origen essentializes pagan prophecy as something fundamentally different from Christian prophecy.[24]

Second, he notes that the Pythia loses control in a very distinctive way: as the Pythia is "sitting at the mouth of the Castalian cave she receives a spirit through her womb" (*Cels.*7.3.25). Origen's sexualized invective against the Pythia is grounded in a physiological understanding of prophecy commonly found in Greco-Roman discourses. Plutarch, in his *On the Obsolescence of Oracles*, for example, famously narrates "the dangers of prophecy," discussing how prophecy is popularly understood as the loss of control, and even penetration and divine rape enacted by a male god on a female seer:[25] she "*surrenders herself to the control of the god*," when she is not completely clean (as if she were a musical instrument, well strung and well tuned), but in a state of emotion and instability" (437 D, emphasis added). Plutarch participates in a broader understanding of *pneuma* as "a physical entity that enters the body and produces a condition free of mental restraint—enthusiasm."[26] In *On the Obsolescence of Oracles*, he posits a more explicitly sexualized understanding of prophecy when he says that "a pure, virgin soul, becomes the associate (*syneimi*) of the god" (405 C). As Dale Martin notes, the better translation of *syneimi* might be "to have sexual intercourse."[27]

In maligning the Pythia, Origen thus draws on sexual invective, a common mode of constructing and denigrating the "Other." Furthermore, Origen has a particular spin on the sexualized polemic that the Pythia "loses control" in arguing that she loses control of consciousness. In this way, she also lacks strength. As Jennifer Knust succinctly sums up, "sexualized invective serves several purposes at once: outsiders are pushed further away, insiders are policed, and morality is both constituted and defined as 'Christian.'"[28] Origen depicts the Pythia and her prophecy as an outsider to the pure practices of "the prophets in Judaea," who are treated as proto-Christian. Contrary to the Pythia, "the one who is inspired by the divine spirit," argues Origen, "ought to possess the clearest vision at the very time when the deity is in communion with him" (*Cels.* 7.3).

Origen levels criticism against the Pythia and her ecstasy, claiming that she is an "alleged prophetess" in order to devalue her. The fact that Origen uses "prophet" to refer to the Pythia, instead of another term such as "diviner," I propose, means that he is directly juxtaposing "pagan" with "Christian" prophecy.

> It is not the work of divine spirit to lead the alleged prophetess into a state of ecstasy and frenzy so that she loses possession of her consciousness. The person inspired by the divine spirit ought to have derived from it far more benefit than anyone who may be instructed by the oracles to do that which helps towards living a life which is moderate and according to nature, or towards that which is of advantage or which is expedient. (*Cels.* 7.3)

Origen drives a wedge between prophets who lose consciousness and prophets who keep clear vision in the moment of communication with the divine. He opines, "Because of the touch, as it were, of what is called the Holy Spirit upon their soul they possessed clear mental vision and became more radiant in their soul, and even in body, which no longer offered any opposition to the life lived according to virtue" (*Cels.* 7.4). Again, Origen tightly connects virtue to possessing clear mental vision in the moment of prophecy, crafting a particular way of prophecy as a right form of prophecy.

Further, he questions, "If the Pythian priestess is out of her senses and has *not control of* her faculties when she prophesies, what sort of spirit must we think it which poured darkness upon her mind and rational thinking?" (*Cels.* 7.4, emphasis added). Origen tightly connects the loss of control of consciousness with the loss of bodily control. Put differently, for Origen, the Pythia is sexually vulnerable both in physical body and in mind.

Analyzing gendered imagery in classical Greek tragedies, Ruth Padel claims, "The mind—like a woman in society, like female sexuality in relation to male—is acted upon, invaded, a victim of the outside world (especially of divinity)."[29] Although Padel's subject matter is in the classical Greek period, her analysis is pertinent for early Christianity as well, in the sense that women prophets were associated with penetration by evil spirits and condemned as sexually polluted.

Tertullian, who in his *Prescription against Heretics* attempts to disclaim the prophetess Philomena, similarly uses the trope of lack of control. He portrays Philomena as one "who permits thoughts and beliefs to penetrate her mind without being scrupulously just as she allows her body to be penetrated by men."[30] Anne Jensen notes that the manuscript traditions of the prophetess depict her as a woman who is passive and unable to resist the approaches of evil spirits.[31]

To conclude, Origen makes those who participate in a rival prophetic practice feminized and pagan/heathen, employing racial and gender dichotomies between "we" and "you." "Your prophets" are feminized: they are irrational and lose control. Emphasis on control along with rationality and morality is a masculine trait.[32] Origen urges the readers and hearers to participate in disciplined training with virtues of courage, justice, and self-mastery. By reading how the true prophet ("our prophets") acts in the texts, the readers and hearers of the text are by extension exhorted to undertake the same practices (such as controlling emotions) and to reject criticized practices (such as ecstasy and possession).[33] As shown above, Origen's *Comm.Rom.* enjoins his readers or hearers to cultivate themselves to pursue prophecy and spiritual gifts. Origen had women pupils, and the readers and hearers of Origen's writings must have comprised both men and women.[34] Thus, women were also potentially encouraged to cultivate a self that is open to the divine, and that is worthy to be a proper instrument and vessel. Does Origen only call men to cultivate a proper self that is worthy of the Holy Spirit's dwelling? Or are men and women assigned different kinds of virtues, when Origen exhorts the audiences to cultivate a particular self?

The construction of the feminine other is also inextricably linked to racial/ethnic reasoning when Origen starkly juxtaposes "our prophets" (as true Christian and Jewish prophets) with "your prophets" (false prophets and pagans). Christians are aligned with "Jewishness," while "your prophets" are in pagan territory. This dichotomy between prophets in Judea and pagan prophets is all the more significant considering that Origen, along with other early Christian writers, takes great pains to distinguish between Jews and the Christians.[35]

We can conjecture that the competing prophets whom Origen problematizes are both outside and inside of Christianity. Reading against the grain of the arguments that obfuscate the presence of women prophets, we can see their historical presence in early Christianity—the very people Origen needed to work so hard to regulate.[36] How many women (and men) who were participating in prophetic experiences in early Christianity were both pushed away and policed, by being labeled Pythia, Philomena, and pagan?

CONTEMPORARY SYNTHESIS IN KOREAN AND KOREAN AMERICAN CHARISMATIC WOMEN

In the previous section, I argued that the two most common rhetorical techniques for controlling prophetic practices in early Christianity were associating "improper" prophecy with women and pagans, two lesser-than categories. These techniques—feminization and paganization—are still used in the contemporary world to delimit prophetic phenomena and those who participate in the prophetic practices.

Specifically, this early Christian strategy of self-definition resonates with Korean and Korean American women prophets in the service of constructing a racialized other. Just as prophecy was highly gendered in the Greco-Roman world and in early Christianity, similar rhetorical strategies result in discrediting certain people by making them appear illegitimate in the Korean Christian context. Origen's rhetorical construction of the competing prophets as others by racializing them as pagan is thus reiterated in Korean Christianity.

DOUBLE COLONIZATION: FEMINIZATION AND PAGANIZATION OF KOREAN CHARISMATIC WOMEN CHRISTIANS

The early Christian strategy of marginalization through deploying feminization and paganization is reinforced particularly in the modern Korean context that can be best explained by the concept of the "double colonization" described by Gayatri Chakravorty Spivak. Robert Young elaborates Spivak's theory:

> [Native subaltern women] were subject to what is today often called a "double colonization"—that is, in the first instance in the domestic sphere, the patriarchy of men, and then, in the public sphere, the patriarchy of the colonial power. . . . Spivak argues that taken always as an object of knowledge, by colonial and indigenous rulers who are as masculinist as each other, the subaltern woman is written, argued about, even legislated for, but allowed no discursive position from which to speak herself. [37]

Spivak's theory is particularly appropriate since Korean and Korean American churches are feminized and paganized by Anglo-European white Christianity. Korean churches (especially Korean Protestant churches) have been heavily influenced by various Anglo-European missionaries (mostly from the United States and Canada), but at the same time, Korean male (nationalist) elites—while internalizing the colonial logic—exercise masculine colonial power in their own homes.

In Asian countries, Christianity is attached to a concept of modernity, and yet white male scholars often "paganize" Korean Christianity because of its close relationship with shamanism. On the other hand, a majority of Korean immigrants to the United States identify themselves as "Christians," but are not white enough, meaning that their Christianity is under surveillance and suspicion.[38]

A case in point is the just-mentioned association of shamanism with Korean charismatic Christianity. Many scholars (both conservative Christians in Korea and some Westerners including Harvey Cox and Walter Hollenweger) have pigeonholed Korean Pentecostal and charismatic Christianity as "shamanistic."[39] For example, Amos Yong, a scholar of Pentecostalism, records scholarship associating Korean Pentecostals with participation in "shamanic spirit possession."[40] Cox points out that many people are asking the question whether shamanism is "compatible with Christianity."[41] He also maintains, "One of the key reasons for Korean Pentecostalism's extraordinary growth is its unerring ability to absorb huge chunks of indigenous Korean shamanism and demon possession into worship."[42]

The association of shamanism with Pentecostal Christianity is not limited to denominational Pentecostals; by way of extension, any charismatic Christian is criticized as shamanistic by this logic. This controlling method is palpable and efficient in demarcating boundaries. Many Korean and Korean American women whom I have met in various churches have told me that they are reluctant to publicly share their charismatic and prophetic experiences, because they have heard of ecstatic and charismatic experiences labeled as shamanic and thus fear that they too would be called shamans (read: heathen and non-Christian).

I argue that the association of shamanism with the ecstatic and charismatic unwittingly reinforces the marginalization of Korean and Korean American charismatic women. Calling charismatic Korean Christians shamanistic is similar to the polemical charge employed by Origen and other early Christians who aimed to regulate the legitimacy of the prophetic practice. Functioning to circumscribe the boundary of proper and acceptable Christian practices, the construction of a "race-of-heathens," as Liew calls it, is reinforced by the label of shamanism. [43]

This argument does not erase and refute the important scholarship on shamanism in Korea. The study of shamanism is highly valuable insofar as it emphasizes emancipatory power for women, and so on. There has been a welcome plethora of studies in this regard. Neither am I, it should also be said, making an argument that researching shamanism is not an important part of investigating prophecy and spiritual experiences.[44] My argument, rather, is that it should be taken into consideration that a too-easy connection between shamanism and charismatic Christian prophecy could stem from a historical and rhetorical agenda that has consistently relegated certain people (especially women) to cultural categories of "lesser than" and the Other. It is important to understand how the claim of shamanism may be used as a polemical tool that brands these people as pagan, heathen, non-Christian, and thus illegitimate members of the Christian community, and serves a politics of exclusion for the sake of delimiting the boundary of a proper Christianity.

Another way in which the ethnic reasoning of race-of-heathens in relation to Korean and Korean American charismatic Christian women functions is the construction of a moral/rational person as an ideal Christian prophet and the concomitant condemnation of a passive/irrational prophet as a heathen and non-Christian. In the Korean ecclesiastical context, the "gendered pulpit" reflects one strand of the strategy, privileging the moral/rational prophet and delimiting interpretation of the scripture as the ideal mode of prophecy.[45] In Korean and Korean American contexts, Christian pastors are still predominantly male, while the majority of the congregation is predominantly female, even though the first Korean female pastor (the late Rev. Mila Chun) was ordained in 1955 in the Korean Methodist Church and the number of female pastors has steadily increased.[46] Meanwhile, discussing the public roles of women prophets in early Christianity, Karen King maintains, "In speaking, preaching, and teaching, women's sexual status was evaluated differently than men's."[47] King's analysis is still valid regarding contemporary Korean and Korean American Christian women's leadership and authority. Whereas the social roles of women have dramatically developed in Korean society, the ecclesiastical roles of women are still far behind.[48]

While Origen's construction of a moral and rational prophet as the ideal functions to delimit women preachers' authority in Korea, Origen's rhetoric of feminization and paganization particularly serves to marginalize charismatic Christians in the Korean and Korean American landscapes. We have seen above how Origen criticizes the understanding of prophecy that views it as passive (and thus feminized) before the divine and denigrates losing one's control in ecstasy, which often means possession by the divine. Ecstasy and possession are the kind of prophecy that Origen criticized in his polemics. As King says, "for Christians, the rhetoric was clear: true prophets were inspired by divine agency; false prophets were inspired by the devil and his demons."[49] Thus, the key move regarding prophecy, used since early Christianity, was to discern which agency works inside the person—whether it is the Holy Spirit or evil spirits. Since prophecy works when the outside agency (i.e., the Holy Spirit or evil spirits) enters a person, the rhetoric of penetration is inextricably connected to sexualizing and feminizing notions of prophecy. Women prophets are considered to be taken by the divine (whether for good or bad). In the polemics of many early Christian writers as we saw above, whereas a male prophet keeps his control, females lose their control and become easily penetrated by evil spirits.

This early Christian rhetorical move is inextricably connected to the assessment of many Christian women's religious activities throughout the centuries. For example, in the nineteenth-century spiritualist movement, Euro-American women prophets were considered to be ideal mediums for the Spirit, being "naturally" passive and open. However, spiritualists ended up playing important roles in promoting women's rights, because they could speak in public since (in theory) it was not the women who really spoke but the Spirit who possessed them.[50]

Although this theme of women being passive and receptive to the Spirit is common in the history of charismatic Christian women, the way that Korean charismatic women are marginalized is particularly elaborated and highlighted by colonial discourse analysis, especially when their experiences are described as shamanic, as shown above. The connection between spirit possession and shamanism is one of the familiar polemics against the Other, silencing and marginalizing religious opponents and relegating them outside of the boundaries of Christianity.

Employing a colonial discourse analysis regarding possession, Mary Keller maintains, "Traditionally in scholarly texts, the possessed woman is valenced negatively as psychologically fragile, permeable, 'less than' a Western, rational agent."[51] She continues, "Possession is more often ascribed to women, the poor, and the religious other the 'primitive,' the 'tribal,' the third-world woman, the black, the immigrant."[52] Keller's analysis of colonial logic is applicable to my study of the Korean and Korean American charismatic women.

In a similar vein, Jin Young Choi succinctly maintains, "The West's traditional conceptualization of gender—men as civilized, rational, and aggressive in contrast to women as primitive, emotional, and passive—is extended to the process of Western colonization. The West needed to establish its economic and political superiority over the East and consequently feminized the East."[53] In this colonial context, wherein moral and rational men are idealized over against passive and emotional women, Korean and Korean American charismatic Christian women are also racialized, relegated to a "race of pagans and heathens," which puts them beyond the acceptable boundary of Christianity. Just as many prophetic women in early Christianity were called Pythia or Philomena, so many Korean prophetic and charismatic women are considered shamans and, according to colonial logic, discredited as Christian prophets.

CONCLUSION

I argued that Origen's discussions of prophecy are powerful instantiations of attempts in early Christianity to *authorize, valorize, and erase* particular forms of prophecy. We have seen an instantiation of the process of ethnic reasoning that constructs the moral/rational prophets as masculine. Then Origen constructs the competing prophets as the feminine Other and also paganizes them. This strategy of normalizing legitimacy also operates in the modern Korean Christian context, reinforced by colonial context.

If prophecy is a gift from God, we cannot normalize a single identity of prophets (that is, male).[54] If prophecy is something that should be cultivated by ethical practice, there should not be improper barriers to entry based on race, class, and gender. If we take seriously both what Paul said in 1 Corinthians 14:1, "Strive for prophecy," and Origen's interpretation that Paul's teaching is for the diachronic community, shouldn't all, regardless of gender, strive for prophecy?

NOTES

1. Mary Keller, *The Hammer and the Flute: Women, Power, and Spirit Possession* (Baltimore: Johns Hopkins University Press, 2002), 4.

2. Tat-Siong Benny Liew, *What Is Asian American Biblical Hermenuetics?: Reading the New Testament* (Honolulu: University of Hawaii Press, 2007); Jin Young Choi, *Postcolonial Discipleship of Embodiment: An Asian and Asian American Feminist Reading of the Gospel of Mark* (New York: Palgrave Macmillan, 2015); Sze-Kar Wan, "Betwixt and Between: Toward a Hermeneutics of Hyphenation," in *Ways of Being, Ways of Reading: Asian American Biblical Interpretation*, ed. Mary F. Foskett and Jeffrey Kah-Jin Kuan, 137–51 (St. Louis: Chalice, 2006). This feeling of ambivalence is multilayered, for I feel it towards the Korean church, the Korean-immigrant church, and the American church.

3. I use the term of "charismatic," rather than "Pentecostal," to refer to modern Korean and Korean American Christians, although the line between Pentecostal and charismatic groups is porous. With Amos Yong, I follow the *Dictionary of Pentecostal and Charismatic Movements*, agreeing that "Pentecostal" marks something closer to a denomination (with its roots in the Azusa Street revival) while the "charismatic" traverses all denominations and groups (Amos Yong, *Discerning the Spirit(s): A Pentecostal-Charismatic Contribution to Christian Theology of Religions* [Sheffield, UK: Sheffield Academic Press, 2000], 21). See Stanley M. Burgess, Gary B. McGee, and Patrick H. Alexander, eds., *Dictionary of Pentecostal and Charismatic Movements* (Grand Rapids, MI: Zondervan, 2002). For the tight relationship between evangelical and Pentecostal Christians, see Timothy S. Lee, *Born Again: Evangelicalism in Korea* (Honolulu: University of Hawaii Press, 2010).

4. See, inter alia, Elisabeth Schüssler Fiorenza, *In Memory of Her: A Feminist Theological Reconstruction of Christian Origins* (London: SCM, 1995); Elizabeth A. Clark, "The Lady Vanishes: Dilemmas of a Feminist Historian after the 'Linguistic Turn,'" *Church History* 67 (1998): 1–31; Ross Shepherd Kraemer, *Her Share of the Blessings: Women's Religions among Pagans, Jews, and Christians in the Greco-Roman World* (New York: Oxford, 1992); Mary Rose D'Angelo and Ross Shepherd Kraemer, eds., *Women and Christian Origins* (New York: Oxford University Press, 1991).

5. Elisabeth Schüssler Fiorenza, *Rhetoric and Ethic: The Politics of Biblical Studies* (Minneapolis: Fortress, 1999), esp. 105–10, 128; Elisabeth Schüssler Fiorenza, "Re-Visioning

Christian Origins: *In Memory of Her* Revisited," *Journal for the Study of the New Testament Supplement Series* (2003): 225–50.

6. For example, George A. Kennedy, *Classical Rhetorics and Its Christian and Secular Tradition from Ancient to Modern Times* (Chapel Hill: University of North Carolina Press, 1980), and Margaret M. Mitchell, *Paul and the Rhetoric of Reconciliation: An Exegetical Investigation of the Language and Composition of 1 Corinthians* (Tübingen, Germany: J.C.B. Mohr, 1991).

7. Liew, *What Is Asian American Biblical Hermeneutics?*, ix.

8. I am indebted to Jin Young Choi for these concepts; see *Postcolonial Discipleship of Embodiment*, 2, 26–27.

9. Maureen Beyer Moser, *Teacher of Holiness: The Holy Spirit in Origen's Commentary on the Epistle to the Romans* (Piscataway, NJ: Gorgias Press, 2005), 143.

10. The critical edition of Origen's *Comm.Rom.* is from Caroline P. Hammond Bammel et al., eds., *Der Römerbriefkommentar des Origenes: Kritische Ausgabe der Übersetzung Rufins Buchs 1–10* (Freiburg, Germany: Herder, 1990–98). References cite the book and chapter number in PG, which Thomas Scheck followed in his English translation. Origen, *Commentary on the Epistle to the Romans, Books 1–5*, trans. Thomas Scheck, The Fathers of the Church 103 (Washington, DC: Catholic University of America, 2001); Origen, *Commentary on the Epistle to the Romans, Books 6–10*, trans. Thomas Scheck, The Fathers of the Church 104 (Washington, DC: Catholic University of America, 2002). English translation follows Scheck unless otherwise noted.

11. Also, see 1 Corinthians 12:31: "But strive for the greater gifts. And I will show you a still more excellent way." The complete verse for 1 Corinthians 14:1 is "Pursue love and strive for the spiritual gifts, and especially that you may prophesy." All biblical quotations are from the New Revised Standard Version (NRSV) unless otherwise noted.

12. For useful discussions about Origen's thoughts on moral inquiry, see Peter W. Martens, "Conduct: Moral Inquiry," in *Origen and Scripture: The Contours of the Exegetical Life* (Oxford: Oxford University Press, 2012), 161–91.

13. Moser, *Teacher of Holiness,* 145.

14. On Origen's understanding of the diachronic and universal audience, see Caroline Bammel, "Augustine, Origen and the Exegesis of St. Paul," *Augustinianum* 32, no. 2 (1992): 341–68; Judith Kovacs, "Servant of Christ and Steward of the Mysteries of God," in *In Dominico Eloquio, In Lordly Eloquence: Essays on Patristic Exegesis in Honour of Robert Louis Wilen*, ed. Paul M. Blowers, Angela Russell Christman, David G. Hunter, and Robin Darling Young, 147–71 (Grand Rapids, MI: Eerdmans, 2002).

15. English translation is taken from Judith Kovacs, trans. and ed., *1 Corinthians: Interpreted by Early Christians Commentators* (Grand Rapids, MI: Eerdmans, 2005), 230.

16. English translation is taken from Kovacs, *1 Corinthians*, 241.

17. Origen, "Homilies on 1 Corinthians (fragments)," ed. Claude Jenkins, *Journal of Theological Studies* 9 (1908): 231–47, 353–72, 500–514; *Journal of Theological Studies* 10 (1909): 29–51. English translation is taken from Kovacs, *1 Corinthians,* 231.

18. Plutarch, "On the Obsolescence of Oracles," especially 418d, 431a, 436f, 437d, 404f; Philo, *Who is the Heir*, trans. F. H. Colson and G. H. Whitaker, *The Works of Philo, vol. 4*, Loeb Classical Library 261 (Cambridge, MA: Harvard University Press, 1932); Christopher Forbes, "Early Christian Inspired Speech and Hellenistic Popular Religion," *Novum Testamentum* 28 (1986): 266.

19. For example, Karen Jo Torjesen argues, "Men were assigned the virtues of courage, justice, and self-mastery. Women were assigned the virtues of chastity, silence, and obedience." Karen Jo Torjesen, *When Women Were Priests: Women's Leadership in the Early Church and the Scandal of Their Subordination in the Rise of Christianity* (San Francisco: Harper San Francisco, 1993), 115. Also, see Mitzi J. Smith, "'Love Never Fails': Rereading 1 Corinthians 13 with a Womanist Hermeneutic of Love's Struggle," in *Theologies of Failure*, eds. Roberto Sirvent and Duncan B. Reyburn, 230–46 (Eugene, OR: Cascade Books, 2019).

20. For important discussions on Montanism, see Christine Trevett, *Montanism: Gender, Authority and the New Prophecy* (Cambridge, UK: Cambridge University Press, 1996); Laura

Salah Nasrallah, *"An Ecstasy of Folly": Prophecy and Authority in Early Christianity* (Cambridge, MA: Harvard University Press, 2003).

21. For example, Lee M. McDonald and James A. Sanders, *The Canon Debate* (Peabody, MA: Hendrickson Publishers, 2002); David Brakke, "Scriptural Practices in Early Christianity: Towards a New History of the New Testament Canon," in *Invention, Rewriting, Usurpation: Discursive Fights over Religious Traditions in Antiquity*, ed. David Brakke, Anders-Christian Jacobsen, and Jörg Ulrich (Frankfurt am Main: Peter Lang, 2012), 263–80.

22. Origen, *Contra Celsum*, trans. Henry Chadwick (Cambridge, UK: Cambridge University Press, 1953). English translation follows Chadwick, unless otherwise noted.

23. Greek *axios* is mostly translated as "worthy of." Latin *mereo*, which is probably used to translate Greek *axios* in Origen's works, has wider linguistic parameters such as "deserve," "earn," "merit," and "be worthy of." Since the majority of Origen's corpus exists in the Latin translation by Rufinus, the textual evidence on *mereo* and its cognates is greater. See *The Oxford Latin Dictionary* (Oxford: Oxford University Press, 2012), s.v. *"mereo."*

24. For the discussion of the Pythian slave girl in Acts 16:16–18, see Mitzi J. Smith, *The Construction of the Other in the Acts of the Apostles: Charismatics, the Jews, and Women* (Eugene, OR: Pickwick, 2011), 39–44. Also see Marianne Bjelland Kartzow, "Talking Pair: Paul and the Fortune-Telling Slave Girls (Acts 16:16–18)," in *Destabilizing the Margins: An Intersectional Approach to Early Christian Memory* (Eugene, OR: Wipf and Stock, 2012), 122–33.

25. Gail Paterson Corrington, "The 'Divine Woman'? Propaganda and the Power of Celibacy in the New Testament Apocrypha: A Reconsidering," in *Women in Early Christianity*, ed. D. Scholer, 169–82, especially 171–72 (New York: Garland, 1993); Dale Martin, *The Corinthian Body* (New Haven, CT: Yale University Press, 1995), 239–42.

26. John R. Levison, *Inspired: The Holy Spirit and the Mind of Faith* (Grand Rapids, MI: Eerdmans, 2013), 92. For a helpful discussion on this topic, see John R. Levison, *Filled with the Spirit* (Grand Rapids, MI: Eerdmans, 2009), 178–201.

27. Martin, *The Corinthian Body*, 240.

28. Jennifer Wright Knust, *Abandoned to Lust: Sexual Slander and Ancient Christianity* (New York: Columbia University Press, 2006), 112.

29. Ruth Padel, *In and Out of the Mind: Greek Images of the Tragic Self* (Princeton, NJ: Princeton University Press, 1992), 111.

30. There are more examples in Karen L. King, "Prophetic Power and Women's Authority: The Case of the Gospel of Mary (Magdalene)," in *Women Preachers and Prophets through Two Millennia of Christianity*, ed. Beverly Kienzle and Pamela J. Walker (Berkeley: University of California Press, 1998), 39; Tertullian, *Prescription against Heretics*, 6.25.30. Philomena is also mentioned in Eusebius, *Ecclesiastical History*, 5.13. For a discussion of Philomena, see Brad Windon, "The Seduction of Weak Men: Tertullian's Rhetorical Construction of Gender and Ancient Christian 'Heresy,'" in *Mapping Gender in Ancient Religious Discourses*, ed. Todd Penner and Caroline Vander Stichele, 457–78 (Leiden, Netherlands: Brill, 2006).

31. Anne Jensen argues that early recensions of the manuscript traditions depict Philomena particularly as a stereotypically passive woman whereas the later recensions have a slightly different portrayal (*God's Self-Confident Daughters: Early Christianity and the Liberation of Women*, trans. O. C. Dean, Jr. [Louisville, KY: Westminster John Knox, 1996], 304).

32. See note 19.

33. For the connection between ecstasy and possession, see Ross Shepherd Kraemer, "Ecstasy and Possession: The Attraction of Women to the Cult of Dionysos," *Harvard Theological Review* 72 (1979): 55–80; Lisa Maurizio, "Anthropology and Spirit Possession: A Reconstruction of the Pythia's Role at Delphi," *Journal of Hellenic Studies* 115 (1995): 69–86; Giovanni B. Bazzana, *Having the Spirit of Christ: Spirit Possession and Exorcism in the Early Christ Groups* (New Haven, CT: Yale University Press, 2020).

34. See John Anthony McGuckin, ed., *The Westminster Handbook to Origen* (Louisville: Westminster John Knox Press, 2004), s.v. "Disciples of Origen," "School of Alexandria," and "School of Caesarea."

35. See Susanna Drake, *Slandering the Jew: Sexuality and Difference in Early Christian Texts* (Philadelphia: University of Pennsylvania Press, 2013).

36. See, inter alia, Antoinette Clark Wire, *The Corinthian Women Prophets: A Reconstruction through Paul's Rhetoric* (Minneapolis: Fortress, 1990); Christine Trevett, *Montanism: Gender, Authority and the New Prophecy* (Cambridge, UK: Cambridge University Press, 1996); Jensen, *God's Self-Confident Daughters*; Beverly Mayne Kienzle and Pamela J. Walker, eds., *Women Preachers and Prophets through Two Millennia of Christianity* (Berkeley: University of California, 1998); Ute E. Eisen, *Women Officeholders in Early Christianity: Epigraphical and Literary Studies* (Collegeville, MN: Liturgical Press, 2000); Smith, *The Construction of the Other in the Acts of the Apostles*; Jill E. Marshall, *Women Praying and Prophesying in Corinth: Gender and Inspired Speech in First Corinthians* (Tübingen, Germany: Mohr Siebeck Verlag, 2017).

37. Robert Young, *Colonial Desire: Hybridity in Theory, Culture, and Race* (London: Routledge, 1995), 162.

38. For a detailed discussion, see Choi, *Postcolonial Discipleship of Embodiment*.

39. Amos Yong, *Discerning the Spirit(s): A Pentecostal-Charismatic Contribution to Christian Theology of Religions* (Eugene, OR: Wipf and Stock, 2019); Walter Hollenweger, *Pentecostals after a Century: Global Perspectives on a Movement in Transition* (Sheffield, UK: Bloomsbury T&T Clark, 1999); Harvey Cox, "Shamans and Entrepreneurs: Primal Spirituality on the Asian Rim," in *Fire from Heaven: The Rise of Pentecostal Spirituality and the Reshaping of Religion in the Twenty-First Century* (Boston: Da Capo Press, 2001); Wonsuk Ma, "Asian (Classical) Pentecostal Theology in Context," in *Asian and Pentecostal: The Charismatic Face of Christianity in Asia*, ed. Allan Anderson and Edmond Tang (Eugene, OR: Wipf and Stock, 2011), 58–59; Timothy Lee, *Born Again: Evangelicalism in Korea* (Honolulu: University of Hawaii Press, 2009), 120–33.

40. Amos Yong, *The Spirit Poured Out on All Flesh: Pentecostalism and the Possibility of Global Theology* (Grand Rapids, MI: Baker Academic, 2005), 51.

41. Cox, "Shamans and Entrepreneurs," 225.

42. Cox, "Shamans and Entrepreneurs," 224.

43. Liew, *What Is Asian American Biblical Hermeneutics?*, x.

44. Sung-Deuk Oak, "Healing and Exorcism: Christian Encounters with Shamanism in Early Modern Korea," *Asian Ethnology* 69 (2010): 95–128; Ma, "Asian (Classical) Pentecostal Theology in Context," 58–59; Andrew E. Kim, "Korean Religious Culture and Its Affinity to Christianity: The Rise of Protestant Christianity in South Korea," *Sociology of Religion* 6 (2000): 117–33; Young-Gi Hong, "The Backgrounds and Characteristics of the Charismatic Megachurches in Korea," *Asian Journal of Pentecostal Studies* 3, no. 1 (2000): 99–118; Mark P. Hutchinson, ed., *The Oxford History of Protestant Dissenting Traditions, vol. 5, The Twentieth Century: Themes and Variations in a Global Context* (Oxford: Oxford University Press, 2018).

45. For discussions of the pulpit as a gendered space, see Roxanne Mount, *The Gendered Pulpit: Preaching in American Protestant Spaces* (Carbondale: Southern Illinois University Press, 2003).

46. Regarding Korean Christian women's ecclesiastical leadership, see Lee, *Born Again*; World Council of Churches, *Resource Book: 10th Assembly Busan 2013* (Geneva: World Council of Churches); Sebastian C. H. Kim and Kirsteen Kim, *A History of Korean Christianity* (Cambridge, UK: Cambridge University Press, 2014); Grace Ji-Sun Kim, ed., *Here I Am: Faith Stories of Korean American Clergywomen* (Valley Forge, PA: Judson, 2015).

47. King, "Prophetic Power and Authority," 28.

48. Lee, *Born Again*; Kim and Kim, *A History of Korean Christianity*; Choi, *Gender and Mission Encounters in Korea*; Hyaeweol Choi and Margaret Jolly, eds, *Divine Domesticities: Christian Paradoxes in Asia and the Pacific* (Canberra: Australian National University Press, 2014); Hyaeweol Choi, *Gender and Mission Encounters in Korea: New Women, Old Ways* (Berkeley: University of California Press, 2009).

49. King, "Prophetic Power and Authority," 29. Denise Kimber Buell similarly notes, "Prophecy and oracle are usually framed in terms of an invisible agency speaking through a human instrument" ("Imagining Human Transformation in the Context of Invisible Powers: Instrumental Agency in Second-Century Treatments of Conversion," in *Metamorphoses: Res-*

urrection, Body and Transformative Practices in Early Christianity, ed. Turid Karlsen Seim and Jorunn Økland [New York: Walter de Gruyter, 2009], 228).

50. Ann Braude, *Radical Spirits: Spiritualism and Women's Rights in Nineteenth-Century America*, 2nd ed. (Bloomington: Indiana University Press, 2001).

51. Keller, *The Hammer and the Flute*, 3.

52. Keller, *The Hammer and the Flute*, 4. Indeed, with Jin Young Choi, I argue that it is important not to reiterate the dichotomy between Western logos/activity and the non-Western or Asian irrationality/passivity. See Choi, *Postcolonial Discipleship of Embodiment*, 138.

53. Choi, *Postcolonial Discipleship of Embodiment*, 26–27.

54. For a discussion of the normalization of a single identity in early Christianity, see Love L. Sechrest, *A Former Jew: Paul and the Dialectics of Race* (New York: T&T Clark, 2009).

WORKS CITED

Anderson, Allan, and Edmond Tang, eds. *Asian and Pentecostal: The Charismatic Face of Christianity in Asia*. Eugene, OR: Wipf and Stock, 2011.

Bammel, Caroline. "Augustine, Origen and the Exegesis of St. Paul." *Augustinianum* 32 (1992): 341–68.

Bazzana, Giovanni, B. *Having the Spirit of Christ: Spirit Possession and Exorcism in the Early Christ Groups*. New Haven, CT: Yale University Press, 2020.

Brakke, David. "Scriptural Practices in Early Christianity: Towards a New History of the New Testament Canon." In *Invention, Rewriting, Usurpation: Discursive Fights over Religious Traditions in Antiquity*, ed. David Brakke, Anders-Christian Jacobsen, and Jörg Ulrich, 263–80. Frankfurt am Main: Peter Lang, 2012.

Braude, Ann. *Radical Spirits: Spiritualism and Women's Rights in Nineteenth-Century America*. 2nd ed. Bloomington: Indiana University Press, 2001.

Buell, Denise Kimber. "Imagining Human Transformation in the Context of Invisible Powers: Instrumental Agency in Second-Century Treatments of Conversion." In *Metamorphoses: Resurrection, Body and Transformative Practices in Early Christianity*, edited by Turid Karlsen Seim and Jorunn Økland, 249–70. New York: Walter de Gruyter, 2009.

Burgess, Stanley M., Gary B. McGee, and Patrick H. Alexander, eds. *Dictionary of Pentecostal and Charismatic Movements*. Grand Rapids, MI: Zondervan, 2002.

Choi, Hyaeweol. *Gender and Mission Encounters in Korea: New Women, Old Ways*. Berkeley: University of California Press, 2009.

Choi, Hyaeweol, and Margaret Jolly, eds. *Divine Domesticities: Christian Paradoxes in Asia and the Pacific*. Canberra: Australian National University Press, 2014.

Choi, Jin Young. *Postcolonial Discipleship of Embodiment: An Asian and Asian American Feminist Reading of the Gospel of Mark*. New York: Palgrave Macmillan, 2015.

Clark, Elizabeth A. "The Lady Vanishes: Dilemmas of a Feminist Historian after the 'Linguistic Turn.'" *Church History* 67 (1998): 1–31.

Corrington, Gail Patterson. "The 'Divine Woman'? Propaganda and the Power of Celibacy in the New Testament Apocrypha: A Reconsidering." In *Women in Early Christianity*, edited by David M. Scholer, 169–82. New York: Garland, 1993.

Cox, Harvey. "Shamans and Entrepreneurs: Primal Spirituality on the Asian Rim." In *Fire from Heaven: The Rise of Pentecostal Spirituality and the Reshaping of Religion in the Twenty-First Century*, 213–41. Boston: Da Capo, 2001.

D'Angelo, Mary Rose, and Ross Shepherd Kraemer, eds. *Women and Christian Origins*. New York: Oxford University Press, 1991.

Drake, Susanna. *Slandering the Jew: Sexuality and Difference in Early Christian Texts*. Philadelphia: University of Pennsylvania Press, 2013.

Eisen, Ute E. *Women Officeholders in Early Christianity: Epigraphical and Literary Studies*. Collegeville, MN: Liturgical, 2000.

Forbes, Christopher. "Early Christian Inspired Speech and Hellenistic Popular Religion." *Novum Testamentum* 28 (1986): 257–70.

Harris, William. *Ancient Literacy*. Cambridge, MA: Harvard University Press, 1991.

Hollenweger, Walter. *Pentecostals after a Century: Global Perspectives on a Movement in Transition.* Sheffield, UK: Bloomsbury T&T Clark, 1999.

Hong, Young-Gi. "The Backgrounds and Characteristics of the Charismatic Megachurches in Korea." *Asian Journal of Pentecostal Studies* 3, no. 1 (2000): 99–118.

Hutchinson, Mark P., ed. *The Oxford History of Protestant Dissenting Traditions,* vol. 5, *The Twentieth Century: Themes and Variations in a Global Context.* Oxford: Oxford University Press, 2018.

Hvidt, Niels C. *Christian Prophecy: The Post-Biblical Tradition.* Oxford: Oxford University Press, 2007.

Jensen, Anne. *God's Self-Confident Daughters: Early Christianity and the Liberation of Women,* translated by O. C. Dean, Jr. Louisville, KY: Westminster John Knox, 1996.

Kannengiesser, Charles. *Handbook of Patristic Exegesis,* vol. 1. Leiden, Netherlands, and Boston: Brill, 2004.

Kartzow, Marianne Bjelland. *Destabilizing the Margins: An Intersectional Approach to Early Christian Memory.* Eugene, OR: Wipf and Stock, 2012.

Keller, Mary. *The Hammer and the Flute: Women, Power, and Spirit Possession.* Baltimore: Johns Hopkins University Press, 2002.

Kennedy, George A. *Classical Rhetorics and Its Christian and Secular Tradition from Ancient to Modern Times.* Chapel Hill: University of North Carolina Press, 1980.

Kim, Andrew E. "Korean Religious Culture and Its Affinity to Christianity: The Rise of Protestant Christianity in South Korea." *Sociology of Religion* 61 (2000): 117–33.

Kim, Grace Ji-Sun, ed. *Here I am: Faith Stories of Korean American Clergywomen.* Valley Forge, PA: Judson, 2015.

Kim, Sebastian C. H. and Kirsteen Kim. *A History of Korean Christianity.* Cambridge, UK: Cambridge University Press, 2014.

King, Karen. "Prophetic Power and Women's Authority: The Case of the Gospel of Mary (Magdalene)." In *Women Preachers and Prophets through Two Millennia of Christianity,* edited by Beverly Kienzle and Pamela J. Walker, 21–41. Berkeley: University of California Press, 1998.

Knust, Jennifer Wright. *Abandoned to Lust: Sexual Slander and Ancient Christianity.* New York: Columbia University Press, 2006.

Kovacs, Judith L. trans. and ed. *1 Corinthians: Interpreted by Early Christian Commentators.* Grand Rapids, MI: Eerdmans, 2005.

———. "Servant of Christ and Steward of the Mysteries of God: The Purpose of a Pauline Letter According to Origen's Homilies on 1 Corinthians." In *In Dominico Eloquio, In Lordly Eloquence: Essays on Patristic Exegesis in Honour of Robert Louis Wilen,* edited by Paul M. Blowers, Angela Russell Christman, David G. Hunter, and Robin Darling Young, 147–71. Grand Rapids, MI: Eerdmans, 2002.

Kraemer, Ross Shepherd. "Ecstasy and Possession: The Attraction of Women to the Cult of Dionysos." *Harvard Theological Review* 72 (1979): 55–80.

———. *Her Share of the Blessings: Women's Religions among Pagans, Jews, and Christians in the Greco-Roman World.* New York: Oxford University Press, 1992.

Lee, Timothy S. *Born Again: Evangelicalism in Korea.* Honolulu: University of Hawaii Press, 2010.

Levison, John R. *Filled with the Spirit.* Grand Rapids, MI: Eerdmans, 2009.

———. *Inspired: The Holy Spirit and the Mind of Faith.* Grand Rapids, MI: Eerdmans, 2013.

Liew, Tat-Siong Benny. *What Is Asian American Biblical Hermenuetics?: Reading the New Testament.* Honolulu: University of Hawaii Press, 2007.

McDonald, Lee M., and James A. Sanders. *The Canon Debate.* Peabody, MA: Hendrickson, 2002.

McGuckin, John Anthony, ed. *The Westminster Handbook to Origen.* Louisville: Westminster John Knox Press, 2004.

Marshall, Jill E. *Women Praying and Prophesying in Corinth: Gender and Inspired Speech in First Corinthians.* Tübingen, Germany: Mohr Siebeck, 2017.

Martens, Peter W. *Origen and Scripture: The Contours of the Exegetical Life.* Oxford: Oxford University Press, 2012.

Martin, Dale B. *The Corinthian Body*. New Haven, CT: Yale University Press, 1995.

Maurizio, Lisa. "Anthropology and Spirit Possession: A Reconstruction of the Pythia's Role at Delphi." *Journal of Hellenic Studies* 115 (1995): 69–86.

Mitchell, Margaret M. *Paul and the Rhetoric of Reconciliation: An Exegetical Investigation of the Language and Composition of 1 Corinthians*. Tübingen, Germany: Mohr Siebeck, 1991.

Moser, Maureen Beyer. *Teacher of Holiness: The Holy Spirit in Origen's Commentary on the Epistle to the Romans*. Piscataway, NJ: Gorgias, 2005.

Mount, Roxanne. *The Gendered Pulpit: Preaching in American Protestant Spaces*. Carbondale: Southern Illinois University Press, 2003.

Nasrallah, Laura Salah. *"An Ecstasy of Folly": Prophecy and Authority in Early Christianity*. Cambridge, MA: Harvard University Press, 2003.

Oak, Sung-Deuk. "Healing and Exorcism: Christian Encounters with Shamanism in Early Modern Korea." *Asian Ethnology* 69 (2010): 95–128.

Origen. *Commentary on the Epistle to the Romans, Books 1–5*, translated by Thomas P. Scheck. The Fathers of the Church 103. Washington, DC: Catholic University of America, 2001.

———. *Commentary on the Epistle to the Romans, Books 6–10*. Translated by Thomas P. Scheck. The Fathers of the Church 104. Washington, DC: Catholic University of America, 2002.

———. *Contra Celsum*, translated by Henry Chadwick. Cambridge, UK: Cambridge University Press, 1980.

———. "Homilies on 1 Corinthians (Fragments)." Edited by Claude Jenkins. *Journal of Theological Studies* 9 (1908): 231–47, 353–72, 500–514; *Journal of Theological Studies* 10 (1909): 29–51.

Padel, Ruth. *In and Out of the Mind: Greek Images of the Tragic Self*. Princeton, NJ: Princeton University Press, 1992.

Philo. *Who Is the Heir, The Works of Philo, vol. 4*. Loeb Classical Library 261. Trans. F. H. Colson and G. H. Whitaker. Cambridge, MA: Harvard University Press, 1932.

Schüssler Fiorenza, Elisabeth. *In Memory of Her: A Feminist Theological Reconstruction of Christian Origins*. London: SCM, 1995.

———. "Re-Visioning Christian Origins: *In Memory of Her* Revisited." *Journal for the Study of the New Testament Supplement Series* (2003): 225–50.

———. *Rhetoric and Ethic: The Politics of Biblical Studies*. Minneapolis: Fortress, 1999.

Sechrest, Love L. *A Former Jew: Paul and the Dialectics of Race*. New York: T&T Clark, 2009.

Smith, Mitzi J. *The Construction of the Other in the Acts of the Apostles: Charismatics, the Jews, and Women*. Eugene, OR: Pickwick, 2011.

———. "'Love Never Fails': Rereading 1 Corinthians 13 with a Womanist Hermeneutic of Love's Struggle." In *Theologies of Failure*, edited by Roberto Sirvent and Duncan B. Reyburn, 230–46. Eugene, OR: Cascade, 2019.

Torjesen, Karen Jo. *When Women Were Priests: Women's Leadership in the Early Church and the Scandal of Their Subordination in the Rise of Christianity*. San Francisco: Harper San Francisco, 1993.

Trevett, Christine. *Montanism: Gender, Authority and the New Prophecy*. Cambridge, UK: Cambridge University Press, 1996.

Wan, Sze-Kar. "Betwixt and Between: Toward a Hermeneutics of Hyphenation." In *Ways of Being, Ways of Reading: Asian American Biblical Interpretation*, edited by Mary F. Foskett and Jeffrey Kah-Jin Kuan, 137–51. St. Louis: Chalice Press, 2006.

Windon, Brad. "The Seduction of Weak Men: Tertullian's Rhetorical Construction of Gender and Ancient Christian 'Heresy.'" In *Mapping Gender in Ancient Religious Discourses*, edited by Todd Penner and Caroline Vander Stichele, 457–78. Leiden, Netherlands: Brill, 2006.

Wire, Antoinette Clark. *Corinthian Women Prophets: A Reconstruction through Paul's Rhetoric*. Minneapolis: Fortress, 1990.

World Council of Churches. *Resource Book: 10th Assembly Busan 2013*. Geneva: World Council of Churches.

Yong, Amos. *Discerning the Spirit(s): A Pentecostal-Charismatic Contribution to Christian Theology of Religions*. Sheffield, UK: Sheffield Academic Press, 2000.

———. *The Spirit Poured Out on All Flesh: Pentecostalism and the Possibility of Global Theology*. Grand Rapids, MI: Baker, 2005.

Young, Robert. *Colonial Desire: Hybridity in Theory, Culture, and Race*. London: Routledge, 1995.

Chapter Six

You Have Become Children of Sarah

Reading 1 Peter 3:1–6 through the Intersectionality of Asian Immigrant Wives, Patriarchy, and Honorary Whiteness

Janette H. Ok

Among the documents collected in the New Testament, 1 Peter is the most revealing about the process of identity formation. This chapter reexamines the exhortation to Christian wives in 1 Peter 3:1–6 through two lenses: the experiences of first-century Christian women addressed in 1 Peter who are married to non-Christian men and that of Asian immigrant women in interracial marriages. The author of 1 Peter offers his women readers a strategy of minimizing unnecessary suspicion and criticism from their husbands and disrupting stereotypes associated with Christians in general and Christian women in particular. While 1 Peter's address to wives in mixed marriages serves both an apologetic and missionary function in response to outside criticism, it also serves an identity-forming function as the author seeks to strengthen ingroup cohesion among his readers and their capacity to cope with prejudice, conflict, and hostility within the domestic sphere.

By characterizing gentile Christian wives as "children of Sarah" (3:6), 1 Peter offers wives a means to elevate their status as children of Sarah irrespective of their husbands' opinion of them or conversion to their religion.[1] The author inscribes them into the great Jewish matriarch's genealogy to remind them of their elect status as God's chosen, royal, holy people (2:9–10) that is not based on shared bloodlines but on shared belief and behavior.

The uniquely intersectional experiences of Asian American women who are married to white American men offers insights into the ways the author

111

of 1 Peter seeks to help his female, married addressees cautiously negotiate their multiple and potentially conflicting commitments to members of their domestic household, specifically their husbands, and members of the "household of God."

Asian American women often experience the cultural homogenization of their identities, despite having immigrated to the U.S. from distinct cultures, and the exoticization of their identities, despite being ethnicized as honorary whites.[2] In a study of racialized sexism and sexualized racism for Asian American women, participants reported intersectional experiences of discrimination that set them apart from Asian American men and other women of color, including white women.[3] The homogenization or reduction of ethnic and gendered diversity among Asian American women has led some to construct their own idealized identities as a way to set themselves apart from white American women and the cultural stereotypes the dominant culture has of them.[4] Their new idealized identities, however, have the potential to be essentialized by others, suggesting both the effectiveness of such a strategy and its liabilities.

First Peter 3:1–6 confronts the essentializing of negative and unwanted stereotypes of Christian women through the idealizing and ethnicizing of certain behaviors. Although the author does not seek to idealize the hierarchical and patriarchal ordering of husband and wife, his advice to wives has been interpreted as an essential and enduring posture and practice of submission that Christian wives are to have across time and cultures. However, as the experiences of some Asian immigrant women suggest, idealizing and ethnicizing certain behaviors as a way to disrupt stereotypes and give a sense of greater personal agency may ironically lead to the further essentializing of racial-ethnic and gender stereotypes and idealization of whiteness and patriarchy. The contemporary experiences of Asian immigrant women subsequently interrogate a universally prescriptive reading of the 1 Peter text through the particular intersectional challenges they face in their marriages and family relationships.

THE EXPERIENCES OF FIRST-CENTURY WOMEN
ADDRESSED IN 1 PETER 3:1–6

In the letter's section known as the *Haustafel* or household code (2:18–3:7), the author of 1 Peter addresses appropriate relationships between slaves and masters, wives and husbands, and husbands and wives. After exhorting addressees to "be subordinate you all to every human creature (*pasē anthrōpinē ktisei*) because of the Lord" (2:13), the author narrows his focus on Christian slaves (2:18–25) and wives (3:1–6) before saying a brief word to believing husbands (3:7).[5] The author shows particular concern for slaves and wives living in unbelieving households because their subordinate status leaves them in a precarious, vulnerable, and potentially hazardous position. His advice to wives reflects a strategy that both complies with and challenges dominant Greco-Roman cultural expectations and values for women, opening the door for evangelistic possibilities, while also helping to forge a stronger sense of their identity as children of Sarah.

The Petrine author offers believing wives the following advice: "Likewise you wives, be subordinate to your husbands so that even if some are disobedient to word, they may be won over without a word by the behavior of their wives when they observe your reverent and chaste behavior" (vv. 1–2).[6] The phrase "even if some" (*kai ei tines*) has led some commentators to conclude that mixed marriages were the exception, not the rule: 1 Peter's injunction applies to all women in all marriages, whether Christian or non-Christian.[7] However, elsewhere in the letter, those who "disobey the word" (2:8) and "the gospel of God" (4:17) starkly contrast those who "believe" (2:7), are the "people of God" (2:10), and belong to the "household of God" (4:17). Furthermore, the restrained missional hope conveyed in 3:1 by the Greek word *kerdēthēsontai* ("may be won over") suggests the possibility for the conversion of "some" husbands.[8] The author's singular address to believing husbands in 3:7 strongly suggests that marriages between believers are the exception, not the rule. The brevity of 1 Peter's exhortation to husbands also reflects that the author's concern in 3:1–6 is not with wifely submission but with helping wives prudently navigate and strategically survive potentially conflictual relationships with their unbelieving husbands as a result of their obedience to Christ. The rest of 1 Peter's household code assumes that those in social and domestic positions of authority over Christians are unbelievers (2:13–3:6). Furthermore, the parallel NT household codes address both husbands and wives as though they are in Christian marriages (Col. 3:18–19; Eph. 5:21–33; cf. Titus 2:3–5) and make no mention of husbands disobeying the word or evoking fear in their wives.

Christian wives were not in a position to win over their husbands by means of coercion. Instead, they had to take a more "winsome" approach by attracting them by their distinctly Christian but attractive way of life (cf. 2:12).[9] The implication in 3:6 that wives have something to be terrified about reflects the author's concern for women in religiously mixed marriages because they are particularly vulnerable to the intimidation of their nonbelieving husbands.[10] While suffering is not explicitly mentioned in 3:1–6, 1 Peter's exhortation that wives be "free from all fear" (3:6) implies the threat of violence.[11] Unbelieving husbands would have likely become antagonistic toward their wives because of their Christian beliefs and activities, as supported by the identification of the letter's recipients in 2:11 as *paroikous kai parepidēmous* ("resident aliens and foreigners") and the multiple references to the negative attitudes toward Christians harbored by non-Christians (e.g., 2:12; 3:13–14, 16; 4:4, 14–16).

First Peter's plea that women subordinate themselves to their unbelieving husbands corresponds to the prevailing norms, expectations, and values concerning the roles and interactions of husbands and wives in the Greco-Roman domestic context. According to Roman writers, the ideal household served as a microcosm of the intensely hierarchical structure of society in which the emperor reigned supreme, while all others held lower status positions largely determined by their birth and gender. The Roman household thus was to function "like an empire writ small: the head of the household, usually a free male, ruled over the other household members subordinate to him."[12] It also served as the site of religious activity where members of the household, which might extend to family members, slaves, employees, and other dependents, worshiped the gods of *paterfamilias* (father of the family).[13] Although masters or husbands usually presided over the domestic cult, slaves and wives often had the role of preparing and carrying out cultic rituals in the household.[14]

The mere suggestion in 1 Peter 3:1 that husbands might adopt the religion of their wives is itself remarkable in light of Greco-Roman societal expectation that a submissive and deferential woman wholeheartedly accept the religion of her husband.[15] So Plutarch warns, "A married woman should therefore worship and recognize the gods whom her husband holds dear, and these alone. The door must be closed to strange cults and foreign superstitions. No god takes pleasure in cult performed furtively by a woman."[16] In 3:1–6, 1 Peter addresses the very women Plutarch has in mind, since from the perspective of their nonbelieving husbands, these wives worshipped and recognized a "foreign" deity of a strange, new cult known as "the Christians."[17]

Whether these Christian women also participated in the worship of their husband's gods is uncertain. Warren Carter argues that 1 Peter does not discourage Christians from participating in Rome's imperial cult nor wives and slaves from participating in the domestic cult because it was their nonparticipation in such socially and religiously sanctioned activities that caused hostility between Christians and non-Christians.[18] He interprets 1 Peter's exhortation to wives as a "strategy of urging civic and domestic submission, including cultic participation, while maintaining inner loyalty to Christ."[19] Because 1 Peter has a "culturally assimilationist agenda," the letter encourages Christians in general and slaves and wives in particular to be publicly compliant, while remaining inwardly resistant.[20] Carter turns to the work of James C. Scott to help illuminate the agency 1 Peter offers slaves and women. Scott argues in *Weapons of the Weak* that calculated measures of public conformity can help cover the tracks of more hidden forms of resistance and noncompliance.[21] Those without the power to overtly resist authority may show public deference as a way to mask their resistance. First Peter's admonition that wives conduct and adorn themselves in a manner that demonstrates their modesty, reverence, and gentle and tranquil spirit enables them to demonstrate outward compliance with socially sanctioned practices, such as cultic participation, while inwardly resisting the authority of their husbands because "their hearts are now given to Christ (3:15)."[22]

Caroline Johnson Hodge similarly argues that 1 Peter urges compliance to traditional social hierarchies as a means to "ease the tensions" between slaves and wives and their unbelieving masters and husbands and also possibly to prevent further persecution and slander against the Christian community.[23] She sees in 1 Peter's advice to women a form of agency "precisely in her subservience."[24] Despite being in a subordinate position, a Christian wife has the potential to wield some influence over her husband's religious allegiance. The very fact that these wives are worshipping a "foreign" deity is itself an act of resistance to their husbands' power, since even religious practice that is "constrained by patriarchal values" still has the capacity to "empower disempowered participants."[25] While the warning against excessive accessorizing and expensive clothing and the encouraging of modesty and other inner virtues in 3:3–4 is not uniquely Christian, the author of 1 Peter offers an explicitly theological rationale for a woman's modesty and inner beauty.[26]

In 1 Peter 3:3–4, the author does not wish to condemn wives for their certain sartorial choices but to safeguard them against being perceived by their husbands or by society at large in ways that could be misconstrued as sexually provocative precisely because they were taking the liberty to come in and out of the home to gather with the "household of God" (4:17). The independent conversions of these women would lead them to attend Christian meetings, neglect their traditional cultic duties, and "negotiate between two communities in conflict."[27] First Peter thus encourages wives to adorn themselves with inner qualities of a "gentle and tranquil spirit" in order to minimize the suspicions and conflict that may ensue from their worshipping a "foreign" deity outside of the home (3:4).[28] By leaving the home unadorned, she would make it clear to her husband that she is leaving to worship her God of the new cult now known as "the Christians" and not leaving for a tryst or to engage in sexual promiscuity (4:16).[29]

David Balch, in arguing for the apologetic function of the household code in 1 Peter, explains that the primary reason the author prescribes his readers to follow conventional Greco-Roman household behavior was "to reduce social-political tension between society and the churches."[30] The letter first addresses slaves and wives because they faced the most intense social tension between the church and Roman society, since Romans believed wives and slaves to be particularly susceptible to the seduction of foreign cults.[31] Clarice Martin likewise asserts that "patriarchally appropriate behavior was enjoined to persuade authorities that Christian communities were not a threat to the state (1 Pet. 2:11–3:12)."[32] Elisabeth Schüssler Fiorenza agrees with

Balch's hypothesis that assimilation to doing what is good in the sight of the larger Greco-Roman community was the main purpose of the Petrine household code, although she questions the actual effectiveness of the strategy hypothesized by Balch to reduce the tension between the Christian community and the patriarchal pagan household.[33]

Betsy Bauman-Martin argues that Balch's highly influential reading of the *Haustafel* in 1 Peter has been too simplistically taken up by feminist interpreters to argue that Christian slaves and women are encouraged to behave in ways that would appease their masters and husbands in order to prevent unnecessary domestic conflict and subsequent persecution.[34] Instead, she interprets 1 Peter's injunctions to wives as addressing the rupture already taking place between masters and slaves and Christian husbands and their wives because of their Christian beliefs and "antipatriarchal activity."[35] With John Elliott, she argues that the purpose of 1 Peter's injunction to wives is not to defend them against accusations that they pose a danger to society and the family but to encourage Christian distinctiveness and particularity from the values of the dominant culture in order to promote greater ingroup cohesion.[36]

The household code in 1 Peter attends to both outgroup and ingroup perceptions and concerns. As Shively Smith explains, the letter's writer has a "double vision" in which Christians remain subject to the social contracts demanded of subordinates in the Greco-Roman social system while being subject to an "alternative social system with its own communal standards."[37] Through the household ethic, 1 Peter attempts to preserve the bonds of intimacy of the household to keep societal peace and also to prevent Christians from reinforcing false and negative stereotypes that Christians are family and society haters. The emphasis the letters places on being a "spiritual household" (*oikos pneumatikos*) and an "house of God" (*oikos tou theou*) provides an alternative family and household *in addition* to their unbelieving families and households. Christians must manage multiple and intersecting commitments (e.g., to their masters, husbands, wives, neighbors, associates, and Christ group) and must navigate multiple ideologies and pressures (e.g., how to honor the emperor without worshipping him, how to live as free people within the laws of Rome, and how to worship God while living under the roof of a master or husband who worships other gods). Their primary and ultimate commitment, however, is to Christ their Lord. The reverence (*en phobō*) expected of a wife is not for her husband but for God (cf. 1:17; 2:17; 2:18, 20). The author does not exhort wives to hold their husband in high regard. Rather, he encourages them to hold themselves in high regard not because of their status as wives but because of their identity as children of Sarah.

The letter's author is not simply concerned with the visibility of a certain way of behaving in the eyes of nonbelievers. When Christians engage "honorable conduct" (*tēn anastrophēn . . . kalēn*), Gentiles may still condemn them as "evildoers" (*kakopoioi*) because of their refusal to participate in the behaviors and values that Gentiles consider appropriate (3:16–17; 4:4; 14, 16, 19) and practice of that which Gentiles consider shameful, such as behaving in a lowly manner patterned after Christ (2:21–23; cf. 3:9). Although the author does not portray unbelievers in a positive light, he does suggest that Gentiles who slander Christians as "evildoers" might nevertheless observe their good deeds and share some common ground with Christians in judging what is "good" (2:14; 3:2), even as the author characterizes the desires and behavior of Gentiles in a negative light elsewhere in the letter (e.g., 4:2–4).

First Peter's admonishment to wives reveals the "boundary-crossing" activities that Christian wives had to maneuver and how they had to tread cautiously, deftly, and strategically between the public and private spheres.[38] Although these women are to accept the authority of their husbands, such authority does not render them completely passive nor prohibit them from taking risks for "doing what is right" (2:12; 3:6; 3:14). Their reverent and chaste behavior may please and even convert their husbands, but it may also put them in continued or escalating conflict with them. Thus 1 Peter attempts to give them a further motivation for their good conduct that does not depend on their husbands' positive or negative evaluation of them. That is, while he seeks to offer wives a strategy to challenge and disrupt negative perceptions that their husbands may have of them as a result of their new way of life and also convert their husbands to this way of life, the author of 1 Peter seeks to change the way wives perceive themselves by offering them the honorary status as Sarah's children.

YOU HAVE BECOME SARAH'S CHILDREN

The apologetic and missionary impulse in 1 Peter 1:1–5 shifts focus when the author appeals to "holy wives" in 3:5–6: "For this is the way the holy wives in former times—wives who put their trust in God—used to adorn themselves by being subordinate to their husbands, like Sarah obeyed Abraham, calling him lord. You have become her children when you do what is right and do not fear any kind of intimidation."[39] The background of 3:6 is notoriously difficult to ascertain as the image of Sarah found in 1 Peter does not harmonize well with her depiction in Genesis and in Midrash of Genesis. The majority of commentators attribute Genesis 18:12 as the OT passage 1 Peter alludes to in 3:6. Mark Kiley shares the majority view that 1 Peter has Genesis 18:12 in mind, but he explains that Sarah's obedience as conveyed in Genesis 12 and 20 enables the Petrine author to "typify what he sees as the commendable attitude of a wife."[40] Sarah and her perilous situation as the wife of Abraham in a foreign land serves as a model to the Gentile Christian women married to nonbelievers in a hostile environment.[41] For Troy Martin, either 1 Peter misinterprets the Genesis tradition regarding Sarah or makes use of noncanonical legend. Martin makes a case for the latter, arguing that the Testament of Abraham best illuminates the probable background of 1 Peter 3:6 because it contains specific instances when Sarah obeys Abraham and calls him "lord," presents Sarah as the mother of the elect, and connects good deeds with fearlessness.[42]

Magda Misset-Van de Weg offers another possibility that does not discount that the author of 1 Peter has the "Abraham-Sarah cycle" of Genesis in mind; she sees the role of Sarah in 1 Peter 3:6 as symbolic. Sarah is the "apogee, the more precise marker, or the sign" that along with the holy woman of the past serves to "situate women's submissiveness within the framework of the sacred tradition."[43] The Petrine author places his female, married addressees on the continuum of ancient Jewish wives, who also submitted themselves to their husbands as a way to inscribe them into the narrative of the Jewish people.[44] When the author of 1 Peter singles out Sarah as the great matriarch of the Jewish people, he brings them into the narrative of the people of God, specifically by means of bequeathing them a spiritual ancestry. The author is reminding his addressees of their status as God's elect children when he says they have become Sarah's children (*tekna*).

The fact that 1 Peter refers to readers in 3:6 as *tekna* (children), not *thygateres* (daughters), is significant.[45] Earlier in 1:14, the author describes his readers as "children of obedience" (*tekna hypakoēs*). The phrase *tekna hypakoēs* describes obedience as a fundamental aspect of his addressees' identity as God's children and thus as a central cultural value as God's people. To be children of God is to be obedient to God. God is holy, and so God's children must also be holy (1:15–16). By identifying wives in 3:6 as Sarah's children, 1 Peter's author reiterates the idea that they are God's children. By recalling the holy character of wives in the past and associating their holiness with their hopefulness in God (3:5), he reiterates the idea that holiness, which characterizes God's children, is possible even in the face of resistance, conflict, and persecution because believers have a "living" and "eschatological hope" (1:3, 13).

In 1 Peter, the idea of shared descent arises as the author establishes his addressees' elect status.[46] In the letter's prescript, he begins to delineate a spiritual genealogy for his predominantly Gentile audience based on the fact that Christians are "chosen (*eklektos*) . . . according to the foreknowledge of God the Father" (1:1–2) and "born anew to a living hope through the resurrection of Jesus Christ from the dead" (1:3b). Such descriptors serve as bases for their identity as "people of God" (2:10). Rather than use the language and logic of adoption (*hiothesia*) by the Spirit to explain how Gentiles are also sons and heirs of God as Paul does, the author links the idea of election to that of spiritual regeneration (*anagennaō*) to explain how his addressees can invoke God as Father and understand themselves as God's children (1:3, 14, 17, 23; cf. Rom. 8:14–17; Gal. 4:6–7).[47]

In 1 Peter 3:6, the author makes a strong connection between his address-ees' obedience and their status as God's children but uses a more explicitly ethnic line of reasoning.[48] Their distinctive "way of life" or "behavior" (*anastrophē*) connects them more specifically to the ancestry of Sarah.[49] By becoming children of Sarah, Christian wives in effect become honorary Jews. Jewishness serves as a means of engendering solidarity for the letter's belea-guered addressees, particularly woman in mixed marriages, who might other-wise feel extremely isolated and alienated in their domestic sphere and alone in their marital suffering.

Why use Sarah imagery here rather than children of God imagery used elsewhere? Through Sarah, the author is able to intersect the various strate-gies for coping with and minimizing, in so far as it is possible, the conflict, risk, and suffering that Christian wives experienced as subordinate members of unbelieving households. Christian wives, despite their precarious positions in the households of their *paterfamilias*, have an honored status as children of obedience, which is another way of saying they are children of Sarah. By ethnicizing his addressees' religious identity, the author is able to essentialize the behaviors associated with Sarah as an indelible part of their identity. By appealing to them as Sarah's children, Christian wives can live in a manner that might appease their husbands and possibly convert them. But moreover, they can live faithful lives that please God regardless of whether husbands are appeased or won over and even in the face of tensions or hostility.

FIRST PETER AND ASIAN IMMIGRANT WIVES

Western feminist, womanist, liberationist, and postcolonial scholarship has given much attention to resistance and agency among the oppressed. This shift from seeing the oppressed as passive victims to active and strategic resistors has served as a much-needed corrective to the prevailing notion in Western scholarship that views the disenfranchised or disempowered as pas-sive victims or completely powerless. It has also helped open the door to the manifold ways and degrees in which the subjugated have resisted their op-pressors. However, there are some downsides to focusing too much attention on resistance as a totalizing strategy or way of being.

For Asian Americans, the impact of the model minority stereotype on the Asian American psyche and experience has been explored by many.[50] While critique of this narrative is vital, Karen Pyke speaks of what she calls the "*model resistor* stereotype," which treats the oppressed as almost superhu-man in their reliance and resourcefulness so as to deny the harsh realities of

their challenges, depression, and oppression.[51] Pyke's point is that an intersectional approach that considers gender in model minority critique helps
avoid relying on an either/or approach to interpreting individual action as
being resistance or complicity. Intersectionality helps nuance simplistic binaries and helps us consider, for example, not only how women respond to
oppression but also what people *do to* women, not only the measures women
take to increase their agency but also how by resisting one form of domination they can inadvertently reproduce other forms of it.[52]

In her book *Where Is Your Body?* legal scholar Mari Matsuda articulates a
very helpful method for understanding intersectionality:

> When I see something that looks racist, I ask, "Where is the patriarchy in
> this?" When I see something that looks sexist, I ask, "Where is the heterosex-
> ism in this?" When I see something that looks homophobic, I ask, "Where are
> the class interests in this?" Working in coalition forces us to look at both the
> obvious and the nonobvious relationships of domination, and, as we have done
> this, we have come to see that no form of subordination ever stands alone.[53]

Pyke, adapting Matsuda's model to her cross-racial study, asks, "Where is
the complicity with racial oppression in this resistance to gender oppression?
Where is the resistance or challenge to gender inequality in this complicity
with racial domination?"[54] Intersectionality opens our eyes to see the overlapping, interdependent, and sometimes contradictory relationships between
domination and subordination. It also helps us consider how strategies to
overcome one thing may rely on structural forms of that very thing one is
trying to overcome.

Experiences of Recent Asian Immigrant Women in Interracial Marriages

In the opening act of Puccini's famous opera, *Madam Butterfly*, U.S. Navy
lieutenant Benjamin Pinkerton describes his soon-to-be Japanese bride, Cio-
Cio San in the following way: "She . . . like a butterfly, hovers and settles,
with so much charm and such seductive graces, that to pursue her a wild wish
seized me—though in the quest her frail wings should be broken."[55] The
opera follows the story of Pinkerton who marries Cio-Cio San, or "Butterfly," with the intention of moving back to U.S. later to marry a "real
American bride," unbeknownst to his ecstatic and naive young wife. Determined to please her husband, Cio-Cio San renounces her family's Buddhist
religion to adopt Christianity. Thus her entire family renounces her. Cio-Cio
San considers this enormous loss of her family and religion as a necessary
sacrifice to follow her true love. Pinkerton, however, goes back to America
and leaves her with the promise that he will return to Japan for both her and
their son. He never does. As a further act of cowardice, exploitation, and

abandonment, he sends his American wife to collect the boy. After realizing that she has relinquished everything only to be left with nothing, she bows to an image of the Buddha one last time before stabbing herself with a knife bearing the inscription, "To die with honour / When one can no longer live with honour."

It is difficult to understand why a play such as *Madam Butterfly* remains so popular despite the orientalism, sexism, and colonial-era stereotypes it employs in order to portray the innocent, beautiful, and sacrificial Asian woman. Psychologist Natalie Porter explains in her study of contemporary relationships between white American husbands and their Asian immigrant wives how historical and social constructions of whiteness continue to create inequality in heterosexual relationships.[56] Porter's case studies shed light on the intersectionality of gender, social class, culture, immigration, and whiteness in shaping the dominant white culture's perceptions of these Asian women and how Asian women constructed their identities in opposition to "the Butterfly myth."[57] They did this, she argues, in order to increase their psychological well-being while simultaneously internalizing the idea that white American culture is superior to their own.

In studies of white men who select mail-order brides, the men often saw themselves as more socially conservative and traditional than other American men and sought less "pushy" and "domineering" American women.[58] They tended to essentialize Asian women as being more submissive, modest (though highly sexual), and family oriented, and Asian wives in turn seemed to have internalized these qualities and essentialized white American women as being more aggressive, less family centered, less attractive, and less self-sacrificing.[59] As a way to set themselves apart from white American wives, Asian immigrant wives dedicated themselves to meeting their husband's expectations of them. This is not only because they internalized these "Butterfly stereotypes"[60] but also because they often lacked family and social support in the U.S. They thus saw themselves as more reliant on their spouses, even as their spouses depended heavily on them for their domestic and financial contributions. When white cultural practices and values serve as universal norms of appropriateness, internalized racism is difficult to overcome.[61] Asian immigrant wives who mimic racialized gender stereotypes in the larger society tend to evaluate whiteness as both normative and superior to their own ethnic values and practices. However, when they seek to resist such stereotypes by attempting to act differently from their own stereotypes of white American wives, they end up relinquishing some of their agency to advocate for themselves.[62]

In one of Porter's case studies, a woman named Daya gave up her successful career as a dentist in India to marry her white American husband.[63] Because she would need to repeat her education in order to practice dentistry in the States, she decided to give up her profession because her husband thought it was too costly and took her attention away from the family. She also chose to do so as a strategy that set her apart from American wives, whom she perceived as less committed to their families and marriages. It was a way for her to interrogate and push back against Western norms of individuality and self-fulfillment. Yet, simultaneously, it caused a dilemma of constructing an identity different from those who viewed her as less American and hence reinforced that stereotype while allowing that form of resistance to prevent her from advocating more for her own interests. In other words, Daya attempted to set herself apart from white American wives by being more domestic than she would have been in India, while resisting the status of honorary white. The fact that her husband expressed displeasure at socializing in the Indian community because it made him feel like an outsider, coupled with his frequent business trips that made it difficult for her to meet with her Indian friends, only increased her sense of isolation and depression. Furthermore, her husband equated American life as a superior life to her experiences in India. This made it difficult for him to consider the alienation and otherness she felt by being an immigrant in an interracial marriage in a location where she had no family support to help with child care, contrary to her experience in India. The way in which Daya and other Indian women experienced a greater sense of well-being was by "maintaining stronger ties with and a sense of superiority about their home cultures" and by entertaining the possibility of returning to their former homes in India to give their children a better quality of life. [64]

When Teresa came to the U.S. from a rural agricultural region of the Philippines, she experienced economic gain and social status relative to women in her home country, unlike Daya, who experienced a loss in economic and social status upon immigrating. [65] Teresa had a successful career as a nurse. Her husband Ned, however, had been unemployed for the past two years. Although they sought therapy for their son, James, what therapy revealed was Teresa's marginalization in the home. Both Ned and James showed little respect for Teresa's culture. James referred to his mother's food as disgusting and painted an image of Filipino society as dangerous, outdated, and lawless but American society as safe, modern, and orderly. He portrayed his father as the breadwinner of the family, when in reality his mother worked to support the family financially. In general, Teresa herself spoke little of her language and culture to her family. In therapy, she remained silent, deferring the therapist's questions to her husband, even when they were directed toward her. As assessed by his therapist, James's overidentification with his father and dismissal of his mother, whom he actually resembled more in attributes and appearance, manifested an "internalized racism." [66] This internalized racism reveals itself in the way he viewed his mother as a second-class, un-assimilated citizen (despite having dual degrees and a respected, well-paying career that supported the family) and referred to similarly biracial and bicultural students as "others" and "Asian-looking."[67]

Whereas Daya gave up her successful career and higher social and economic status in India to marry her white American husband and raise her family in the U.S., Teresa gained a successful career in the U.S. and attained a higher social and economic status by marrying her white American husband. Both women accepted the normativity of the white American for their husbands and children. They did not, however, accept all of American life for themselves. In fact, they rejected the values and customs they perceived as belonging to white American women, such as being more career oriented and self-serving.[68] While these women did not see themselves as white nor express the desire to be white, they did like Cio-Cio San aim to please their husbands and give primacy to their American heritage over their own. The biracial and bicultural children of these Asian women fully identified with white culture.[69] Both Daya and Teresa essentialized themselves as more family oriented and self-sacrificing than their white American counterparts, even though Daya grew up in India with much more independence and social and familial support than in the States and Teresa worked as the primary wage earner while her husband stayed home. Their adherence to "traditional gender roles" led to their invisibility in the family and to a lack of awareness from their spouses of how much these women had to assimilate in order to raise white children rather than biracial and bicultural children.

CONCLUSION

Teresa's case study suggests that assimilating at the expense of honoring one's own ethnic and cultural heritage in order to please her husband has a negative impact not only on her well-being and sense of self-worth but on the way her spouse and son perceive her. Earning the respect of her husband and son and elevating their appreciation of her culture proved difficult when she herself was reluctant to share her language or culture. In other words, winning them over without a word led to her marginalization and invisibility in her household. Daya's case study suggests the benefits of maintaining not only strong ties with one's interracial family but also with the larger community of one's home culture. The alienation felt by Asian immigrant wives and their need to affirm their ethnic identity and community resonate with the situation of Christian wives in 1 Peter, who are vulnerable to feelings of hopelessness amid hostile and precarious domestic circumstances and whose sense of Christian identity needs strengthening.

In view of the self-loathing felt by ethnic women who accept the hegemonic normativity of the values of the dominant culture, I suggest that we consider seeing the Petrine author's appeal to Sarah as an attempt to elevate the status of the wives suffering from a low sense of self in domestic contexts where their values and identity as Christ followers are marginalized and denigrated. By recalling the holy women of the past and establishing their identity as children of Sarah, the author places wives within the genealogy of the chosen, holy, royal people of God as a way to elevate their sense of self-respect and give them a stronger sense of ingroup identity as God's children. These wives had little choice but to subordinate themselves to their husbands, but they could actively entrust themselves to their faithful creator and do what is right, even if it inevitably results in their suffering (4:19). The author of 1 Peter offers a less potentially devastating and more realistic approach to navigating marriage in non-Christian households by not equating faithfulness to God with wholesale submission to their unbelieving husbands nor with outright resistance to their authority.[70] Rather, he seeks to engender in Christian wives a resilient sense of their chosen status not as wives or mothers but as children endowed with a spiritual heritage that cannot be taken away from them.

By examining how race/ethnicity, gender, religion, and culture intersect in the experiences of women in both ancient Greco-Roman and contemporary U.S. contexts, I seek to further nuance the way the injunctions to wives in 1 Peter 3:1–6 have been understood as way to alleviate unnecessary and potentially violent conflict between Christian wives and their pagan husbands and offer a form of agency. Gentile Christian women faced stereotypes of being family haters. Furthermore, Christian wives managed multiple commitments and had to navigate multiple ideologies and pressures. The author of 1 Peter seeks to disrupt and resist the essentializing of Christian women as threats to family cohesion by exhorting them to be more chaste, virtuous, and family oriented than their Greco-Roman counterparts and behave as children of Sarah. In doing so, he offers them a way to identify with an entirely separate system of honor that comes not from being the wife or mother but by being children who are inscribed into the narrative of Israel through the great matriarch and given a new ethno-religious identity. First Peter does not characterize or idealize a woman's subordination to her husband as a God-ordained principle. Rather, he presents the Christian wife's willingness to accept and submit to the authority of her husband—though not at all costs—as a necessary strategy for survival and avoiding unnecessary conflict. While the author expresses the hope that the behavior of believing wives may eventually lead to the conversion of their husbands, his primary concern is that wives possess the kind of quiet aplomb and fearlessness that is precious before God and befits their new status as Sarah's children.

NOTES

1. While it is impossible to know the precise ethnic-religious makeup of 1 Peter's actual audience, the letter gives us clues to his imagined audience and writes to them as if they are Gentiles (1:14; 1:18; 2:10; 4:3–4).

2. Natalie Porter, "The Butterfly Dilemma: Asian Women, Whiteness, and Heterosexual Relationships," *Women & Therapy* 38, no. 3–4 (2015): 211.

3. Themes of discrimination directed at Asian American women included assumptions that they are "exoticized and fetishized (e.g., comments like, 'You look like a China Doll' or 'I have a thing for Asian women'), not a leader, submissive and passive, cute and small, invisible and silent, and service providers" (Shruti Mukkamala and Karen L. Suyemoto, "Racialized Sexism/ Sexualized Racism: A Multimethod Study of Intersectional Experiences of Discrimination for Asian American Women," *Asian American Journal of Psychology* 9, no. 1 [2018]: 42).

4. Porter, "Butterfly Dilemma," 211.

5. Both John Elliott and Paul Achtemeier translate *anthrōpinē ktisei* "every human creature." Unlike "every human institution" (used by the NRSV and ESV), the translation "every human creature" more clearly conveys the common humanity emphasized by the imperatives *hypotagēte*, in verse 13 and *timēsate* in verse 17 that form an *inclusio*. The translation "every human creature" also limits the authority and power even of the emperor, who in the Roman social order was superordinate to all. Furthermore, the phrase *anthrōpinē ktisei* prepares readers for the list of other social superordinates to whom the author instructs Christian slaves and wives to subordinate themselves (2:18–3:6). See John H. Elliott, *1 Peter*, AB 37B (New York: Anchor Bible, 2001), 484, 486; Paul J. Achtemeier, *1 Peter*, Hermeneia (Minneapolis: Augsburg Fortress, 1996), 179–80.

6. Translations mine unless otherwise noted. The verb *hypotagēte*, a compound of the preposition *hypo-* ("under") and the verb *tassō* ("order, place, station"), occurs six times in 1 Peter (2:13, 18; 3:1, 5, 22; 5:5). "Subordinate," rather than "submit" or "obey," helps convey the positional sense advocated by 1 Peter. Rather than demand unconditional obedience to civil authority, masters, and husbands, the author advocates for a more nuanced approach in which one must find his/her proper place in the social order and household and act accordingly (Achtemeier, *1 Peter*, 182).

7. E.g., Wayne A. Grudem, *1 Peter*, TNTC (Grand Rapids: Eerdmans, 1998), 137.

8. Cf. 1 Pet. 2:12. *Kerdainō* appears in Matthew 18:15 in reference to "convincing" a brother who has sinned against a person of his wrongdoing and in 1 Corinthians 9:19–22 in reference to Paul's "convincing" or "winning over" others for the cause of the gospel. See David Daube, "Κερδαίνω as a Missionary Term," *HTR* 40 (1947): 109–20; Greg W. Forbes, *1 Peter* (Nashville, TN: B&H Academic, 2014), 99.

9. Elliott, *1 Peter*, 558.

10. Elliott, *1 Peter*, 574.

11. Caroline E. Johnson Hodge, "'Holy Wives' in Roman Households: 1 Peter 3:1–6," *Women and Spirituality* 4, no. 1 (2010): 10.

12. Johnson Hodge, "Holy Wives," 4–5.

13. Johnson Hodge, "Holy Wives," 5–7.

14. Johnson Hodge, "Holy Wives," 7–8, who cites Plautus's plays *Trinummus* and *Rudens* and Cato's *de Agricultura*.

15. J. Ramsey Michaels, *1 Peter*, WBC (Waco, TX: Word, 1988), 171.

16. Plutarch, *Advice to the Bride and Groom* 19, trans. from Sarah B. Pomeroy, ed., *Plutarch's Advice to the Bride and Groom and A Consolation to His Wife: English Translations, Commentary, Interpretive Essays and Bibliography* (New York: Oxford, 1991), 7.

17. Johnson Hodge, "Holy Wives," 9.

18. Warren Carter, "Going All the Way? Honoring the Emperor and Sacrificing Wives and Slaves in 1 Peter 2:13–3:6," *A Feminist Companion to the Catholic Epistles and Hebrews*, ed. Amy-Jill Levine with Maria Mayo Robbins (London: T&T Clark, 2004), 14–33.

19. Carter, "Going All the Way," 31.

20. Carter, "Going All the Way," 33.

21. James C. Scott, *Weapons of the Weak: Everyday Forms of Peasant Resistance* (New Haven, CT: Yale University Press, 2008), 284, cited in Carter, "Going All the Way," 32.

22. Carter, "Going All the Way," 28, 32.

23. Johnson Hodge, "Holy Wives," 11.

24. Johnson Hodge, "Holy Wives," 3.

25. Johnson Hodge, "Holy Wives," 20.

26. The views against excessive outward attention to beauty espoused in 1 Peter 3:3–4 agree with the values of the OT (e.g., 1 Sam. 16:7; Prov. 31:30; Isa. 3:18–24) and of Greek and Jewish moralists (e.g., Dio Chrysostom, *Or.* 7.117; Juvenal, *Satire* 3.180–81; Plutarch, *Mor., Con. pr.* 141E; Philo, *Virt.* 7.39; 39–40).

27. Betsy Bauman-Martin, "Women on the Edge: New Perspectives on Women in the Petrine *Haustafel*," *JBL* 123, no. 2 (2004): 273.

28. Johnson Hodge, "Holy Wives," 9, 11.

29. Karen H. Jobes, *1 Peter*, BECNT (Grand Rapids, MI: Baker Academic, 2005), 205.

30. David L. Balch, *Let Wives Be Submissive: The Domestic Code in 1 Peter*, SBLMS 26 (Chico, CA: Scholars Press, 1981), 81.

31. Balch, *Let Wives Be Submissive*, 96–97.

32. Clarice J. Martin, "The *Haustafeln* (Household Codes) in African American Biblical Interpretation: 'Free Slaves' and 'Subordinate Women,'" in *Stony the Road We Trod: African American Biblical Interpretation*, 206–23 (Minneapolis: Augsburg Press, 1991), 213.

33. Elisabeth Schüssler Fiorenza, *In Memory of Her: A Feminist Theological Reconstruction of Christian Origins* (New York: Crossroads, 1983), 253–62, cited in Betsy Bauman-Martin, "Women on the Edge," 257.

34. Bauman-Martin, "Women on the Edge," 256–57.

35. Bauman-Martin, "Women on the Edge," 258, 264.

36. Bauman-Martin, "Women on the Edge," 264 n. 39.

37. Shively T. J. Smith, *Strangers to Family: Diaspora and 1 Peter's Invention of God's Household* (Waco, TX: Baylor University Press, 2016), 77–78.

38. Bauman-Martin, "Women on the Edge," 268, 273, and Margaret Y. MacDonald, *Early Christian Women and Pagan Opinion: The Power of the Hysterical Woman* (Cambridge, UK: Cambridge University Press, 1996), 203.

39. Translation adapted from Magda Misset-Van de Weg, "Sarah Imagery in 1 Peter," in *A Feminist Companion to the Catholic Epistles and Hebrews*, ed. Amy-Jill Levine with Maria Mayo Robbins, 50–62 (London: T&T Clark, 2004), 50.

40. Mark Kiley, "Like Sara: The Tale of Terror behind 1 Peter 3:6," *JBL* 106, no. 4 (1987), 691.

41. Kiley, "Like Sara," 692. See also Michal Beth Dinkler, who sees Sarah's situation in Genesis 12 and 20 as parallel to that of the women addressed in 1 Peter ("Sarah's Submission: Peter's Analogy in 1 Peter 3:5–6," *Priscilla Papers* 21, no. 3 [2007], 10) and Aída Besançon Spencer, who also concludes that Genesis 12 and 20 is most apropos to 1 Peter's context ("Peter's Pedagogical Method in 1 Peter 3:6," *Bulletin for Biblical Research* 10, no. 1 [2000], 106).

42. Troy W. Martin, "The TestAbr and the Background of 1 Pet 3:6," *ZNW* 90 (1999): 139–46. Spencer also argues, as does Martin, that Genesis 18:12 does not fit 1 Peter's description of Sarah ("Peter's Pedagogical Method," 106).

43. Misset-Van de Weg, "Sarah Imagery in 1 Peter," 62.

44. Work from the field of narrative psychology offers some insight. Julie Beck explains that, "the way a person integrates those facts and events internally" is how one makes meaning, and "this narrative becomes a form or identity, in which the things someone chooses to include in the story, and the way she tells it, can both reflect and shape who she is" ("The Story of My Life: How Narrative Creates Personality," *The Atlantic*, August 10, 2015. https://www.theatlantic.com/health/archive/2015/08/life-stories-narrative-psychology-redemption-mental-health/400796/).

45. For others who translate *tekna* in 3:6 as "children" not "daughters," see, e.g., Michaels, *1 Peter*, 166, and David G. Horrell, "Ethnicisation, Marriage and Early Christian Identity: Criti-

cal Reflections on 1 Corinthians 7, 1 Peter 3 and Modern New Testament Scholarship," *NTS* 62 (2016): 455.

46. I have argued in my dissertation, the author of 1 Peter characterizes Christian identity as a kind of ethnic identity because doing so has the potential to engender a powerful sense of solidarity for his largely Gentile addressees who experienced social alienation, estrangement, and hostility from the wider society *as a result* of their conversion. Janette H. Ok, "Who You Are No Longer: Constructing Ethnic Identity in 1 Peter," PhD diss., Princeton Theological Seminary, 2018.

47. Rom. 8:15–17; 23; Gal. 4:1–7; cf. Eph. 1:3–6. Caroline Johnson Hodge addresses how Paul uses the metaphor of adoption by the Spirit to reconstruct the origins of Gentiles in *If Sons, Then Heirs: A Study of Kinship and Ethnicity in the Letters of Paul* (New York: Oxford University Press, 2007), 67–77. The meaning of *anagennaō* conveyed in 1 Peter 1:3 appears by implication in John 3:3–8 when Jesus tells Nicodemus that "no one can see the kingdom of God without being born from above" (*ean mē tis gennēthē anōthen, ou dynatai idein tēn basileian tou theou*).

48. Denise Kimber Buell intentionally deploys the terms "race" and "ethnicity" interchangeably in her examination of Christian strategies of self-definition, as represented in her use of the phrase "ethnoracial." *Why This New Race: Ethnic Reasoning in Early Christianity* (New York: Columbia University Press, 2005).

49. Horrell, "Ethnicisation," 453. The aorist verb *egenēthete* denotes the event of conversion or "new birth" (1:3, 23) The participle phrase *agathopoiousai kai mē phoboumenai mēdemian ptoesin* conveys both a sense of exhortation and conditionality (455), not in the sense that they are saved by works but that wives demonstrate their identity as children of Sarah by doing what is good even in the face of intimidation or terror (cf. 1:6–7).

50. E.g., Nicholas Daniel Hartlep, *The Model Minority Stereotype: Demystifying Asian American Success* (Charlotte, NC: Information Age, 2013); Victor Bascara, *Model-Minority Imperialism* (Minneapolis: University of Minneapolis Press, 2006); Claire Jean Kim, "The Racial Triangulation of Asian Americans," *Politics & Society* 27, no. 1 (1999): 105–38; Peter Turnley, "The Effects of Seeing Asian-Americans as a 'Model Minority,'" *New York Times*, October 16, 2015, https://www.nytimes.com/roomfordebate/2015/10/16/the-effects-of-seeing-asian-americans-as-a-model-minority; Janette H. Ok, "Myth of Model Minority," *Intersecting Realities: Race, Identity, and Culture in the Spiritual-Moral Life of Young Asian Americans*, ed. Hak Joon Lee, 121–33 (Eugene, OR: Cascade, 2018).

51. Karen Pyke, "An Intersectional Approach to Resistance and Complicity: The Case of Racialised Desire among Asian American Women," *Journal of Intercultural Studies* 31, no. 1 (2010): 83. The trope of the impervious "strong black woman" serves as an example of how the "*model resistor* stereotype" downplays and/or dismisses the multiple discriminations of gender, race, and class that many black women suffer. Another problem with the "*model resistor* stereotype" is that overidealizing resistance tends to normalize domination (83). See also Karen Pyke, "Defying the Taboo on the Study of Internalized Racism," *Global Migration, Cultural Transformation, and Social Change*, eds. Emory Elliott, Jasmine Payne, and Patricia Pluesch, 101–20. (New York: Palgrave Macmillan, 2007).

52. Pyke, "An Intersectional Approach," 81, 83.

53. Mari J. Matsuda, *Where Is Your Body? And Other Essays on Race, Gender and the Law* (Boston: Beacon Press, 1996), 64–65.

54. Pyke, "An Intersectional Approach," 83.

55. L. Illica and G. Giacosa, *Madam Butterfly: A Japanese Tragedy,* trans. R. H. Elkin (New York: G. Ricordi & Company, 1906), 11. Illica and Giacosa's libretto serves as the script for Giacomo Puccini's musical composition.

56. Porter, "Butterfly Dilemma," 207–8.

57. Porter, "Butterfly Dilemma," 211.

58. Porter, "Butterfly Dilemma," 216.

59. Porter, "Butterfly Dilemma," 216–17.

60. Porter, "Butterfly Dilemma," 211.

61. Joe L. Kincheloe, "The Struggle to Define and Reinvent Whiteness: A Pedagogical Analysis," *College Literature* 26 (Fall): 162–97.

62. Gayatri Spivak's concept of "strategic essentialism" may be helpful to consider how immigrant wives might express agency in such a way that "essentializes" them in order to set themselves from the predominant narrative of femininity. Donna Landry and Gerald MacLean, eds., *The Spivak Reader* (New York and London: Routledge, 1996), 214.
63. Porter, "Butterfly Dilemma," 213–14.
64. Porter, "Butterfly Dilemma," 214.
65. Porter, "Butterfly Dilemma," 212.
66. Porter, "Butterfly Dilemma." 212.
67. Porter, "Butterfly Dilemma," 212.
68. Porter, "Butterfly Dilemma," 216.
69. Porter, "Butterfly Dilemma," 216.
70. James W. Aaegeson, "1 Peter 2.11–3.7: Slaves, Wives and the Complexities of Interpretation," *A Feminist Companion to the Catholic Epistles and Hebrews*, ed. Amy-Jill Levine with Maria Mayo Robbins, 34–49 (London: T&T Clark, 2004), 44.

WORKS CITED

Aaegeson, James W. "1 Peter 2.11–3.7: Slaves, Wives and the Complexities of Interpretation." In *A Feminist Companion to the Catholic Epistles and Hebrews*, edited by Amy-Jill Levine with Maria Mayo Robbins, 34–49. London: T&T Clark, 2004.
Achtemeier, Paul J. *1 Peter*. Hermeneia. Minneapolis: Augsburg Fortress, 1996.
Balch, David L. *Let Wives Be Submissive: The Domestic Code in 1 Peter*. SBLMS 26. Chico, CA: Scholars, 1981.
Bascara, Victor. *Model-Minority Imperialism*. Minneapolis: University of Minneapolis Press, 2006.
Bauman-Martin, Betsy. "Women on the Edge: New Perspectives on Women in the Petrine *Haustafel*." *JBL* 123, no. 2 (2004): 253–79.
Beck, Julie. "The Story of My Life: How Narrative Creates Personality." *The Atlantic*, August 10, 2015. https://www.theatlantic.com/health/archive/2015/08/life-stories-narrative-psychology-redemption-mental-health/400796/.
Carter, Warren. "Going All the Way? Honoring the Emperor and Sacrificing Wives and Slaves in 1 Peter 2:13–3:6." In *A Feminist Companion to the Catholic Epistles and Hebrews*, edited by Amy-Jill Levine with Maria Mayo Robbins, 14–33. London: T&T Clark, 2004.
Daube, David. "Κερδαίνω as a Missionary Term." *HTR* 40 (1947): 109–20.
Dinkler, Michal Beth. "Sarah's Submission: Peter's Analogy in 1 Peter 3:5–6." *Priscilla Papers* 21, no. 3 (2007): 9–15.
Elliott, John H. *1 Peter*. AB 37B. New York: Anchor Bible, 2001.
Fiorenza, Elisabeth Schüssler. *In Memory of Her: A Feminist Theological Reconstruction of Christian Origins*. New York: Crossroads, 1983.
Forbes, Greg W. *1 Peter*. Nashville, TN: B & H, 2014.
Grudem, Wayne A. *1 Peter*. TNTC. Grand Rapids, MI: Eerdmans, 1998.
Horrell, David G. "Ethnicisation, Marriage and Early Christian Identity: Critical Reflections on 1 Corinthians 7, 1 Peter 3 and Modern New Testament Scholarship." *NTS* 62 (2016): 439–60.
Illica, Luigi, and Giuseppe Giacosa. *Madam Butterfly: A Japanese Tragedy*, translated by R. H. Elkin. New York: G. Ricordi & Company, 1906.
Jobes, Karen H. *1 Peter*. BECNT. Grand Rapids, MI: Baker, 2005.
Johnson Hodge, Caroline E. "'Holy Wives' in Roman Households: 1 Peter 3:1–6." *Women and Spirituality* 4, no. 1 (2010): 1–24.
———. *If Sons, Then Heirs: A Study of Kinship and Ethnicity in the Letters of Paul*. Oxford: Oxford University Press, 2007.
Kiley, Mark. "Like Sara: The Tale of Terror behind 1 Peter 3:6." *JBL* 106, no. 4 (1987): 689–92.
Kim, Jean Claire. "The Racial Triangulation of Asian Americans." *Politics & Society* 27, no. 1 (1999): 105–38.

Kimber Buell, Denise. *Why This New Race: Ethnic Reasoning in Early Christianity.* New York: Columbia University Press, 2005.

Kincheloe, Joe L. "The Struggle to Define and Reinvent Whiteness: A Pedagogical Analysis." *College Literature* 26 (1999): 162–97.

MacDonald, Margaret Y. *Early Christian Women and Pagan Opinion: The Power of the Hysterical Woman.* Cambridge, UK: Cambridge University Press, 1996.

Martin, Clarice J. "The *Haustafeln* (Household Codes) in African American Biblical Interpretation: 'Free Slaves' and 'Subordinate Women.'" In *Stony the Road We Trod: African American Biblical Interpretation,* edited by Cain Hope Felder, 206–23. Minneapolis: Augsburg, 1991.

Martin, Troy W. "The TestAbr and the Background of 1 Pet 3:6." *ZNW* 90 (1999): 139–46.

Matsuda, Mari J. *Where Is Your Body? And Other Essays on Race, Gender and the Law.* Boston: Beacon, 1996.

Michaels, J. Ramsey. *1 Peter.* WBC. Waco, TX: Word, 1988.

Misset-Van de Weg, Magda. "Sarah Imagery in 1 Peter." In *A Feminist Companion to the Catholic Epistles and Hebrews,* edited by Amy-Jill Levine with Maria Mayo Robbins, 50–62. London: T&T Clark, 2004.

Mukkamala, Shruti, and Karen L. Suyemoto. "Racialized Sexism/Sexualized Racism: A Multimethod Study of Intersectional Experiences of Discrimination for Asian American Women." *Asian American Journal of Psychology* 9, no. 1 (2018): 32–46.

Ok, Janette H. "Myth of Model Minority." In *Intersecting Realities: Race, Identity, and Culture in the Spiritual-Moral Life of Young Asian Americans,* edited by Hak Joon Lee, 50–62. Eugene, OR: Cascade, 2018.

———. "Who You Are No Longer: Constructing Ethnic Identity in 1 Peter." PhD diss., Princeton Theological Seminary, 2018.

Pomeroy, Sarah B., ed. *Plutarch's Advice to the Bride and Groom and A Consolation to His Wife: English Translations, Commentary, Interpretive Essays and Bibliography.* New York: Oxford, 1991.

Porter, Natalie. "The Butterfly Dilemma: Asian Women, Whiteness, and Heterosexual Relationships." *Women & Therapy* 38, no. 3–4 (2015): 207–19.

Pyke, Karen. "Defying the Taboo on the Study of Internalized Racism." In Global Migration, Cultural Transformation, and Social Change, edited by Emory Elliott, Jasmine Payne, and Patricia Ploesch, 101–20. New York: Palgrave Macmillan, 2007.

———. "An Intersectional Approach to Resistance and Complicity: The Case of Racialised Desire among Asian American Women." *Journal of Intercultural Studies* 31, no. 1 (2010): 81–94.

Scott, James C. *Weapons of the Weak: Everyday Forms of Peasant Resistance.* New Haven, CT: Yale University Press, 2008.

Smith, Shively T. J. *Strangers to Family: Diaspora and 1 Peter's Invention of God's Household.* Waco, TX: Baylor University Press, 2016.

Spencer, Aída Besançon. "Peter's Pedagogical Method in 1 Peter 3:6." *Bulletin for Biblical Research* 10, no. 1 (2000): 107–19.

Spivak, Gayatri. *The Spivak Reader,* edited by Donna Landry and Gerald MacLean. New York and London: Routledge, 1996.

Tuan, Mia. "Honorary White." *Encyclopedia of Diversity in Education,* edited by James A. Banks. Thousand Oaks, CA: Sage, 2012. http://dx.doi.org/10.4135/9781452218533.n349.

Turnley Peter. "The Effects of Seeing Asian-Americans as a 'Model Minority.'" *New York Times,* October 16, 2015. http:// https://www.nytimes.com/roomfordebate/2015/10/16/the-effects-of-seeing-asian-americans-as-a-model-minority

Index

Abraham, 5, 5–6, 34, 59, 62, 117–118
Africa, ix; Egypt, vii, 2, 6, 10, 11, 12;
Ethiopia, vii
African ancestry, x, 45; descent, x, 61,
64n29
African American(s), xii–xiii, xiv–xv, 24,
26, 27, 27–28, 46, 63n7, 66n57, 67, 68,
72, 142; biblical interpretation, 65n45,
67, 68, 126n32, 129, 141; church, 72;
community, 35; experience, 23, 30, 42,
42n45, 67, 142; spirituals, 84n4, 86;
women, 63n3, 66n65, 69. *See also*
black people
Africans, ix, 26, 27, 51, 52, 53, 55, 56, 57,
64n29, 80, 81; Egyptians, vii;
Ethiopians, vii; eunuch, xixn28. *See
also* slave/enslaved
Ahmed, Sara, 15, 20n69–20n70, 25,
40n8–40n11
alien, 60, 80; resident, 113. *See also*
foreigner; stranger
alienated, 14, 119
alienation, 51, 121, 123, 127n46
alterity, 23, 24–25, 25, 26–27, 29
Ambrosiaster, 93
American South, ix, 53, 65n40. *See also*
antebellum
androcentric,
antebellum, 45, 47, 52, 53, 57, 64n17,
65n39, 68
Apollos, 74, 75, 77

Asia Minor, 41n33, 43, 50, 62
Asian, xii, xixn29, 20, 20n67, 99, 102n2,
105n39, 105n44, 106, 106n52, 107,
108, 121, 122–123, 125n2, 141, 142;
American, xii–xiii, xviiin16, xx, 20,
20n67, 102n2, 103n7, 105n43, 106,
107, 108, 111–112, 119, 121, 125n3,
127n50–127n51, 128, 129, 141, 142;
immigrant, xvi, 65n48, 67, 111, 112,
120, 121, 123
Asians, x. *See also* Korean and Korean
American Women

babies, 12, 13, 19n59. *See also* infants
baptism, 59
baptismal formula, 34, 36, 58–59, 61, 74
baptismal creed, 37, 59
baptized, 15, 34, 61
Bathsheba, 9, 15
Bhabha, Homi, 29–30, 33, 40n3,
41n20–41n21, 42, 42n36, 54, 65n32,
65n35, 66; ambivalence, 32, 40n3, 54,
57; colonial mimicry, 29–30, 54, 57;
hybridity, 32, 54
binaries, xiv, 32, 35, 47, 58–59, 61, 119
black (people), vii, x–xi, 15, 20n66, 20n67,
21, 27, 29, 45, 61, 64n23, 64n29, 68,
72, 82, 86, 101; bodies, ix, x, 45;
community,. *See also* African
Americans
black Baptists, 142

67, 68, 73, 74–75, 78, 80, 81

Galatians, xiv–xv, 23–24, 26, 30–31, 32,
32–34, 34–36, 37–38, 39, 40n3, 41n26,
41n30–41n31, 42, 42n34–42n35,
42n40, 42n42, 42n45, 42n48, 43,
45–47, 48–51, 51–53, 54–55, 56–57,
57–59, 60–61, 62, 63n6, 64n13, 64n20,
65n34, 65n37, 65n44, 66n57–66n59,
66n66–66n68, 67, 68, 85n24, 86; Gal.
3:28, xiv–xv, 19n47, 21, 23, 34, 47, 55,
57–59, 61, 62, 65n49, 66n58, 68, 74,
84n15
gender, xi, xii, xiii, xiv, xvi, xvii, xixn28,
xx, 2, 9, 12, 16n13, 20, 23, 29, 30, 36,
50, 58–59, 65n39, 65n50, 67, 72,
84n17, 87, 89, 97, 101, 102, 103n20,
104n30, 105n36, 105n48, 106, 107,
108, 112, 114, 119, 120, 121, 123, 124,
127n51, 127n53, 129, 141
gendered, 9, 72, 97, 98, 100, 105n45, 108,
112
genealogy, 2, 5, 5–6, 6, 9, 17n31, 18n45,
24, 111, 118, 123
Gentiles, xviiin7, 1, 3, 7, 9, 11, 13, 17n24,
17n30, 18n34, 19n61, 32, 36–37, 45,
48, 51, 53, 54, 58–59, 60, 61, 62,
66n59, 116, 118, 125n1, 125n4
geopolitical, 4, 8, 19n61, 29, 62
Giddings, Paula, xviiin10, xx
global, xiv, xvii, 15, 20n66–20n67, 21, 30,
41n22, 42, 78, 105n39–105n40,
105n44, 107, 109, 127n51, 129

Hagar, xv, 45, 47, 61–62, 62, 66n65
Hall, Jonathan M., viii, xviiin8
Ham, curse of, 27–28, 41n14, 41n17, 42,
43. *See also* children
Harris-Perry, Melissa, 77, 85n28–85n29
Hasmonean, 4, 7, 17n21, 17n24
Herod, 7, 8, 9, 10, 10–11, 11, 15, 19n54
Herodotus, vii, xviiin1, xx, 17n27
Hockey, Katherine M., xviiin24, xix,
xixn27, xx, 16n2, 20
Horsley, Richard, 4, 17n22, 42n37, 64n15,
67
household(s), 7, 19n47, 21, 57, 62, 111,
112–113, 114, 115, 116, 119, 123,
125n6, 125n11, 129; code(s), xvi,

65n47, 65n49, 68, 112–113, 115, 116,
126n32, 129; *paterfamilias*, 81, 114,
119
Hsu, Madeline Y., xviiin16, xx
husband(s), 71, 82, 111, 112, 112–115,
116, 117, 117–118, 119, 120–123,
123–124, 125n6; of Mary, 5; pagan,
xvi, 124. *See also* marriage
Hyrcanus, 3, 16n14, 18n41

immigrant(s), 61, 128; Asian women, xvi,
65n48, 67, 111, 112, 119, 120, 121,
128, 128n62. *See also* Asian; Korean
Indian, vii, xiii, 121. *See also* South Asian
indigenous, xiii
infanticide, 19n58, 21
infantilizing, 77
infants, 12, 13, 15, 19n59. *See also* babies
intersectional, xi–xii, xiv–xi, xixn28, xx, 1,
4, 9, 15, 17n25, 19n47, 21, 58,
65n49–65n50, 67, 68, 107, 111–112,
119, 125n3, 126n24, 127n51–127n52,
127n54, 129
intersectionality, xiii, xviiin26, xx, 9, 21,
41n25, 43, 63n2, 65n48, 66n64, 67, 68,
111, 119–120, 120, 121, 141
Isaac, Benjamin, 2, 16n6, 16n8, 16n11,
17n15–17n17, 21
Ivy League schools, xv, 53; Harvard
University, 53, 55

Jacobs, Harriet, 57, 65n46. *See also* Brent,
Linda
Jeremiah, 12, 12–13
Jesus (Christ), xiv, 1–2, 5, 18n35–18n36,
18n44–18n45, 19n48, 19n50–19n52,
19n58–19n59, 20, 20n68, 21, 23, 30,
31, 34, 35, 36–37, 37, 40n4, 41n26, 46,
47, 48, 49, 51, 54–55, 59, 61, 62, 63n5,
64n16, 66, 69, 73, 76, 78, 79, 80, 81,
81–82, 82, 84n4, 85n35, 85n37, 86,
118, 127n47; ethnic identity of, 1–2, 4,
5, 6–7, 8; the Galilean, 1, 6, 8, 9; King
of the Jews, 1, 6–7, 8, 9, 10, 11, 15;
Messiah, 5, 6, 7, 8, 10, 18n36, 51, 72;
movement, xii, xviiin7, 8, 32, 34, 35,
36, 39, 47, 51, 60; son of David, 5, 5–6,
6; as ultimate slave master, 53
Jewish identity, 3, 4, 23, 31, 33, 81, 82

136   *Index*

neighbor: love, 49; neighbor's children, 15;
  neighbors, 49, 116
New Testament, xii–xiii, xiii, xx, 27, 28,
  58, 63n7, 65n34, 65n37, 66n57, 67, 68,
  89, 102n2, 102n5, 104n21, 104n25,
  106, 108, 111, 113, 126n45, 128, 141,
  142
Noah, 35
normalization, 89, 92, 106n54
normalize, 55, 59, 102, 127n51

Occident, 23
Ok, Janette H., xvi, 142
Orient, 23
Oriental(s), 80
Orientalism, 29, 41n18–41n19, 43, 121
Origen, xv, xvi, xviiin7, 90–96, 97, 98, 99,
  100, 102, 103n9–103n10, 103n12,
  103n14, 103n17, 104n22–104n23,
  104n34, 106, 107, 108
other, the, vii, xii, xiv, xvi, 2, 8, 14, 23–24,
  24–25, 25, 26, 29, 29–30, 39, 54, 66,
  95, 99, 101, 104n24, 105n36, 108. *See
  also* alterity
othering, viii, xi, 26, 29, 49
otherness, 24–25, 25, 26, 28, 31, 39, 121;
  discourse of, 24, 31; embodiment of,
  29; racialization of, ix

pagan, 90, 94, 96, 97, 98, 99, 126n38, 129;
  household, 115; husbands, xvi, 124;
  mantic practices, 95; prophecy, 94, 95;
  prophets, 97
paganism, 90
paganization, xvi, 90, 94, 98, 100
paganize, xvi, 98–99, 102
pagans, xvi, 17n21, 97, 98, 101, 102n4,
  107
paidagōgos, 55, 64n28, 77. *See also* slave
paidiskē, 62. *See also* slave girl
Palestine, xiv, 3, 4, 7, 15, 17n22, 21
Parker, Angela N., xv, 38, 42n48, 43, 56,
  65n44, 68, 71, 85n24, 86, 142
Patterson, Orlando, ix, xviiin3, xviiin15,
  xx, 64n14, 68
Paul, Apostle: authority of, 31, 47, 51, 60,
  74; antislavery, 47, 53, 54, 57;
  Europeanization of, xv, 71, 80, 82,
  83n2, 85n35; feminized, 71, 72, 74, 75,

76, 76–77, 79, 82, 85n23; gospel of,
  41n26, 48, 50; identity of, 54, 76;
  letters/epistles of, 26, 36, 42n43, 43, 48,
  52, 63n8, 64n12–64n13, 68, 73, 91,
  127n47, 128; matrix of domination, xv,
  72; mimetic power of, xv, 71;
  opponents of, 46, 48–49, 49, 50, 60;
  and proslavery, 47, 53, 54, 57; rhetoric
  of, xv, 45–48, 50, 51, 54–55, 57, 59, 62,
  71–72, 73, 74, 75–76, 76–77, 78–79,
  79, 82, 84n16; Roman citizen, 47, 63n8,
  65n31; slave of Christ, xv, 48, 54, 56;
  and slavery, use of, 45, 55, 56. *See also*
  counterterror; First Corinthians;
  Galatians
Pentecostal, 99, 102n3, 105n39, 105n44,
  106, 107, 109
Pentecostalism, 99, 105n40, 109. *See also*
  Korean
performance, xiv, xvii, xixn32–xixn33, xx
performative, xiv, xvii
Philo, 3, 103n18, 108, 126n26
Philomena, 97, 101, 104n30–104n31
Plutarch, 95, 103n18, 114, 125n16,
  126n26, 129
polemic, 95, 96
polemical, 99
polemicize, 93
polemics, 90, 94, 100, 101
poor, 46, 50, 57, 58, 61, 74, 101
Porter, Natalie, 121, 125n2, 125n4,
  127n56–127n60, 128n63–128n69, 129
postcolonial: discipleship, 20, 20n68,
  102n2, 103n8, 105n38, 106, 106n52,
  141; hermeneutic, 29, 30, 32, 40n3,
  41n23–41n24, 43; Jesus, 19n52, 20;
  scholarship, xvi, 89, 119; theology,
  19n52, 19n60, 20; theorists, xiv, xix,
  xixn30, 24, 25, 29; theory, 29, 30, 142
postcolonialism, viii
power, vii, xi–xii, xiv, xv, xvii, xixn33, xx,
  8, 8–10, 11, 12, 14, 15, 18n42, 19n64,
  29, 30, 31, 32, 33–34, 36–37, 39,
  41n33, 45, 50, 51, 52, 54, 60, 63n1, 68,
  71–73, 74, 75, 76, 77, 78–79, 79,
  81–82, 82–83, 84n5, 84n7,
  84n14–84n15, 85n38, 86, 89, 91, 98,
  99, 102, 102n1, 104n25, 104n30,
  105n47, 105n49, 106, 107, 114–115,

20n67, 120

sexuality, xi, xii, xixn28, 23, 58, 75, 82, 83, 97, 104n35, 106; heterosexuality, 85n23, 86

sexualized, 95–96; sexualized racism, 112, 125n3, 129

Shaman, 99, 101, 105n39; shamanic, 99, 101; shamanistic, 99, 105n41–105n42, 106; shamanism, 99, 101, 105n44, 108

shame, 75, 76, 76–78, 85n28, 86; shameful, 116

shaming, 75, 77, 78–79

Sims, Angela D., 63n1, 68

slave, vii, 34, 52, 54–55, 55, 60, 61, 62, 66n58, 67, 74, 76; children, 61, 62; girl, xixn28, 8, 65n46, 104n24; enslaved, ix, x, xv, xviiin12, 26, 27, 29, 45, 46–47, 48, 49, 50, 51, 52, 52–53, 53, 55–57, 57–59, 60, 61–62, 63n9, 65n39–65n50, 67, 72, 75; master, 46, 52, 53, 55, 56, 57, 60, 62; narratives, xv, 47, 57; plantations, 53; religion, 64n17, 68; societies, ix, 52, 54, 58, 62. *See also* Brent, Linda; Douglas, Frederick; Paul, Apostle

slavery, xiv, xv, xviiin3, xviiin15, xx, 27, 41n14, 41n16, 42, 43, 45, 46, 51, 52, 53, 55, 56, 57, 59, 62, 63n7, 64n14, 64n26–64n27, 64n29, 65n33, 65n42–65n43, 65n47, 66n61–66n62, 66n69–66n70, 67, 68, 69, 85n24, 85n30, 86, 142; abolition of, 53; abolitionists, 57; antislavery, xv, 47, 53–54, 57; enslavement, ix, x, xv, 20n67, 45–47, 49, 50, 52–53, 54–55, 56–57, 57, 62, 64n29, 65n37, 68; proslavery, xv, 47, 53–54, 57; as social death, ix, xviiin3, xviiin15, xx, 64n14, 68

Smith, Mitzi J., xv, xviiin25, 15, 18n45, 20n66, 21, 41n25, 43, 63n2–63n3, 64n21, 64n23, 65n45, 66n62, 67, 68, 69, 84n4, 103n19, 104n24, 108, 141

Smith, Shanell T., 40n3, 43

Smith, Shively, 116, 126n37, 129

solidarity, 15, 25, 38, 51, 119, 127n46

South Asian, xiii. *See also* Indian

spirit, xv, 15, 34, 35, 36, 37, 39, 74, 75, 84n15, 86, 94–95, 95–96, 96, 97,

100–101, 102n1, 103n9, 104n26, 104n33, 105n40, 106, 107, 108, 109, 114, 115, 118, 127n47; possession, 99, 101, 102n1, 104n33, 106, 107, 108. *See also* shamanic

spirits, 38, 102n3, 106, 106n50, 109; demonic, 90; evil, 97, 100

spiritual, 27, 39, 47, 53, 59, 99, 116, 118; freedom, 53; genealogy, 118; gifts, 91, 92, 97, 103n11; heritage, 123; moral life, 127n50, 129

spirituality, 104n33, 106, 125n11, 128

spiritualist movement, 101

spiritualized, 80, 81

Spirituals, 84n4, 102

Spivak, Gayatri Chakravorty, 98, 128n62, 129

stereotype, xvi, xviiin8, 17n15, 27, 29, 30, 33, 85n28, 86, 111, 112, 116, 119, 121, 124, 127n50–127n51

stranger(s), 23, 24–25, 26, 29, 40n5–40n11, 126n37, 129. *See also* alien; foreigner

submission, 65n48, 112, 113, 114, 123, 126n41, 128

suffering, 2, 14, 15, 45, 84n4, 87, 113, 119, 123

Sugirtharajah, R. S., 41n30, 43, 83n2, 85n35, 86

Tamez, Elsa, 51, 53, 64n22, 65n30, 68

Terrell, JoAnne Marie, 85n38, 86

Townes, Emilie, 84n4, 87

trauma, 1, 15, 46, 55

traumatize, 46, 58, 64n23, 68

violence, xviiin26, xixn28, xx, 28, 29, 33, 55, 56, 58, 67, 113

Wan, Sze-kar, 32, 41n30, 43, 102n2, 108

Weems, Renita, 45, 63n3, 69

whiteness, xi, xiii, xvi, xviiin24, xix, 7, 45, 111, 112, 121, 125n2, 127n61, 129

wife, 9, 83n1, 112, 113, 115, 116, 117, 120, 124, 125n16, 129. *See also* marriage

wives, xvi, 62, 111, 112, 112–116, 117, 117–118, 119, 121, 123–124, 125n5, 125n11–125n14, 125n17–125n18,

About the Editors and Contributors

Mitzi J. Smith, PhD (Harvard University), is the J. Davison Philips Professor of New Testament at Columbia Theological Seminary, Decatur, Georgia. Her recent book *Toward Decentering the New Testament: A Reintroduction* was coauthored with Yung Suk Kim. She is the author of *Womanist Sass and Talk Back: Social (In)Justice, Intersectionality and Biblical Interpretation* and *Insights from African American Interpretation*. Smith self-identifies as a womanist biblical scholar. She is coeditor of the monograph series Womanist Readings of Scripture (Rowman & Littlefield).

Jin Young Choi, PhD (Vanderbilt University), is professor of New Testament and Christian origins and the Baptist Missionary Training School professorial chair for biblical studies at Colgate Rochester Crozer Divinity School in Rochester, New York. She was a Louisville Institute postdoctoral fellow. Choi is the author of *Postcolonial Discipleship of Embodiment: An Asian and Asian American Feminist Reading of the Gospel of Mark*. Her current work focuses on the intersection of race/ethnicity, gender, empire, and early Christianity, employing postcolonial feminist criticism and diaspora studies. Choi has served the Society of Biblical Literature in several compacities and currently is a cochair of the Minority Criticism and Biblical Interpretation Group and a member of the editorial boards of Semeia Studies and International Voices in Biblical Studies.

* * *

Jung H. Choi, ThD (Harvard University), is assistant professor of religious studies at North Carolina Wesleyan College, Rocky Mount, North Carolina. She was a Woman of Color Scholar in the General Board of Higher Education and Ministry of the United Methodist Church. Choi is currently working on a monograph on discourses on prophecy, scriptural practices, and the cultivation of the self in early Christianity. She also contributes to the volume *The New Testament in Color: A Multiethnic Commentary on the New Testament*. Choi is on the steering committees for Korean Biblical Colloquium of the Society of Biblical Literature and for Wesleyan and Methodist Studies Unit of the American Academy of Religion.

Jennifer Kaalund, PhD (The Theological School at Drew University), is assistant professor of religious studies at Iona College, New Rochelle, New York. Her book *Reading Hebrews and 1 Peter with the African American Great Migration: Diaspora, Place, and Identity* explores the constructed and contested identities in Hebrews and 1 Peter through the lens of the "New Negro," a similarly vulnerable identity formed during the Great Migration in the U.S. in the early twentieth century. Kaalund serves on the editorial board for the Journal of Feminist Studies in Religion.

Janette H. Ok, PhD (Princeton Theological Seminary), is associate professor of New Testament at Fuller Theological Seminary, Pasadena, California. She is the coeditor of the forthcoming volume *The New Testament in Color: A Multiethnic Commentary on the New Testament* and is writing a commentary on 1–3 John. Her forthcoming book *Constructing Ethnic Identity in 1 Peter: Who You Are No Longer* examines how and why the author of 1 Peter depicts Christian identity as an ethnic identity. Ok serves as the cochair of the Asian and Asian American Hermeneutics group of the Society of Biblical Literature. She also serves as a pastor at Ekko Church in Orange County, California.

Angela N. Parker, PhD (Chicago Theological Seminary), is assistant professor of New Testament and Greek at Mercer University's McAfee School of Theology in Atlanta, Georgia. In additional to her doctorate, Parker earned a BA in religion and philosophy from Shaw University and an MTS from Duke Divinity School. Parker's research interests include the Gospel of Mark, Pauline literature, postcolonial theory, and womanist hermeneutics of the Bible. Ordained in the Missionary Baptist tradition, Parker is currently researching Paul's language of flesh, slavery, and surrogacy and how various streams of black Baptists engage these Pauline ideas.

Made in the USA
Columbia, SC
03 November 2024

45546936R00100